Stand-up Comedy and Contemporary Feminisms

Library of Gender and Popular Culture

From *Mad Men* to gaming culture, performance art to steampunk fashion, the presentation and representation of gender continues to saturate popular media. This series seeks to explore the intersection of gender and popular culture, engaging with a variety of texts – drawn primarily from Art, Fashion, TV, Cinema, Cultural Studies and Media Studies – as a way of considering various models for understanding the complementary relationship between 'gender identities' and 'popular culture'. By considering race, ethnicity, class and sexual identities across a range of cultural forms, each book in the series adopts a critical stance towards issues surrounding the development of gender identities and popular and mass cultural 'products'.

For further information or enquiries, please contact the library series editors:

Claire Nally: claire.nally@northumbria.ac.uk
Angela Smith: angela.smith@sunderland.ac.uk

Advisory Board:

Dr Kate Ames, Central Queensland University, Australia
Dr Michael Higgins, University of Strathclyde, UK
Prof Åsa Kroon, Örebro University, Sweden
Dr Andrea McDonnell, Emmanuel College, USA
Dr Niall Richardson, University of Sussex, UK
Dr Jacki Willson, University of Leeds, UK

Published titles:

The Aesthetics of Camp: Post-Queer Gender and Popular Culture By Anna Malinowska

Ageing Femininity on Screen: The Older Woman in Contemporary Cinema By Niall Richardson

All-American TV Crime Drama: Feminism and Identity Politics in Law and Order: Special Victims Unit By Sujata Moorti and Lisa Cuklanz

Are You Not Entertained?: Mapping the Gladiator across Visual Media By Lindsay Steenberg

Bad Girls, Dirty Bodies: Sex, Performance and Safe Femininity By Gemma Commane

Conflicting Masculinities: Men in Television Period Drama By Katherine Byrne, Julie Anne Taddeo and James Leggott (Eds)

Fat on Film: Gender, Race and Body Size in Contemporary Hollywood Cinema By Barbara Plotz

Fathers on Film: Paternity and Masculinity in 1990s Hollywood By Katie Barnett

Feel-Bad Postfeminism: Impasse, Resilience and Female Subjectivity in Popular Culture By Catherine McDermott

Film Bodies: Queer Feminist Encounters with Gender and Sexuality in Cinema By Katharina Lindner

From the Margins to the Mainstream: Women On and Off Screen in Television and Film By Marianne Kac-Vergne and Julie Assouly (Eds)

Gay Pornography: Representations of Sexuality and Masculinity By John Mercer

Gender and Austerity in Popular Culture: Femininity, Masculinity and Recession in Film and Television By Helen Davies and Claire O'Callaghan (Eds)

Gender and Early Television: Mapping Women's Role in Emerging US and British Media, 1850–1950 By Sarah Arnold

The Gendered Motorcycle: Representations in Society, Media and Popular Culture By Esperanza Miyake

Gendering History on Screen: Women Filmmakers and Historical Films By Julia Erhart

Girls Like This, Boys Like That: The Reproduction of Gender in Contemporary Youth Cultures By Victoria Cann

'Guilty Pleasures': European Audiences and Contemporary Hollywood Romantic Comedy By Alice Guilluy

The Gypsy Woman: Representations in Literature and Visual Culture By Jodie Matthews

Male and Female Violence in Popular Media By Elisa Giomi and Sveva Magaraggia

Masculinity in Contemporary Science Fiction Cinema: Cyborgs, Troopers and Other Men of the Future By Marianne Kac-Vergne

From the Margins to the Mainstream Women in Film and Television By Marianne Kac-Vergne & Julie Assouly (Eds)

Positive Images: Gay Men and HIV/AIDS in the Culture of 'Post-Crisis' By Dion Kagan

Postfeminism and Contemporary Vampire Romance By Lea Gerhards

Queer Horror Film and Television: Sexuality and Masculinity at the Margins By Darren Elliott-Smith

Queer Sexualities in Early Film: Cinema and Male-Male Intimacy By Shane Brown

Screening Queer Memory: LGBTQ Pasts in Contemporary Film and Television By Anamarija Horvat

Steampunk: Gender and the NeoVictorian By Claire Nally

Television Comedy and Femininity: Queering Gender By Rosie White

Tweenhood: Femininity and Celebrity in Tween Popular Culture By Melanie Kennedy

Women Who Kill: Gender and Sexuality in Film and Series of the Post-Feminist Era By David Roche and Cristelle Maury (Eds) *Wonder Woman: Feminism, Culture and the Body* By Joan Ormrod

Young Women, Girls and Postfeminism in Contemporary British Film By Sarah Hill

Stand-up Comedy and Contemporary Feminisms

Sexism, Stereotypes and Structural Inequalities

Ellie Tomsett

BLOOMSBURY ACADEMIC
LONDON • NEW YORK • OXFORD • NEW DELHI • SYDNEY

BLOOMSBURY ACADEMIC
Bloomsbury Publishing Plc
50 Bedford Square, London, WC1B 3DP, UK
1385 Broadway, New York, NY 10018, USA
29 Earlsfort Terrace, Dublin 2, Ireland

BLOOMSBURY, BLOOMSBURY ACADEMIC and the Diana logo are trademarks of Bloomsbury Publishing Plc

First published in Great Britain 2023
This paperback edition published 2025

Copyright © Ellie Tomsett, 2023

Ellie Tomsett has asserted her right under the Copyright, Designs and Patents Act, 1988, to be identified as Author of this work.

For legal purposes the Acknowledgements on p. xi constitute an extension of this copyright page.

Cover design: Ben Anslow
Cover image: Woman pulling face
(© Tim Robberts / Getty Images)

All rights reserved. No part of this publication may be reproduced or transmitted in any form or by any means, electronic or mechanical, including photocopying, recording, or any information storage or retrieval system, without prior permission in writing from the publishers.

Bloomsbury Publishing Plc does not have any control over, or responsibility for, any third-party websites referred to or in this book. All internet addresses given in this book were correct at the time of going to press. The author and publisher regret any inconvenience caused if addresses have changed or sites have ceased to exist, but can accept no responsibility for any such changes.

A catalogue record for this book is available from the British Library.

ISBN: HB: 978-1-3503-0228-0
PB: 978-1-3503-0232-7
ePDF: 978-1-3503-0230-3
eBook: 978-1-3503-0229-7

Series: Library of Gender and Popular Culture

Typeset by Deanta Global Publishing Services, Chennai, India

To find out more about our authors and books visit www.bloomsbury.com and sign up for our newsletters.

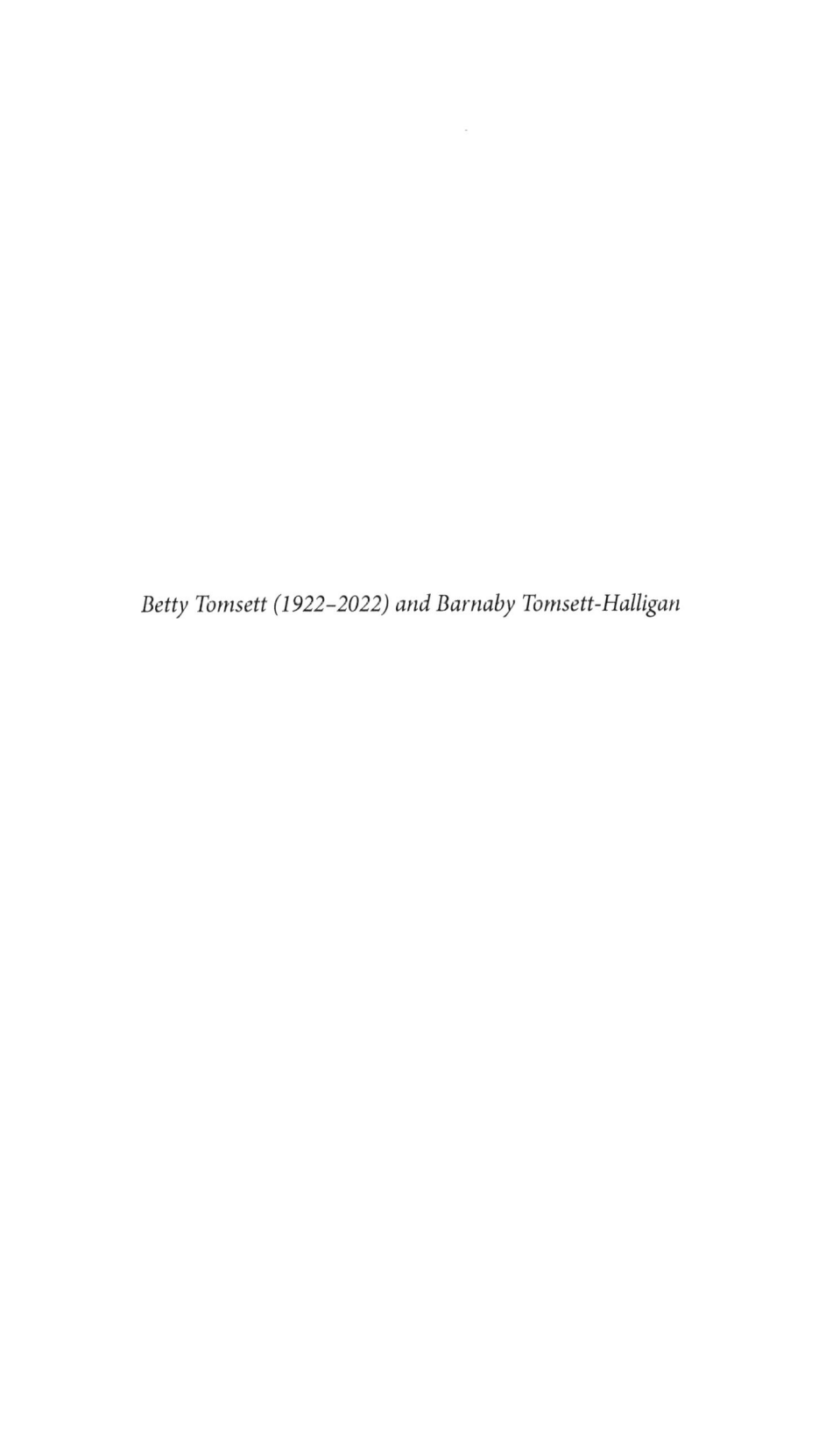

Betty Tomsett (1922–2022) and Barnaby Tomsett-Halligan

Contents

List of illustrations	x
Acknowledgements	xi

Introduction: Welcome to the stage		1
1	How did we get here? The gendered evolution of the UK comedy circuit	29
2	Where are we now? Challenges today for women comics	49
3	Women-only comedy spaces: Addressing inequality on the UK comedy circuit	79
4	Online to IRL: The impact of social media on stand-up comedy by women	111
5	Bodies on stage: Feminisms on the comedy circuit post-2013	137
6	An (un)equal and opposite reaction: The backlash and barriers facing feminist comedy	173
7	Comedy too	193
8	Conclusion: Reflections on UK comedy's glass ceiling	211

Notes	231
References	236
Index	253

Illustrations

Figures

1	Image of Women in Comedy Festival Poster from 2016	23
2	Image of Women in Comedy Festival Poster from 2017	87
3	Image of publicity for Manchester Arenas comedy offer, as seen in public spaces across Manchester in 2018	93
4	Image of author and friends with comedian Joe Lycett after a work-in-progress show of *More, More, More, How Do You Lycett? How Do You Lycett?* at Midlands Arts Centre March 2022	118
5	Image of Jo Brand in conversation with Dr Kate Fox at Manchester Literature Festival 2018	188

Tables

1	Gender Identity of Survey Respondents	88
2	Sexuality of Survey Respondents	88
3	Age of Survey Respondents	89
4	Disability of Survey Respondents	89
5	Ethnicity of Survey Respondents	90
6	Professional Area of Survey Respondents	91
7	Characteristics of Sampled Participants for the Interview Stage of Audience Study	97

Acknowledgements

I would like to thank the following people for their support and guidance whilst completing this book and the underlying research it is based upon: Dr Suzanne Speidel, Dr Chi-Yun Shin and Jon Bridle at Sheffield Hallam University. Colleagues at Birmingham City University's Centre for Media and Cultural Research, including Dr Poppy Wilde, Marverine Duffy, Dr Hazel Collie, Dr Karen Patel, Dr Gemma Commane and Professor Kirsten Forkert. My Mixed Bill colleagues, Dr Kate Fox, Lisa Moore, Dr Sarah Ilott and Dr Natalie Diddams and collaborators Dr Nathalie Weidhase and Dr Rosie White.

Special thanks to both my partner Dr Ben Halligan (and our cats Frida and Valerie), who, due to a quirk of timing, had to put up with me completing this manuscript whilst also being eight months pregnant, and my mother who provided childcare when I was indexing the book and caring for a new baby.

Finally, thanks to all my contributors for giving up their time to participate in this project by being interviewed – Hazel O'Keefe, Lynne Parker, David Schneider, Zoe Lyons, Sophie Willan, Janice Connolly, Soula Notos, Daphna Baram, Kerry Leigh, Dana Alexander, Allyson June Smith, Kiri Pritchard-McLean, Ali Hendry Ballard, Lara A. King, Dotty Winters and Kate Smurthwaite – as well as all the audience members who completed surveys and participated in interviews.

Introduction
Welcome to the stage

'Isn't being funny and a feminist an oxymoron?'

'Funny women? That'll be a short study then'

. . . and adjacent sentiments are comments I heard multiple times across the course of my research into women and comedy in the UK. These remarks were universally from cisgender men, many of whom were working within academia. Comments were often followed up with, as will be explored in this volume, the familiar 'just joking' defence as a way of both undermining the topic (and thus me, and my research) and preventing the opportunity to 'legitimately' (in their eyes) be offended. When not being overtly dismissive, I would also often get to hear about how much people 'love Sarah Millican and Miranda Hart' as if they were the only British women comedians I could possibly be concerning myself with. So, with these experiences in mind, I'd like to start this book by acknowledging those naysayers who made this kind of comment to me during the last ten years. It was helpful to see my argument be made for me so often and so clearly – that sexism around comedy and humour is still very much alive and well, and that there is significant ignorance of the diversity of talented women comics in the UK. It is these key issues that this volume will examine.

I commenced my investigation into women and comedy in 2013, a year during which several explicitly feminist comedy shows won the prestigious Edinburgh Festival Comedy Awards. Although the very act of standing on a stage and expressing your opinions as a woman could be considered a feminist act, the winning shows of

2013 went further, covering complex issues and deconstructing fixed gender roles. Although prior to this date there had been many British comedians engaging with feminism (Jenny Lecoat during the 1980s, for example), this peak in public and critical acclaim for feminist comedy in 2013 was also a high point in media consideration of modern feminisms. The public exposure of feminist initiatives such as Everyday Sexism, No More Page 3 and Vagenda Magazine, as well as Caroline Criado-Perez's high-profile campaign for Jane Austen to appear on banknotes, resulted in widespread press interest in the exclusion of women's achievements from public recognition.[1] This wider (white-centric) feminist context in Britain coincided with the success of a new generation of women-led comedy in America which has been made accessible to UK audiences via the increased use of digital platforms. The critical attention gained by HBO's *Girls* (2012–17) provoked TV executives and journalists to ask where the UK's Lena Dunham-esque 'voice of a generation of women' would come from (Cooke 2014). The continued success of Tina Fey, Amy Poehler, Maya Rudolph and the rising star of Amy Schumer contributed to a perceived disparity between the success of funny women in America and the UK. The public interest in contemporary feminist campaigns and the journalistic discussion about the UK's top female comedy talent meant that an academic exploration of these areas felt timely.

The motivation for the research that underpins this book was therefore to expose and interrogate the ways in which women's comic voices have been both integrated and marginalized within the UK comedy industry. The specific focus of this book will be the live stand-up comedy environment over the last ten years (2013–23). As existing research into comedy created and performed by women has focused overwhelmingly on American examples, I have sought to redress this by focusing squarely on what is happening in Britain. The notable differences in the cultural, industrial and performance contexts between the US and UK comedy industries, as it relates to women, have to date been somewhat underplayed. This book addresses this gap by identifying various structural and ideological barriers facing women comedians when attempting to break through the UK comedy industry's glass ceiling.

Comedy research as a field of study has tended to foreground analysis of the content and performance style of comedy; this is often at the expense of a full consideration of the *contexts* within which comedy is created by comedians and received by audiences. This book is concerned with the content of live comedy (the texts) as they explicitly relate to the social, political, technological and performance contexts within which they originate.

The ethos of my research was underpinned by a feminist approach to enquiry in line with discussions found within the work of Helen Roberts (1981), Sandra Harding (1987), Liz Stanley (1990), Christina Hughes (2002), Gail Letherby (2003), Brooke Ackerly and Jacqui True (2010) and Yasmin Gunaratnam and Carrie Hamilton (2017). Feminist research remains an evolving and contested area due to the fact that, as Harding highlights, the specific methods used by feminist researchers, for example, 'listening to (or interrogating) informants, observing behaviour or examining historical traces and records' (1987: 2), are not unique to this approach to enquiry. However, how feminist researchers 'carry out these methods of evidence gathering is often strikingly different' (Harding 1987: 2) from traditional approaches. It is the way in which the deployment of generic research methods by feminist researchers starts 'with the political commitment to produce useful knowledge that will make a difference to women's lives through social and individual change' (Letherby 2003: 4) that sets feminist research apart.

As feminist research includes the 'incorporation of the researcher's personal feelings and experiences into the research process' (Neuman 2014: 118), it is important to consider my own position in relation to the topic of study. In broad terms, this means that it was important, as a white, able-bodied, middle-class heterosexual cisgender woman, that I remained aware of my positioning in relation to the subject at hand whilst conducting the underlying research for this book. More specifically, in relation to the context of my research, I have been an audience member for comedy for around twenty years and whilst the vast majority of those experiences were for enjoyment only, rather than research purposes, this gave me a foundation of knowledge upon which to build my argument. I am not a comedian (a repeated nightmare I have is that I am invited to talk at a conference under the misapprehension that I'm a comic and I am going to do a set) and so I took steps to ensure I engaged extensively with the contexts and content under consideration before drawing conclusions. In addition to my relation to comedy, it is important to highlight that my personal understanding of feminism is an intersectional and trans inclusive one. This research was conducted from my position, as will become clear during the following chapters; however, I maintained an awareness that in the current cultural context, there are multiple feminist perspectives and that the very word feminism may be interpreted differently by participants of all genders. My use of the term 'feminisms' throughout this book corresponds with this awareness. Whilst conducting the research for this volume it was necessary to recognize my own privilege within feminism, in that voices like mine are better represented than other far more marginalized perspectives.

Harding stresses that for feminist researchers an awareness that 'women come only in different classes, races and cultures: there is no "woman" and no "woman's experience"' (1987: 7) is vital. Thus, whilst I wish to foreground my position as researcher here I will not be universalizing findings in a way that ignores the way that race, ability, sexuality and class intersect with gender to create specific forms of oppression and disadvantage. The use of the term 'woman' within this book should be read as inclusive of trans women. I wish it was not necessary to make this explicit declaration as it should be commonly accepted, but 'we are where we are' in UK academia. There are of course additional and specific barriers that trans women face when trying to integrate into all industries and comedy is no different. Whilst I do not wish to obscure or ignore these additional oppressions, I want to be clear that both I and indeed the specific organizational examples I am exploring in this book (Funny Women, Laughing Cows and the UK Women in Comedy Festival) are trans inclusive.

Situating the study in relation to gender stereotypes

Just as the comedy industry itself, in terms of venues, forms and the ideological content of jokes, has developed over time, so too has the wider cultural understanding of women and humour. These understandings have shifted significantly during the rise of stand-up comedy as a form. In terms of the stereotypes about women that may be limiting participation in stand-up comedy, we can see two central thought patterns in operation: conceptions regarding what women are capable of (or incapable of) due to their gender, and what is considered culturally appropriate behaviour and knowledge for women to demonstrate or possess per se. These gendered assumptions often intersect with racial stereotypes about women of colour, creating additional layers of exclusion.

There is a well-worn stereotype that women are incapable of being funny and the notion that somehow the ability to be humorous is inherently a male trait continues to be popular. This idea impacts not only on those working within the industry (including industry gatekeepers) but on audiences too. It is clear that even when a more diverse array of comedians take to the stage, as had started to occur in the 1980s with the alternative movement, audiences and promoters cannot just switch off any internalized biases they have developed. Stereotypes about gender are culturally ingrained and, as Cordelia Fine discusses in her work *Delusions of Gender: The Real Science Between Sex Differences* (2010):

> Even if you, personally, don't subscribe to these stereotypes, there is a part of your mind that isn't so prissy. Social psychologists are finding

that what we can consciously report about ourselves does not tell the whole story. (2010: 4)

Thus, even when, as individuals, we may think we hold progressive views about gender, race or sexuality, and even actively work towards equality in our speech and conscious behaviours, our unconscious minds will still refer back to the stereotypical views we were exposed to when growing up and the views that are reinforced in our day-to-day experiences.

In 2015, I discussed this issue with (now multi-BAFTA award-winning) comedian Sophie Willan, who had also been considering the way these stereotypes impact on her work:

> I wrote a poem about this, years ago [. . .]. It's something like 'Every time she speaks, her femininity does but reek, the stagnant perfume of the past.' because it does! Because every time she [a woman comic on a panel show] speaks you go [makes shocked face] 'woman!'. [. . .] And all that backlog that you've got, all the file, the Google file in your brain of all those debates about 'are women funny?' is going through your head, you're gripping your couch, or you're gripping your chair, thinking 'can she do it?'. So already that's not funny is it? You know, already she is set up to fail.

Willian touches on the way in which the debate about humour is articulated in terms of gendered characteristics or the biological determinism of 'male' or 'female' brains. This stereotype regarding humour has been pervasive for many years and has been of central concern for many academic studies across numerous humanities and social science fields, including the work of Frances Gray (1994), Louis Franzini (1996), Joanne Gilbert (2004), Helga Kotthoff (2006), Regina Barreca (2013) and Linda Mizejewski (2014). The idea that women cannot be funny *because* of their gender (or their biological sex) is only one small step away from more troubling assertions about the capabilities of women, such as their suitability to work in certain industries or to hold positions of power. Fine, whose work seeks to challenge this reductive use of the currently available science on male and female brains, warns:

> The neuroscientific discoveries we read about in magazines, newspaper articles, books and sometimes even journals tell a tale of two different brains – essentially different – that create timeless and immutable psychological differences between the sexes. It's a compelling story that offers a neat, satisfying explanation, and justification, of the gender status-quo. (Fine 2010: xxii)

The science then, packaged as popular rhetoric or sound bites, helps to reinforce stereotypes, without the limitations of any research findings or data being fully explained or made clear to the casual reader. The work of scientists Simon Baron-Cohen (2003) and Louann Brizendine (2007, 2010) provide examples of 'male or female brain' related research that is regularly watered down or rehashed to support outdated gender norms in the popular press. Both Brizendine and Baron-Cohen's focus is on studying the in utero testosterone levels in human foetuses, a crucial factor in the determination of biological sex, resulting in a 'male' or 'female' brain.[2] Much of their work is critiqued by Fine as insufficient, in that the methods used to measure these testosterone levels are unreliable, and also the animal subjects used to prove an equivalence across mammals, such as rats, have numerous other behavioural differences that have not been accounted for in the findings (Fine 2010: 99–118). The reductive uses of information taken from these scientific studies feed into the collective subconscious and become part of our cultural memory, building up unconscious biases and contributing (to use Willan's term) to the 'Google files' in our brains. As Fine highlights:

> The principle behind learning in associative memory is simple: as its name suggests, what is picked up are associations in the environment. Place a woman behind almost every vacuum cleaner being pushed around a carpet and, by Jove, associative memory will pick up this pattern. (2010:5)

The level of exposure we have to these restrictive notions of (binary) gender does not go unnoticed by our unconscious minds; we start to form associations. Put a white man behind every microphone on a comedy club stage and an association of a comedian *as* a white male is formed in our collective memory as a result. These limiting attitudes regarding women's capabilities, or 'natural' qualities, create barriers for women across all industries, not only creative ones. Attitudes about women being overly emotional and naturally submissive (and therefore poor leaders) influence, consciously or unconsciously, decisions that prevent women directing big-budget films, participating in competitive sport, achieving equal representation in boardrooms or gaining political power (see Robins 2017 in relation to Hilary Clinton by way of example). Even though progress is being made in challenging gender stereotypes, and British society is slowly coming around to a more nuanced understanding beyond a gender binary, these attitudes, which now are no longer to be articulated verbally for fear of reproach, are still shockingly prevalent.

In addition to the biological determinism, or neurosexism, of the 'women aren't funny' debates, the inherent linking of comedy to sexual promiscuity and sexualized behaviour has also resulted in the idea that comedy is unsuitable for women. This is arguably the case because comedy is seen to encourage or enable women to publicly display knowledge of sexuality that women should simply not have. When reflecting on her childhood in 1970s America, Regina Barreca comments that to be capable of producing humour was also to impinge on an active masculine behaviour, as '[t]his relationship to joking put girls in a position similar to the sexual dilemma that proposed we be attractive but unavailable, caught between being cheap and being prudish' (2013: 7). She discusses how Western society has historically expected women to placate men by laughing at jokes that victimize them, to avoid male discomfort, equating faking laughter to faking an orgasm. Further to the idea of required responses to humour being linked to social roles, power and superiority, Lisa Merrill, writing in the late 1980s, at roughly the same time as Barreca's first edition, comments that historically mainstream male humour has alienated women by forcing any female audience member to 'devalue her own experience' (1988: 279). It is easy to see in the light of so many criticisms of feminists as devoid of a sense of humour, how historically women perhaps have chosen the easier route, to laugh along, rather than challenge sexist jokes and confirm the 'humourless feminist' stereotype. This is an especially pertinent observation when we consider the way sexual joking or double entendre formed a significant amount of the comedy of the working men's club era in the UK.

In relation to gender expression, space is an important factor. Janet Bing's 2007 research 'Liberated Jokes: Sexual Humor in All-Female Groups' explored the way sexual joking operates differently in women-only spaces. In relation to the prevailing stereotype that women's humour is less sexual than male's humour, she highlights that 'because academic humor theorists have historically been predominantly male, the sexual jokes collected, published and analysed have generally been those told in all-male groups' (Bing 2007: 338). Bing sets about considering the work on sexual humour patterns undertaken by Victor Raskin (1985) whose semantic approach to humour proposes that sexual jokes rely on the incongruous switch from a non-sexual script, or set-up, to a sexual conclusion. Bing concludes that sexual jokes delivered by and for women are more prevalent than at first thought. Liberated women's humour according to Bing's analysis switches between the two scripts in a different way (from sexual to non-sexual) in contrast to mainstream male humour (which changes from non-sexual to sexual).

Although Bing advocates the positive features of sexual humour for and by women, which she identifies as predominantly existing in all-female groups, she is also keenly aware of the potential negative impacts of jokes that rely on sexual knowledge. Bing's work highlights the impact engagement with sexual joking has on women's perception as promiscuous or sexually available. In addressing this difficulty for women in possessing sexual knowledge, or more accurately publicly *demonstrating* possession of sexual knowledge by laughing at a joke that requires this awareness, she comments:

> As in many other situations, women are in a double bind. If they don't tell or laugh at sexual jokes, even those directed against them, they have no sense of humor. If they do, they are available. Most males do not operate under such restrictions. (343)

Women's ownership as well as enjoyment of sexuality has laboured under a variety of taboos or, at the very least, has been less socially acceptable than male equivalents.

Due to the way the debates and stereotypes about women and comedy draw on sexist stereotypes, women's ability, or licence, to be the creators of humour is inextricably linked to feminism and the women's rights movement. In her work on American humour, Rebecca Krefting explores topics related to superiority and social power dynamics in what she terms 'charged humor' (2014). She considers the way certain types of humour that aim 'to represent the under-represented, to empower and affirm marginalized communities and identities' can be a way of 'enacting cultural citizenship' (Krefting 2014: 21) bonding and unifying social groups together through laughter. She contends that by engaging with charged humour American comedians from marginalized positions, for example, along gender, class, racial, ability or LGBTQ+ lines, they make themselves less marketable in comparison to those who do not seek to challenge social hierarchies or drag uncomfortable truths into the light. Katelyn Hale Wood's work on Black feminist comedy in America also comments on how power structures are central to the comedy of Black women, both historically and in the current day. She explores this in relation to the work of comedians Moms Mabley and Mo'Nique. Wood comments that 'as an artist, public intellectual, and cultural worker, the Black feminist comic uses the mic to "talk back" to dominant narratives that caricaturize Black culture and Black women, and to express how systemic racism, sexism, and heterosexism are imposed on the everyday lives of Black women'; this therefore 'demonstrates the joke as a powerful way to resist and insist on the vital presence of Black feminist action and community' (Wood 2018: 324).

In a UK context, in 1994 Frances Gray undertook the task of analysing classical humour theory in relation to feminism in her work *Women and Laughter*. Gray's writing provides a vital touchstone for discussion of comedy and feminism. Her consideration of sitcom and the stand-up comedy scene in both America and Britain demonstrates clearly how the work of early 1990s comedians evidenced a shift in feminist engagement with humour and performed comedy. By discussing the ways in which historically society has disenfranchized women of their humour, shutting them out of the comic arena by dismissing female humour whenever it has been undeniable, Gray manages to open a complex debate around women and laughter. She contends that '[m]ost feminist activity has been centrally concerned with silence, and with its breaking' (1994: 13). It is this breaking of the silence imposed through a suppression of comedy by women that is of concern to this book, as feminists labour under additional stereotypes that relate to humour. Feminists have famously been satirized as humourless and unable to take a joke, as '[t]o object to a specific joke, in a specific context, is to be perceived as an enemy of laughter in general' (Gray 1994: 4).

The potential for humour and performed comedy to have a feminist impact has been explored by Cynthia and Julie Willett in their article with Yael D. Sherman 'The Seriously Erotic Politics of Feminist Laughter' (2012). They highlight how the tools of humour have long been established as a way of maintaining gender divides and patriarchal control and that by 'turning the master's tool (so to speak) against him' (Willett, Willett and Sherman 2012: 222) humour can be reclaimed by women to promote equality and critique injustice. Willett and Willett explore this further in *Uproarious: How Feminists and Other Subversive Comics Speak Truth* (2019) through an extensive critique of how humour operates within the cultural landscape of America in relation to comedians 'othered' due to their gender, race, sexuality and religion.

The character of Millie Tant created for adult comic *Viz* (1979 to present), which was particularly popular in the UK in the 1990s, provides an obvious touchstone for the ridiculing of feminist activism in British cultural traditions. As David Huxley observes when discussing representations of gender and class in *Viz*, Millie's narratives:

> [N]ormally involve arranging protests against non-existent or redundant threats (such as phallic pillar boxes) and misinterpreting innocent remarks. The results [. . .] almost inevitably some type of swift retribution in the form of humiliation or physical violence or both. (Huxley 1998: 287)

Millie is an amalgamation of a variety of feminist stereotypes used to discredit both individual women and the collective action of the women's movement. In Millie's physical depiction (as large, butch and braless), humourless attitude and aggressive behaviour, we can find a perpetuation through comedy of negative assumptions about feminists. The way comedy has been used to ridicule the feminist position as an overreaction maintains stereotypes about women and more specifically feminists not being able to 'take a joke'. This has been integrated into popular culture in the UK for a long time. It is the way in which women's sexual identities and women's abilities as comedians have been combined and silenced, which makes stand-up comedy such a rewarding and important area to consider through a feminist lens.

In the late 1990s, when *Viz* remained popular, British popular culture saw the explosion of 'Cool Britannia', at a time when Britain's cultural exports, such as music and fashion, were seen as the benchmark of cool in the Western world. Significantly, this moment facilitated the rise of the 'ladette'. As Angela Smith observes, 'the term "ladette" is commonly thought to have been coined by the men's magazine *FHM* in 1994 to describe young women who adopt "laddish" behaviour in terms of boisterous assertiveness, heavy drinking session and sexual promiscuity' (2013: 139). During this period it became normalized, fashionable even, for women to replicate behaviour more commonly associated with working-class men. This behaviour was arguably an attempt to demonstrate that equality had been achieved and that women could now do everything to the same standard as their male counterparts. The poster girls of this (overwhelmingly white) cultural movement included many high-profile models, musicians, presenter and DJs of the time, such as Denise Van Outen, Sara Cox, Zoë Ball and Sarah Cawood (Nally and Smith 2013). In general, the 1990s saw a shift away from the collective feminist campaigns of the 1970s and 1980s, such as the Greenham Common protests, to a position within pop culture that focused on women's individual freedoms. As Angela McRobbie comments when writing in the early 2000s:

> Post-feminism positively draws on and invokes feminism as that which can be taken into account, to suggest that equality is achieved, in order to install a whole repertoire of new meanings which emphasise that it is no longer needed, it is a spent force. (McRobbie 2004: 254)

'Ladette' culture typified this, as the individual women enjoyed some of the freedoms afforded them by the progression of women's rights (e.g. body autonomy, control of their own money, property and reproductive choices), turning a blind eye to continuing systemic injustices by maintaining that further fighting for rights was unnecessary. During this period, the focus was very much on the individual choices afforded women, rather than institutional or collective gains as a group (Gill 2007a). Women could now drink men under the table but still found it hard to get a seat at one in boardrooms.

The journalism during this time united both the stereotypes of women being incapable of being funny and the position that somehow comedy was inappropriate for women due to its link with sexual knowledge. With these new social freedoms, women might now drink like men and be promiscuous like men, but could they tell a joke? There was clearly a disparity between allowing women to conduct masculine behaviour (that arguably made them more available as sexual objects for men) and verbalizing challenging attitudes that needed to be silenced. Christopher Hitchens' *Vanity Fair* article 'Why Women Aren't Funny' (2007), set about explaining, or 'mansplaining' (before the term came to prominence via the work of Rebecca Solnit, 2014), the limits of female comic capability. This article provides a high-water mark for the problematic attitudes of the time. In his article, Hitchens argues that men have evolved to be funny in order to attract a sexual partner, whereas women have no need to do anything other than exist in order to be found attractive by men.

The article is drenched in heteronormativity and male privilege and is unrelenting in its homogenizing of 'men' and 'women' into unquestioned and binary positions. Women, explains Hitchens, do not need to be funny to be attractive to men (phrased throughout as their unquestioned life purpose), and so they simply are not funny. Those women who have had to develop a sense of humour have done so as their bodies are fundamentally unattractive to men, and thus they must adapt to find other ways to attract a mate, or they are lesbians, in which case men are irrelevant. Here we can see Hitchens drawing on the evolutionary neurosexist approaches prevalent at the time. This argument is, in many ways, resonant with stereotypes historically levelled at the feminist movement – the rationale seemingly being if you're not physically attractive to men, turn to women's rights, lesbianism or comedy. As Linda Mizejewski comments in the opening of her consideration of women in comedy in America, 'this bias "pretty" versus "funny" is a rough but fairly accurate way to sum up the history of women in comedy' (Mizejewski 2014: 1). Hitchens' article provoked significant feminist retaliation, his intention, as can be surmised by the sheer level of provocation on offer within the article. His writing paved the way for numerous articles that sought to redress the balance by discussing the many funny women he had overlooked. Most significantly, at the time, Alessandra Stanley wrote a direct response to Hitchens in her 2008 *Vanity Fair* article 'Who Says Women Aren't Funny?', in which she interviewed, amongst others, Tina Fey, Amy Poehler and Sarah Silverman to highlight the obvious flaws in his argument. This attitude and public airing of debates around the topic of 'women aren't funny', epitomized by Hitchens was very much at its peak in the late 2000s.

The current discussion around women and comedy follows on from this period of blatant sexism ten or fifteen years ago. Awareness of sexist attitudes and the impact they have on audiences was regularly discussed with my interviewees as part of this research, and the sexism still evident on the circuit will be discussed in more detail in the following chapters. In my discussion with the comedy promoter Hazel O'Keefe, she notes that it was around 2012/13 that she felt the focus of debate shifted away from this essentialist argument:

> [T]he debates have moved. [...] That's [the women aren't funny debate] not a debate, that's not a question anymore. If you ask that question you're quite frankly a knob-head. It's that simple. [*laughs*][...] If you asked, 'are black people funny?' you know it would be completely challenged, so why say that about females? So, I think because the debate has moved on, it has stepped things up a little bit.

We appear to have moved from a cultural moment of 'women aren't funny' to a position where this attitude is seen as manifestly sexist. Rebuttals of this comment are often articulated in a way that equates the assumptions at the heart of the statement to the problematic assumptions of racism. However, although I share O'Keefe's optimism regarding increased awareness about the unacceptable nature of the debate, I would argue that society has moved to an equally challenging position. The first of these new attitudes can be summed up as 'women are funny, but maybe only to other women'. This has then arguably further developed, especially for some who work within the industry and identify as women, to 'women are funny, and we shouldn't talk about this topic anymore'.

Post-Hitchens, when journalists or comedians, or those who operate in both roles such as Bridget Christie, contend that 'The "Are Women Funny?" debate is as dead as Christopher Hitchens' (Christie 2013), what needs to be considered is whether his attitude, displayed so openly in 2007, is still present in the public unconscious. When it is no longer appropriate to express sexist or racist ideas publicly, does this mean that these attitudes have disappeared overnight? Does something have to be spoken about publicly to exist and therefore impact on the opportunities for women? Does less vocal or overt sexism or racism mean that the structures created by those who held these attitudes have been dismantled? The answer to all of these questions is, surely, 'no'. It is, therefore, too soon to celebrate the eradication of the stereotypes, even if the 'debate' as such has abated.

Many of the articles written post-Hitchens sought, admirably, to highlight the work of the many women comics on both sides of the Atlantic who had been very successful within comedy.[3] However, much of the tone of these articles fed into an attitude that women's comedy was a genre in and of itself and that somehow the gender of the performer would directly affect whether something could be found amusing by others. The idea that women create comedy only for other women is deeply frustrating and belittles the wealth of talent present on the current circuit. There is no male equivalent of this attitude as society considers white, cisgendered heterosexual male perspectives to form a basic universally understandable baseline from which everything else conforms or deviates.

The comedians on the current circuit who identify as women perform various genres of comedy such as sketch, absurdist, character, observational, political or musical comedy. As part of this research, I interviewed comedians who perform many different styles of live comedy in an attempt to reflect this range. Often the journalistic (and occasionally academic) writing around women performers throws together a variety of genres of performance, with a total erasure of the differences between live and recorded forms, seemingly asserting that these performers have more in common with each other as women than they do with their contemporaries across the gender spectrum in their particular fields. This research, which has been conducted from an intersectional feminist perspective, in line with how Kimberlé Crenshaw (1991) theorized overlapping aspects of oppression, categorically rejects this idea. It is more problematic to push together and attempt to make a single cohesive narrative for these performers that does not account for other aspects of their identities or the differences between their comic approaches. As an example, the comedy of Janice Connolly, who performs the character Barbara Nice, has more in common with Al Murray's Pub Landlord character or Steve Delaney's Count Arthur Strong, than she does with, say, Kate Smurthwaite, whose comedy is political satire.

In recent years, where women can be funny and achieve success within the industry, a defensive attitude about discussing 'being a woman in comedy' has also developed. Comics are now unwilling to discuss their gender in relation to their material as they feel that by doing so they are perpetuating stereotypes. I can appreciate why this topic might be annoying for comedians to discuss, and an additional burden to carry when people are simply 'humans in comedy' irrespective of their gender (Izade 2016). However, I would argue that this displays a postfeminist attitude about the context. The argument that discussing gender is more problematic than sexism itself, in any industry, must be understood to be deeply flawed (Gill 2014). This approach throws out constructive discussion that could help progress the industry, alongside the more reductive exasperating aspects of it too. Sexism has not gone away, even if 'no one ever says' problematic things out loud (which is patently not the case in some environments). Therefore, advocating that people should not talk about gender is a counter-productive approach. Most of the performers interviewed as part of this research could easily recall sexist interactions with audiences, comedians or promoters that linked with the 'women aren't funny debate'. Even if those exact words were not said aloud, the behaviour women still encounter betrays the long-term influence this has had on the way they are received within the industry. Feminist and anti-racist scholar Sara Ahmed, who writes extensively on the double bind of those who highlight a problem (namely racism, sexism or homophobia) becoming the problem, comments:

> When you name something as sexist or as racist you are making that thing more tangible so that it can be more easily communicated to others. But for those who do not have a sense of the racism or sexism

you are talking about, to bring them up is to bring them into existence. **When you expose a problem you pose a problem.** (2017: 37, original emphasis)

Gender is not a genre. Comedy performed by women is not 'women's comedy', just as music created and performed by women is not 'women's music'. With this contemporary attitude, we seem to have now moved to a position where talking about gendered challenges or sexism is more of a problem, for those working at the top of the comedy industry at least (from those who have successfully navigated themselves through the system), than the sexism itself. This is also an issue that American screen comics have addressed (Evans 2015). That said, the reductive discourse around the industry evidenced in journalism, reviews and think pieces has impacted on my own awareness as a researcher as to why people are sometimes resistant or weary of discussing these topics.[4]

It has been important to set out in detail the stereotypes surrounding women in comedy early on in this book, as they form a significant part of the cultural context of the performers and performances under discussion. Gender stereotypes still matter, even if it is no longer acceptable to articulate them aloud in certain contexts, because they form a key part of the cultural landscape which influences the unconscious biases of audience members. These stereotypes also have the potential to impact on any women-performing comedy. Awareness of stereotypes also influences behaviour, as individual understanding of the self can be impacted upon by what we think others believe about us. This is often referred to as 'stereotype threat' and is the focus of the work of Toni Schmader (2001), Schmader et al. (2008) and Christian Wheeler and Richard Petty (2001). Activating awareness of a stereotype to an individual, before asking them to perform a task related to that stereotype, can impact on how well they perform. For example, Schmader's work focuses on the way women perform worse in mathematics tests if the stereotype that 'women can't do maths' is activated before they take the test. This effect is not specific to gender; similar studies, including those conducted by Claude Steele and Joshua Aronson (1995) and Jean-Claude Croziet and Theresa Claire (1998), have considered the impact racial and class stereotypes have on participants' performance of related tasks. Whilst no studies yet exist that explore stereotype threat for women in a comedy club environment, the concept clearly has a relevance to this context. If a woman comedian goes on stage after a comedian or compère (of any gender) has used gendered stereotypes in their routine, then the stereotypes have been activated. In this circumstance, these comedians then start their set at a disadvantage. Sophie Willan articulated this when she argued that often women in comedy are 'set up to fail'. As Fine argues, 'the boundary of the self-concept is permeable to other people's conceptions of you (or, somewhat more accurately, your perceptions of their perceptions of you)' (2010: 10). So, with an awareness of the stereotypes at play in the comedy club environment in relation to gender, both in the minds of the audience and often other comedians, women performers can feel additional pressure not to conform to these stereotypes or inadvertently confirm anyone's bias. This is not a pressure exerted on male comedians who operate without these additional expectations.

Methodology

The methodology of this book's underlying research was designed to counter a bias within the study of comedy towards content analysis and the overwhelming focus on male comedians. Additionally, the existing literature on comedy (and, more specifically, where it exists, literature on comedy by women) is very America-centric. This may be because the United Kingdom is seriously lagging behind the United States in relation to women at the top of the comedy industry. As this book will explore, Black women especially have felt the need to leave the UK and head to America to stand a chance of breaking through – as considered by Lenny Henry in his discussion with London Hughes and Gina Yashere for his chapter in *Black British Lives Matter: A Clarion Call for Equality*, a book he co-edited with Marcus Ryder in 2021.

The methods I have used to explore women in UK comedy re-centre the discussion on women's experiences to enable opportunities for contextual consideration in relation to industrial, performance and social contexts. This move away from content or textual analysis in isolation is justified because it is only through a thorough analysis of these contexts that a real understanding of the challenges and achievements defining women's experience in the UK comedy industry can be fully understood. As such my work considers the industrial structures and organizations of the UK comedy industry and is neither limited to a consideration of the comedy produced (the texts) nor the individual witness testimonies or audience data (the people), but exists to unify these isolated aspects into a cohesive argument. My research was conducted using an approach inspired by Joanne Gilbert's (2004) performance contexts and content analysis, with engagement with comedy audiences informed by the work of Sharon Lockyer and Lynn Myers (2011). This interdisciplinary approach enables a deeper understanding of current comedy performed by women than could be achieved through content analysis alone.

This book does not attempt to position any of the qualitative information gathered as objective. Rather, it seeks to collate a narrative of various subjective experiences, my own included, without universalizing. The impact that ethnicity, ability and sexuality, amongst other factors, have upon lived experience and levels of marginality has also been considered. In relation to this I have reflected upon the tension between what Letherby describes as '*authorized knowledge*', that which is considered legitimate (or legitimated) by institutions, and '*experiential knowledge*', which is developed through lived experience (2003: 22). This distinction is significant to this book in several ways, first in that comedy as an area of academic study itself is very easy to dismiss due to its subjective nature. The understanding that something is comic is rooted in experiential knowledge – what one person claims to be comedy, another may not experience as such – and thus it has been easy to disparage studies of comedy as being subjective to the point of meaninglessness. Arguably to study stand-up comedy effectively requires an awareness of multiple perspectives and interpretations that inherently resist being turned into authorized knowledge.

In addition to this issue of subjectivity and what can be known about comedy, history has predominantly been filtered through male perspectives and articulated through the words of men, and 'as women were excluded from organized religion, law and politics and from entering educational institutions for many centuries, *authorized knowledge* has historically meant masculinized knowledge' (Letherby 2003: 22). Consequently, even when comedy as a subject of study has gained traction within academia, in order to legitimize the field researchers have often relied upon connections to more authorized approaches or theoretical frameworks, which have overwhelmingly been male. I have lost count of the times people have suggested or assumed that my work must relate in a significant way to Henri Bergson, Sigmund Freud or Pierre Bourdieu. The underlying implication here is (or seems to be) that articulating these connections to well-known male scholarship would legitimize or justify my research's status as an academically suitable topic of study. I reject this idea that situates authorized (predominantly male and white) knowledge as above the experiential. Therefore, in addition to the gendered bias in what is considered legitimate knowledge, the research that underpins this book has been conducted with (or motivated by) an awareness that the historical recording and analysis of artistic endeavour has often omitted, obscured or failed to take seriously the contributions of women. Wherever possible I have sought to engage with the existing work of women and attempted, in line with the work of Sara Ahmed (2013), to practise feminist citation. Ahmed comments that academic citation is 'a rather successful reproductive technology, a way of reproducing the world around certain bodies' (Ahmed 2013). Comedy studies as a discipline has arguably fallen into this trap as part of an attempt to gain traction within the academy. It is my intention to disrupt this by engaging with the work of women scholars in relation to key concepts wherever this is possible. This is to ensure their work is not overlooked in favour of works by male scholars (in many instances about comedy produced solely by men) which have benefitted by proximity to existing understandings of authorized knowledge.

A key part of the underlying research for this book is my time spent as a participant-observer with the UK Women in Comedy Festival in Manchester. In October 2013, I approached the founder and then director of the Festival, Hazel O'Keefe, with the suggestion that I volunteer with them as part of my research. Initially I was invited along to a volunteer meeting in January 2014 (the purpose of which was to reflect on the first iteration of the festival which I engaged with from an audience perspective). In this meeting I explained my area of study to all present and was invited following that to attend all meetings with all other volunteers.[5] O'Keefe, who prior to this interaction I had not met, suggested a few months in that it would be easier if I had a specific title for this project and I was thereafter referred to as the festival's 'Researcher in Residence'. I contributed in numerous ways, from glass collecting and chair stacking at events to designing the festivals logo, posters and brochures (see Figure 1). It was made clear to all that my role was not to study the other volunteers but to engage with the process of the festival and interview performers about their experiences of performing in spaces such as the context provided by the festival.

Participant observation is of course inherently linked to ethnographic practices. When describing feminist ethnography, Beverley Skeggs comments:

> It usually combines certain features in specific ways: fieldwork that will be conducted over a *prolonged period of time*; utilizing different research techniques; conducted *within the settings* of the participants, with an understanding of how the context informs the action; *involving the researcher in participation* and observation. (2001: 426, original emphasis)

Figure 1 Image of UK Women in Comedy Festival Poster from 2016, designed by the author.

I am not claiming that my approach was ethnographic as such, although the term remains contested and porous to new ways of approaching social research. However, it is clear that in relation to engaging with the volunteer group there are aspects of similarity to feminist ethnography as I worked alongside this group of people for a significant time period and participated in their work. As Letherby notes, 'the research process is a complex endeavour, and the researcher's status as "insider" and "outsider" is subject to constant negotiation between all parties' (2003: 133). My focus for this book was on capturing information from people who passed through this context either as a performer or as an audience member. Therefore, my status on the spectrum of participant (volunteer for the festival) and observer (as a researcher) was in constant flux.

A central aspect of the methodology of this research involved interviewing people with varying connections to and experiences of the social, performance and industrial context being considered. I undertook qualitative semi-structured lifeworld interviews with comedians and promoters in order to establish if there were any themes that united individual experiences from the perspective of those working within the field (Brinkmann and Kvale 2015). My interviews were not conducted solely to access 'data' in the form of these descriptions of lived experiences but in order to broadly inform my own awareness and approach when constructing the discursive content of this book. I was not looking to assess the 'intent' of any comedians in terms of their comic material (e.g. what they hoped to achieve, as was the case with Rebecca Krefting's [2014] work), but to understand their experiences of working within the contexts under consideration. Each comedian or promoter included in this aspect of the research was approached as an expert in their field and selected because of their experience within the context under consideration by the research. It was made explicitly clear to my performer and promoter participants that they would not be anonymized as the strength of their input required the reader to comprehend their experience of the industry being considered.

As part of writing this book, I observed 170 separate performances by women comedians, attending the Edinburgh Festival and various comedy environments in Manchester, Sheffield, Salford and London. I was careful to watch comedy in a variety of spaces and venues to account for varied performances and audiences. The majority of my observations occurred in Manchester as part of the Women in Comedy Festival. The purpose of attending so many performances was to ensure my own experience of the wider circuit was current and my wider contextual understanding evolved alongside the project.

With a unique level of access to a new women-only comedy event, the opportunity to ask audiences about their motivations for attending these kinds of performances or spaces provided potential for new information. Having identified a lack of consideration of contexts when exploring the existing literature and finding nothing that looked specifically at women-only spaces, I was aware how much potential this research had to shine light on an unexplored area. A significant amount of audience studies relating to comedy have been conducted, but many consider audiences for different media forms such as screen comedy, for example, the work of Ketan Chitnis et al. (2006), Giselinde Kuipers (2006) and Inger-Lise Kalviknes Bore (2017) or seek to make an argument about the functions or appreciation of comedy such as Dolf Zillmann and Joanne Cantor (1972), Lawrence Mintz (1985) and Robert Stebbings (1993). It was not my intention to attempt to make claims about *all* audiences' understandings or reasons for appreciating comedy performed by women or to try and categorize the purpose or functions of comedy by women.

The purpose of the audience engagement aspect of the research was to collect data so that both the appeal of women-only live comedy for audiences and motivations for attending women-only live comedy events could be considered. The opportunity to capture this data organically arose as a result of my role as participant-observer with the Women in Comedy Festival and was not an originally intended part of my research project. As the festival had no core funding and the continuation of the project from year to year was always (and continues to be) tenuous, I captured this data early on in my research (in 2014). The methodology of this audience research paralleled that of Lockyer and Myers' (2011) study '"It's About Expecting the Unexpected": Live Stand-up Comedy from the Audience's Perspective', which considered the motivations of audiences to attend live comedy. This was to enable comparison of the collected data with their findings relating to the motivations of audiences to attend live comedy in general. My efforts were concerned with capturing the general attitudes of the audience about women comedians and women-only performance spaces in order to inform my understanding of why they attend women-only comedy nights and how they understood and made sense of these spaces. I wanted to establish whether attendance at the event had something to do with audience perceptions about what would be encountered within these gendered spaces and whether audiences felt these encounters would be different to mainstream or mixed-gendered nights. Without an understanding of why audiences attend the events, it is impossible to understand whether these events have the potential to make changes to the industry.

In addition to my engagement with live comedy from the contexts under consideration, my engagement with online social media as part of this project can be seen as an extension of my role as participant-observer with the Women in Comedy Festival. Having joined the social networking platform Twitter in order to access information about women comedians (practical information such as tour dates and venues), I became increasingly aware that the online environment was a fundamental component of the context within which women comics were already working. Therefore, as part of this project, I was able, through the use of social media, to observe the online behaviours of comedians I had seen in a live arena.

My approach to considering the online context for women comics is broadly in line with what Robert Kozinets (2015) describes as netnography. Netnography is a form of online ethnography that interprets interpersonal interactions online using the frameworks associated with the existing ethnographic practice. With digital netnography 'interpretation can be personal, introspective and focused on subjectivities and subjective positions' (Kozinets 2015: 198), and therefore I felt this complemented the feminist research ethos of my work. I engaged and participated in these platforms, focusing mainly on Twitter, as an individual under my own name in line with a digital ethnographic approach. Ahmed et al. also make the astute point that 'It is also important to note that Twitter profiles and tweets are by default set to public visibility and, consequently, Twitter could be considered more of a public space compared to Facebook' (2017: 6). Whilst I make broad observations about comedians' use of both social media platforms the majority of specific examples discussed originate from Twitter. This aspect of my research evolved alongside the project as I followed comedians on the site as and when they came to my attention. I started by following all comedians associated with or performing at the 2014 Women in Comedy Festival and continued to build upon this during the period of the research.

Structure of the book

This book is broken into eight chapters and will progress from an exploration of the gendered histories of UK stand-up comedy through various contexts and examples towards a consideration of the current live context for women performers and what might come next.

The opening chapter explores in detail how stand-up comedy has been gendered through the performance, industrial and cultural contexts of the form's development in the UK. Specific attention will be paid to the period subsequent to the 1980s, where many small steps towards wider inclusion originated. The second chapter will build on this foundation by setting out the key barriers for women comics identified through interviews with performers and promoters across the mid-2010s. The book then moves on to examine how women-only comedy spaces and events can alleviate or challenge some of the barriers women face, both when entering the industry and when trying to create a sustainable career in comedy. Following this, the discussion progresses by considering how online spaces such as social media, and the opportunities to share user-generated content online, provide a way around some of these barriers for marginalized groups. This is not uncomplicated, however, and the chapter will also discuss how online spaces can be seen to reinforce barriers for women comics or indeed create new barriers instead.

After a thorough examination of comedy contexts, the book then considers some of the specific comedic devices associated with comedy performed by women. This will be completed through an exploration of how self-deprecatory joking responds to the current feminist context of empowerment narratives and the way certain body and sex-positive comedians have rejected this mode of address since 2013. The difficulties of finding a wider mediated platform for explicitly feminist comedy, outside of the live environment, are then examined in addition to the backlash feminist comedy has encountered whereby certain male comics have retaliated through a reassertion of essentialist stereotypes and overt sexism in their comic material.

To close the book and bring the discussion right up to date, I will reflect on why sexual misconduct and abuse within the live comedy industry continues to be so prevalent and why the comedy industry's structure and processes create spaces where this behaviour can continue unchecked. I will also look at what is being done in the UK to try and prevent this continuing abuse of women and marginalized groups. To conclude, the final chapter will provide an overall summary and offer suggestions as to what needs to be done to make the UK live industry more accessible and inclusive to all women.

1

How did we get here?

The gendered evolution of the UK comedy circuit

This opening chapter will explore how the UK comedy industry's structures and spaces, as well as the content of comic material, reflects and is inherently linked to gender stereotypes. The central area of focus of this book is the UK comedy industry of the last ten years (2013–23); it is vital, however, to consider how the industry evolved to its current state and what each stage of this evolution meant for inclusion. This chapter will discuss the evolution of stand-up comedy as a form, enduring gender stereotypes that relate to comedy, and the ways in which the current comedy circuit maintains gender divisions. This chapter expands upon existing UK comedy-history research by providing original insight into the role women-only comedy organizations have played in the development of stand-up since the 1990s.

Historically women, whilst being present at all stages, have always been considered a minority group within the British comedy industry, as explored by Frances Gray (1994), Laraine Porter (1998), Stephen Small (1998) and Sam Beale (2020). This is the case even before we consider the ways that age, race or ability intersect with gender to create different and multiple forms of exclusion. Many of the techniques and subversive strategies that women have developed in order to be included within the male-dominated industry have their roots in the historical spaces and approaches to live comedy. The spatial aspects of stand-up comedy's development are important because as post-colonial theorist Edward Saïd notes in his work *Culture and Imperialism* (1993):

Just as none of us are beyond geography, none of us is completely free from the struggle over geography. That struggle is complex and interesting because it is not only about soldiers and cannons but also about ideas, about forms, about images and imaginings. (6)

Saïd is of course highlighting how the project of colonialism not only stole and controlled physical spaces but impacted ideological conceptions that grew from these spaces too. The early struggle to be included within the spaces of comic performance has had a direct impact on the way the industry currently operates, and on the images and imaginings found in comic performance of all kinds. The comedy industry as a whole sector is a structure created almost universally by, and for the benefit of, white cisgender men. In order to clearly explore this point, the following overview of the UK comedy circuit is organized in chronological order and briefly outlines the early stages of the form's development. Following this, a more detailed consideration of the contexts emerging from the 1980s onwards is undertaken, as this was when the overwhelming majority of inclusive industry practices originated. Additionally, recollections of the 1980s form part of the living memory of many performers still working on the comedy circuit today.

The evolution of stand-up comedy

Live comic performance can be considered a sub-category of theatre. We can see this not only in terms of the form's origins but also in terms of the way data about live comedy is collected in the modern environment (often subsumed within a live performance or theatre category). When reflecting on broader theatrical history, it is clear that the traditions and structures of the performance industries have often excluded women, as noted by Michael Shapiro (1996) and Andrew Stott (2005). Any changes to the exclusion of women from public performance, of all kinds, are inextricably linked to, and reflective of, the cultural role of women in wider society at the time. Sam Beale (2020) in her reweaving of the history of music hall, argues that women were much more present as 'serio-comics' on the stage during the 1880s–1920s than is well known or documented and that despite the available numbers demonstrating a somewhat gender-balanced industry during that period, most of the women have been written out of history (2020: 2). When we reflect upon the long-term development of the performing arts, what has been considered 'appropriate' for women to participate in, in terms of onstage performance, has changed slowly but significantly. These changes have been in line with the progression of rights for women and women's inclusion in the labour market outside of the home.[1]

Despite the ancient origins of comic theatrical tradition, the language used to describe the comparatively new form of stand-up comedy performance is startlingly recent. Oliver Double makes the case for the term 'stand-up', in relation to how we would understand the term in the present day, originating in the late 1940s, stating:

> What does become clear is that the term *stand-up* being used to define a style of comic performance seems to be of American origin. After its first occurrence in 1948, it was common in the American trade press throughout the 1950s. By contrast, it did not appear in the British trade press until the following decade. Before this point, what we would call stand-up comedians were known as *front cloth comics*, referring to the staging in variety theatres, in which performers like Max Miller would do their turns in front of the stage cloth hung closest to the front of the stage. (Double 2017: 107, original italics)[2]

The period of comic performance that preceded the time when 'stand-up comedy' became known as a distinct (and named) form differs in the UK from the American context. In America, stand-up comedy grew out of vaudeville, a type of theatre-based entertainment that 'took the form of a mixed bill of acts, which might include singers, dancers, speciality acts and comedy quartets' (Double 2014: 23). Performers who communicated straight to the audience without recourse to a fourth wall were called monologists. Concurrently in the British context the music hall tradition, which marginally pre-dates vaudeville, had provided a space for a similar comic form to evolve.

With the Theatres Act of 1843 comedy in Britain 'began to resemble a distinct field of cultural production' (Friedman 2014: 15). During the music hall period, which followed the Theatres Act, public entertainment moved into dedicated performance venues from taverns. The performers, who were mainly singers and musicians were still 'performing to male-dominated, largely working-class audiences who drank and ate as they watched' (Double 2014: 35). At the start of the twentieth century, the line-ups became shorter and were repeated several times a night, becoming popularly known as variety rather than music hall.

Variety survived as a form of popular entertainment until the late 1950s and contrary to popular depictions of this time, women were included as comedic performers throughout this period, as explored by Huxley and James (2012), Beale (2020) and Tomsett and White (2024). The manner in which comedy developed in these formative settings is significant to consider in terms of the way comedy has been framed as a male-dominated industry. The involvement of women with musicianship and singing has historically been socially acceptable and interlinked with class status. Music provided a way into the music hall spaces of early comic performance enabling women to move from music to comic songs and then increasingly engage in direct address with the audience and comic patter. The work of performer Marie Lloyd (1870–1922) during this period provides an example here. Lloyd is the best-known British woman performer from this era and, as Beale observes, within her comic songs had a distinctive 'conspiratorial tone' which created an 'intimate rapport based on audiences' collusion with her suggestiveness' (2020: 206).

In the early 1960s due to the decline of variety in specialist theatrical and music hall venues, entertainment of all kinds, but most significantly stand-up comedy, moved into the working men's clubs. These clubs were communal spaces designed to facilitate the socializing of working-class men; they became a focal point for industrial communities. This was concurrent to the satire boom in radio, television and theatrical environments, as discussed in the work of Stephen Wagg (2002). The working men's clubs, whilst owned and run locally, were 'governed by the Club and Institute Union' (Friedman 2014: 17). It is of course relevant to note that 'the clubs were set up specifically by and for men' (Gray 1994: 134), or more precisely white, cisgender, heterosexual, able-bodied men. Thus, it is the 1960s and working men's club comedy spaces where a very clear interconnection of class, race and gender in the policing of space comes to the fore. It is during this period of stand-up comedy's evolution that the physical spaces of performances clearly create barriers to inclusion and impact upon, or prevent the development of, the content of stand-up comedy. The space of the working men's club was heavily gendered, and a significant number of clubs would only allow male members and so any woman in the audience had to be the guest of a man. It wasn't until 2007, and long after the heyday of the venues, that women were granted the same rights as men to these spaces (Condron 2007).

It is during the 1960s that we can most clearly see comedians explicitly maintaining hegemonic notions of gender, race and class through the jokes being told on stage through the emergence of 'a new genre of comedy known as traditional or trad stand-up' (Friedman 2014: 17). This traditional stand-up comedy was performed with very little alternative position or opposition, as those who would be able to offer a different perspective or approach were unwelcome in the spaces of performance. As Frances Gray argues when considering the content of comic performance from this time 'The point was not to radically change the audience's perceptions but to get a reflex response' (1994: 135). In order to achieve this, reflexive response originality of material was unimportant. Gray comments that the best way to achieve a laugh 'was to be aggressive' and that 'misogyny, along with racism and homophobia, was an easy way' (1994: 135). It was a complex negotiation process for people who identified as one (or more) of the popular targets for humour, to make a transition from the object or 'butt of the joke' to the role of performer themselves.

From the 1960s variety also became a fixture of broadcast television. This meant that many of the comics from the working men's club circuit managed to reach a broader audience, having their voices heard outside the confines of the clubs too. Several high-profile club comics, including Bernard Manning and Frank Carson, featured on Granada Television's series *The Comedians* (1971–93) in the early 1970s (Double 2014). *The Comedians* was recorded in front of a live audience and enabled a mediated form of live comedy, complete with the live audiences' reactions, to make its way into the homes of the general public. In this way jokes based on gender stereotypes of women became prevalent outside of the live comic environment too (White 2018). As *The Comedians* also acted as a showcase for the performers who took part, it resulted in club comics being integrated more broadly across the television schedules. Notably, this was the case for Russ Abbot, who went on to mainstream success with *The Russ Abbot Show* (1980–96), and Les Dennis with *The Laughter Show* (1984–6), which became the *Les Dennis Laughter Show* (1986–91) after the death of his comedy partner impressionist Dustin Gee. Both Abbot and Dennis became mainstays of the 1980s and 1990s British television.

The televising of stand-up performances in the 1960s and 1970s was complemented by narrative television comedy and the continued rise of the situational comedy or sitcom.[3] These different forms of television comedy worked together to reinforce stereotypes about women, presenting as they did, an unchallenged and united front. Women within comedy, in both live and recorded forms, had little opportunity to *define themselves*. During this period women were represented either as the masculinized, de-sexualized monster or the sex-crazed object within mainstream comedy shows, written overwhelmingly by men. As Laraine Porter observes, 'What unites the narrow spectrum of female types in the traditional modes of popular British comedy of this period is their *a priori* definition by physicality and sexuality' (Porter 1998: 70). Therefore, in the 1960s and 1970s when not being described as wives, mothers-in-law, dumb blondes or spinsters in the punchlines of jokes, or even visually represented by male comics 'dragging up' as old women by stand-up comics on television, women actors could be seen playing these roles themselves in sitcoms, furthering these gender stereotypes. Les Dawson and Roy Barraclough's 'Cissie and Ada' sketches, as performed on the sketch show *Sez Les* (1969–76), provide an example of the upholding of gender stereotypes through comic cross-dressing during this period. The grotesque characters of Cissie and Ada often depicted in the laundrette or around the kitchen table were working-class northern women with a passion for gossip and low-level neighbourhood scandal. The mother-in-law, her-indoors and dumb blonde jokes typified by the likes of Bernard Manning, whose comedy was also notoriously racist and homophobic, have become synonymous with this era of the UK comedy industry and traditional stand-up form.

We can see that physical barriers (the spaces themselves) prevented women from equal access to stand-up comedy, especially during the working men's club era. This is in many respects comparable to the way contemporary comedy spaces are often physically inaccessible to those with disabilities, as thoroughly explored in the work of sociologist Sharon Lockyer (2015).[4] It was in reaction to the traditional stand-up scene's style and content, prevalent during the working men's club era, that the alternative comedy scene was established. It is in the 1980s that we start to see greater efforts to include women in live comedy.

Alternative comedy and the 1980s

In 1979, in the wake of America (where the LA Comedy Store opened in 1972), Britain finally got its first dedicated comedy club in the form of The Comedy Store in Dean Street, Soho, London. The shift between traditional stand-up taking place in working men's clubs to comedy-specific venues, as part of the alternative movement across the 1980s, cannot be underestimated in terms of inclusion, despite being a far from perfect solution to gendered and racial inequalities. From the start, the politics of the alternative comedy scene was distinctly anti-establishment, defining itself in opposition to the kind of 'trad' comedy produced by the club comics. Arriving at a time of national tension, when Britain was governed by the divisive Thatcher-led Conservative government (Vinen 2013), the alternative comedy scene rebelled against the sexist, racist and homophobic aspects of the working men's club era. The comedy club became a space to blow off steam and rebel against the Tory government, a space to be critical and political, to be entertained but also challenged, rather than only to drown one's sorrows or socialize. The physical and ideological barriers to women's participation in the traditional spaces meant that the opportunity to perform in a more inclusive environment, such as The Comedy Store, literally and metaphorically opened many doors for women.

It was at this stage of the development of stand-up comedy in the UK that a broader range of voices started to be more formally included and encouraged. Comedians who were central to the comedy scene of this period include Dawn French and Jennifer Saunders, Rik Mayall, Adrian Edmonson, Ben Elton, Alexei Sayle and Jo Brand (who initially performed under the name 'The Seamonster'). As Sam Friedman notes, they offered much more variation in performance style and content than had been the case with traditional stand-up. Despite this variation the comics 'were united by an experimental approach to comedy that self-consciously attempted to push beyond the "low brow" styles that had previously dominated the field' (Friedman 2014: 19). It is at this stage in British comedy history that (white) women's voices start to be included in a more meaningful way, as they are finally able to get onto stage more easily, providing women an opportunity for self-definition through comedy. Crucially, this did not, however, result in equal remuneration for work, as Dawn French (2008) and Jennifer Saunders (2013) explore in their autobiographies. Both comedians note how they were paid approximately half of what their male Comic Strip colleagues took home, highlighting that simply adding women into a flawed and unequal system does not magically fix underlying structural inequalities.

It is worth considering here the Soho context of The Comedy Store. When looking back on this era academic discourse has tended to focus on the increased inclusion of women during this period, which is understandable as this moment was incredibly important in that regard. However, the opening of The Comedy Store in Soho, a district of London synonymous with sex work, porn theatres and gentlemen's clubs should not be overlooked (Mort 2007). Whilst women were included on stage at The Comedy Store from the very start, when leaving the club they were still presented with a very stereotypical and sexualized version of women. Soho at this time would not have been a gender-neutral space – if it is possible for any city space to be gender neutral, or indeed work beyond the binary, as explored in the work of Petra Doan (2010). The industry Soho has become known for pre-gentrification and, booming in the 1980s, was reliant upon the marketization and objectification of women's bodies. Having worked (in the film education sector) in Soho myself during the late 2000s, I find this specific geographic context highly relevant to this period in UK comedy history. Stepping out of the confines of my office onto Berwick Street, a few yards away from the famous (now former) Raymond's Revue Bar, the environment I encountered provided a constant reminder about the way society objectifies and commodifies women's bodies. Thus, over twenty years earlier than my own experiences of Soho, whilst the space of comic performance itself became more inclusive and welcoming, the wider geographic context of that space was still starkly gendered and sexualized.

When comedy was performed in working men's clubs, women were rarely onstage and, if they did perform, were mostly there to be objectified sexually. This is most obviously the case with stripping which was somewhat commonplace in this context. This objectification may well have started to make its way off the stage during the alternative comedy movement of the 1980s, but society still saw women as sexual commodities. Perhaps the radical new comedy of the alternative scene, seeking a non-mainstream environment from which to challenge norms, could only initially exist in this marginalized space of sex work?

Isolated within a very specific part of London, the opportunities for this new comedy to infiltrate industrial regions of the UK, where many of the working men's clubs existed, were limited.

The 1990s and comedy as the new rock and roll

Britain in the 1990s saw comedy become known as the 'new rock and roll' with the rise of a new group of superstar comedians. Wider fan bases, facilitated by television and radio, meant that comedy tours moved up from small venues and regional theatres to arenas. Those comics who had found success in broadcast mediums now toured with their material, normally incorporating both a live rendition of televised material to keep the fans happy, with small sections of new material. These tours started to take place in larger and larger venues, eventually reaching sports stadiums and arenas capable of seating thousands. This was a new, and in every respect much bigger, experience for comedy audiences. In 1993, the famously fractious comic double act of David Baddiel and Rob Newman sold out the 12,000-seat Wembley stadium with their tour, becoming the first act to ever do so (Thompson 2004: 73–4). For those who could not attend these huge live shows, recordings were made and sold on VHS, and latterly DVD, so that performances could be kept and enjoyed for future. This moved the commodification of comedy from being objectified as vinyl records and audio recordings to a much more visual artefact.

Arena comedy arrived concurrently to what would come to be known as the 'Cool Britannia' period of the mid-1990s. This cultural moment was cemented by a change in British government, from the 'grey man' (John Major) led Conservatives to New Labour in 1997. The optimism of a cool, British, international-facing future was epitomized by the young Tony Blair, who saw, and exploited, the value of Britain's cultural industries in shaping awareness of the UK's identity on the international stage. It was also a time when the increasing inclusion of women in politics was part of mainstream discourse. The Labour majority government was formed with just over 100 female MPs, and this was seen as a victory for women's inclusion in society – even though the press at the time undermined this by regularly referring to the elected MPs as 'Blair's Babes' (Harman 2017).

The concept of comedy as the new rock and roll is actually a very apt way to capture this moment in comedy history, as many of the gendered assumptions about popular music easily translate to comedy. The term originated in the late 1980s when comedian and writer Dave Cohen included the phrase within a review, citing a throwaway comment made by a comedian on stage. This phrase was subsequently picked up by Janet Street Porter, who used it on television, popularizing the expression (Cohen 2013). The exceptionalism used when discussing women in bands, especially women musicians, is comparable to the way women in comedy are discussed. This is possibly due to the way both performing music and comedy are embodied art forms, where the physical person who holds the creative talent or skill performs in front of the audience (unlike say, fine art or sculpture). This means that the gender of the performer is often noted and assessed in some way as part of their skills.

In the early 1990s, the UK's Black comedy circuit also started to emerge. Black comedians who were excluded from mainstream comedy nights and the increased profile of the comedy industry (explicitly, or through structurally racist booking practices, implicitly) started creating their own opportunities and organizing tours around British cities such as London, Birmingham and Leicester (Small 1998). These nights provided the opportunity to produce comic material that focused on a more uniquely Black British experience. Stephen Small notes that central to this development of a British Black comedy scene was the desire to work outside of mainstream spaces, and as part of his interviews found that 'several comics said they did not want to change their comedy, or to dilute it, in order to appeal to non-black audiences' (Small, 1998: 238). Subsequent to Small's writing, the Black comedy scene continued to boom across the 2000s in large theatre venues across the country and provided a platform for many Black British comics, including Eddie Nester, John Simmit, Felix Dexter, Angie Le Mar and Llewella Gideon, as explored in current comedian Mo Gilligan's documentary *Black, British and Funny* (Channel 4, 2020). Despite these comics attaining undeniable success in the context of this circuit, they were still not afforded the same opportunities as their white peers in mainstream comedy spaces.

Alongside the developments of the live comedy scene and the rise of arena comedy, British television comedy, especially that produced by the BBC and Channel 4 during this era, was booming. Many comedians enjoyed a live presence on the circuit as well as television work on sketch and panel shows. In terms of women's presence on screen during this boom in television comedy, Channel 4 produced *Smack the Pony* (1999–2003), written by and starring Doon Mackichan, Sally Phillips and Fiona Allen. The significance of *Smack the Pony*, in terms of the queering of gender roles, has been explored extensively in the work of Rosie White (2018). *Spaced* (1998–2000), a sitcom that has now achieved cult status, was co-written by Simon Pegg and Jessica Hynes and offered women a new comic role model in the form of the awkward Daisy Steiner, defying the sexual stereotypes of previous eras of sitcom outlined by Porter (1998). In 1998 a significant impact was made in terms of racial diversity in televised comedy, with the South Asian British sketch show *Goodness Gracious Me* (1998–2001) created by Sanjeev Bhaskar, Meera Syal and Anil Gupta and broadcast by BBC2 following a successful run on BBC Radio 4. Ben Thompson's *Sunshine on Putty: The Golden Age of British Comedy from Vic Reeves to the Office* (2004) includes a humorous 'chronological timeline' of this period which provides an insight into just how male (and white) UK comedy was at the time. Within the book, which is just over 450 pages, there are only 25 women comedians and performers listed in the index, only one referencing a woman of colour, Meera Syal. Thus, whilst we can see the significance of this period in broadening the range of comedy available on UK television, things were still very far from equal.

This, notably minimal, inclusion of women and minority perspectives from mainstream comedy on television did not go unnoticed and, around this time, the UK saw the establishment of two separate high-profile organizations created to address gender inequality on the live circuit. Both Funny Women and Laughing Cows were established to champion parity for women in live comedy. Interventions into the live circuit during this period were seen as a way to make changes higher up in the industry. As is the case for a significant amount of women's creative labour, this particular aspect of comedy history is not well documented.[5]

Laughing Cows Comedy was founded by promoter Hazel O'Keefe, who started to produce all-women line-ups in 1998. When discussing how the organization came into being and the attitudes on the circuit at the time, O'Keefe said that she

> started asking questions of certain promoters, you know 'Why are you not booking this person, why are you not doing that? Why do you only at the most ever have one female on the line-up?' and it was just a common response, and this was back in 1998, that promoters would not take the risk of booking more than one female. As a feminist, [. . .] running a lesbian bar I was just thinking, 'this is ridiculous'. For me, for my market an all-female line-up would work perfectly. So yeah that's how Laughing Cows started quite simply [. . .] at The Vesper Lounge in November 1998.

The motivation for the establishment of Laughing Cows was a reaction to the idea that having more than one woman on a bill would be a risk. Additionally, O'Keefe had identified a ready-made and under-served audience for comedy performed by women in the context of a lesbian environment. Much of the male-dominated comedy, which, as a hangover from the origins of stand-up, still contained casual homophobia and fixed ideas of gender roles, would not have been appropriate for that setting and so O'Keefe sought to find acts that were a better fit for her audiences.

At around the same time, Lynne Parker, director of the organization Funny Women, had started to think about comedy in a similar way. Funny Women is an organization that runs competitions and live events and provides training to up-and-coming women comedians. Parker had been working in public relations for a group trying to establish a new comedy club in central London. She reflects on Funny Women's origin story as follows:

> Towards the end of the 1990s, so about '97, '98, I was working for a comedy promoter who was launching a club in London and they were a very well-known brand from America called The Improv. [. . .] So, I was spending two or three nights a week in a comedy club environment, which I was fairly familiar with [. . .] it was all going really well and we talked about the fact that they never booked any women, and I was told by the other partner that was because there weren't any. And I thought well this is a bit odd because there are women out there doing stand up, I know there are. I think it was also at the time [. . .] and people like Jo Brand and Jenny Eclair were all probably in the middle of bringing up their kids and there was a wee bit of a lull. I think it's true to say that there weren't perhaps as a many visible women gigging on the circuit. And I just said I think it'd be really good for the club if we could do something to promote women, hence Funny Women was born effectively. No sooner had we got the whole idea up and running, and we were going to have a charity night, and were looking at some of the other clients that I had in the fashion industry and that to sponsor it, the partner, the guy who came over from LA, fell out with the guy here and he hightailed it back to America never to be seen again. [. . .] The one thing I had that I felt really passionate about was this idea of doing something under the banner of Funny Women, so I decided I would do it myself. So, I [. . .] protected it as much as I could and then spent two years nearly to get the whole thing off the ground. Its first manifestation was a big charity comedy night in September 2002.

It is clear that with Funny Women the opportunity to go ahead with a women-only line-up needed more planning and consideration, as they did not have a specific venue in which they could experiment. In 2003, having successfully run one charity night, Funny Women also started to run the Funny Women Awards, an annual event (still running today), that seeks to highlight and promote the work of stand-up comedians who identify as women. The awards started out with a single category and have now developed into an annual event that runs heats across the country (and during the pandemic of 2020/21 internationally online) and rewards writing, performing and film-making talent. Former winners of the Funny Women Awards include Zoe Lyons (2004), Debra Jane Appleby (2005), Andi Osho (2007), Katherine Ryan (2008), Jayde Adams (2014), Desiree Burch (2015) and Thanyia Moore (2017). The runners-up list read like a *Who's Who* of the current comedy circuit and includes amongst many others Bridget Christie, Susan Calman, Diane Morgan, Sara Pascoe, Sindhu Vee and Sofie Hagen. What is evident when looking at this list is the huge variety of both comic approaches and content.

In this way the late 1990s was incredibly significant in terms of the evolution of comedy in the UK, in that we see at this point significant proactive attempts to address the lack of representation for women in comedy, through the establishment of women-only line-ups. Women audiences were now seen as an untapped demographic, as observed by Elaine Aston and Geraldine Harris (2015). These interventions in the live comedy circuit by and for women occurred in the context of the first few female-led screen comedies being televised, such as the aforementioned *Smack the Pony*. Brett Mills, writing in 2009, comments, 'The dominance of masculine comedy can be seen by the tiny proportion of sitcoms which have women as the leading roles, and a minority of sitcom writers, producers and performers are female' (Mills 2009: 21). The slow inclusion of women into television comedy during this period, in a way that was not as reductive as in previous eras, arguably drew attention to the lack of exposure for women on the live circuit, provoking women like O'Keefe and Parker into action.

2000s' comedy scene

Throughout the 1990s and early 2000s, dedicated comedy venues had sprung up across the UK. The Comedy Store opened a new venue in Manchester in 2000 and Jongleurs, which initially started out in London in 1993, expanded rapidly to have eight venues across the country by the millennium. After Jongleurs was bought out in 2000 by the Regent's Inn organization, which then collapsed, it underwent a complex series of buyouts and rebranding. Finally, the company went into administration in 2017. The Glee Club, established in Birmingham in 1994, whilst notably less mainstream than other chains, now also runs venues in Oxford, Cardiff and Nottingham.

It was this expansion of big comedy brands and their refocus on the commercial nature of the form that resulted in the dedicated venues, which were so vital in the establishment of the alternative comedy scene, slowly *becoming* the mainstream. The targeting of 'stag and hen' parties, the group discounts and drink offers meant that, again, the balance had shifted from a concentration on the performance occurring on stage, back to a 'good night out' facilitated by alcohol. In many ways this refocus on comedy as a backdrop to socializing is reminiscent of the working men's club era.

Alongside the comedy clubs' subsummation into a populist mainstream in the mid-2000s, a 'new alternative', or 'DIY' comedy, started to emerge. Double characterizes DIY comedy as 'loose, quirky, folksy, homemade, autobiographical, politically liberal and full of geeky pop culture references' (2014: 59). The DIY or new alternative approach is best seen in the comedy of Pappy's Fun Club, Josie Long, Robin Ince, David O'Doherty and more recently comics such as Mae Martin, Ivo Graham, Alison Spittle, Claudia O'Doherty, Simon Amstell and James Acaster.

Double argues that these acts were inspired by comedians such as Stewart Lee and Daniel Kitson, both of whom eschewed the mainstream circuit and fostered a cult audience by repeatedly touring live material to develop more personalized relationships with audiences (Double 2014: 58). Lee recalls the mood of the early to mid-2000s in his book *How I Escaped My Certain Fate: The Life and Deaths of a Stand-up Comedian* as follows:

> If the phrase hadn't lost its meaning once already, you could almost say we were witnessing the birth of a new Alternative Comedy, in opposition to the crowd-pleasing composite that the old Alternative Comedy had become. [. . .] [T]he ubiquity of these big chains meant that in every city that had a Franchised Laff Retail Outlet™, at least one alternative venue seemed to be thriving in opposition to it, such as XS Malarkey in Manchester, The Glee Club in Birmingham, or The Comedy Box in Bristol, none of which had much crossover with the franchises in terms of acts or audiences. (Lee 2010: 36)

It is clear that during the 2000s a more obvious division was emerging on the live circuit, a split that is still evident in the contemporary industry (Quirk 2018). For an audience member for comedy in Manchester in the present context, there is a distinct difference between certain venues. Comedy at The Comedy Store or The Frog and Bucket (a mid-sized comedy club) on Thursday, Friday or Saturday nights is very commercially focused and frequented by stag and hen parties. XS Malarkey, which runs on Tuesday nights (in, until recently The Bread Shed pub's back room), or the irregular Group Therapy nights at the Gorilla club strike a more alternative tone. The latter nights both define themselves in opposition to the big clubs, cultivate a personal relationship with their audiences through mailing lists and social media and intentionally programme a more alternative selection of comedians than the more mainstream circuit.

In the 2000s, comedy nights in pubs were nothing new. However, the way that the comedy clubs were marketing themselves to appeal to a wide commercial audience meant that often these smaller nights became the only place for voices that did not chime with the commercial ethos that the clubs now fostered. The more challenging, political or niche comedy found its way into smaller nights and regional arts centres rather than existing comedy club venues, and this is a division still in evidence on the UK circuit now (Quirk 2018). It is important to note that even when an individual comic, comedy club or comedy night defines in opposition to the mainstream, economic viability remains essential. As Friedman comments regarding the current circuit:

> While the field retains a strong 'alternative' arm devoted to more autonomous production, there is no public funding for comedy and even those operating in the restricted domain must generate enough money to earn a living. Thus in comedy, all actors straddle the divide between culture and economy in some way. (2014: 146)

The current context has now developed beyond this mid-2000s split between mainstream and new alternative. The arrival of more digital, mediated options for engaging with and developing an audience has provided additional spaces for non-mainstream voices to be heard. The impact that the internet and streaming services have had on the current circuit is significant in that it provides access to an audience irrespective of geography or the need to engage with a physical performance context. It has also enabled more of a crossover directly between DIY or 'new alternative' live comedy to screen comedy via streaming services. This has enabled those who wish to adopt a more alternative approach or tone to eschew the big comedy clubs or mainstream spaces and present their work online through recordings for online services or by posting their own user-generated content (UGC) on sites such as YouTube and Vimeo. Comedian James Acaster provides a relevant example of someone who has attained a good level of success through numerous nominations for the Edinburgh Festival Comedy Awards and has then developed an international audience and profile through recording his alternative comedy shows for Netflix.

It is clear from this brief history of British comedy that there has been inclusion of some women (almost universally white women) at all points, and their achievements cannot be forgotten or dismissed. However, whilst the current industry includes a much more diverse range of comics than ever before, white cisgender male comics have been the norm for a significant part of the industry's history and continue to dominate, especially in the commercial circuit.

Reflecting on the evolution of the stand-up comedy industry, the exclusion of women, as well as people of colour, LGBTQ+ performers and those with differing abilities, from participating in earlier iterations of the form has created a gap which is now slowly being addressed. This gap is not specific to comedy but is potentially made more acute for stand-up due to the way the form itself interacts with other stereotypes about women. Comedy as an *industry* labours under the weight of these stereotypes, but so too does the very *comedic material* being produced by comedians. What is particularly notable about the previous exclusion of women from comedy (in both live and broadcast environments) is that this lack of exposure in performed comedy is central to reinforcing the wider social stereotype that impacts on all women. When discussing the way women were historically excluded from education, Cordelia Fine comments that '[d]espite such – to our modern eyes – obvious impediments to women's intellectual development, they were widely assumed to be naturally inferior by many' (Fine 2010: xxii). This is comparable to the way women within the comedy industry are often viewed in a contemporary context. In the past there have been fewer women than men working as comics and this is often produced as *evidence* that women are not funny (or are less funny than men). This line of argument completely eradicates the fact that women were excluded from participation in this form, and in many cases from the physical spaces of performance, for the majority of stand-up comedy's development.

It is clear, through observation of the current circuit, reviewing relevant literature regarding the UK comedy industry and a consideration of the wider political climate in relation to gender, that the *spaces* of comic performance influenced, or arguably dictated, the *content* of material of stand-up comedy. This is particularly noticeable from the mid-1950s onwards when comedy developed in the spaces of working men's clubs. The exclusion (explicit and implicit) of certain groups from performing in these spaces not only prevented women and minority groups from pursuing a career as comedians but also inhibited the kind of material developed during this period. Put simply, the 'where' of stand-up comedy influenced 'who' became performers and thus the content of 'what' was covered. Thus, this period of live comedy played a significant role in reinforcing the wider notion that comedy is fundamentally a male pursuit. The proliferation of humour within these spaces that targeted women as the butt of the jokes, or those contingent on gender stereotypes, was no doubt influenced by the male dominance of the performance and industrial context of the time. Whilst there can be no doubt that gendered issues on the American circuit exist, as recently explored in the work of Stephen Olbrys Gencarella (2017), the explicit 'maleness' of the UK's formative comic spaces is distinct to Britain.

Jokes from the UK's 'traditional' stand-up era were developed for performance within male-dominated spaces which then, through a wider exposure on television, went on to normalize this male dominance. Stand-up comedy therefore *both contributed to and was influenced by* gender stereotypes from the wider social context during the development of 'traditional' approaches. Following on from these formative spaces, stand-up comedy continues to be uniquely susceptible to gender stereotypes due to the way comic material relies on shared cultural knowledge, to ensure audiences can access humour. This is exacerbated as comic performance also provides an arena for taboos to be explored and thus tends to engage with more controversial topics – topics that cannot be accommodated as easily in other non-comic forms.

2

Where are we now?

Challenges today for women comics

In order to consider the current barriers facing women comics on the UK circuit, beyond the gendered stereotypes that have developed alongside the form, this chapter will start by considering the role of gatekeepers in deciding the fate of many new performers, and how the processes enacted still disadvantages women.

Sam Friedman's 2014 book *Comedy and Distinction: The Cultural Currency of a 'Good' Sense of Humour* explored the role of comedy scouts, critics and producers in the maintaining of current comedy industry's practices. His work focused on the annual Edinburgh Fringe Festival and how this event provides an entry point to wider comic success for performers. Whilst other entry points are emerging, for example, by capitalizing on social media success, a significance is still placed on a successful Edinburgh run of shows, and participation in the festival still attracts industry attention. Irrespective of the prestige of winning an award at Edinburgh, it is often the very basic practicalities of being seen in action by scouts and critics that is a key motivator to participate. The rationale to scout for talent at the festival is clear: Why try and make it along to regional venues and ad hoc performances to source new talent when you could spend several weeks in Edinburgh and have the talent come to you? There are obviously several significant issues related to inclusion that this way of thinking overlooks. For example, the sheer cost of participation in the festival (accommodation, potential room hire, subsistence, promotional costs etc.) immediately removes from the pool of talent under review any comic without the economic means to support themselves. This is a notable contributory factor to some of the existing and long-standing class barriers to getting in and getting on in UK comedy.

Friedman's critical approach to the Edinburgh Fringe analysed who is involved in deciding what 'good' comedy looks like and what role these gatekeepers and tastemakers play in the success of comedians attempting to attain mainstream success. In addition to the patent class barriers, I'd argue that his findings indicate specific challenges for women comedians on the current circuit too.

Drawing on the work of Pierre Bourdieu (1993), Friedman considers the way comedy can operate with varying degrees of cultural capital. His research found that critics of comedy have become increasingly important, concluding:

> Despite previous research indicating that comedy critics possess little cultural influence, the results [. . .] demonstrate that the legitimacy of such influencers has grown considerably in recent years. (Friedman 2014: 141)

The British press, as part of arts coverage, still produce reviews of comedy and often pull together annual articles about 'hot picks' for the Fringe. Alongside this there are organizations with online platforms that operate year-round such as Chortle and The British Comedy Guide.[1] These sites are dedicated specifically to comedy and host reviews alongside interviews, articles and tour announcements. They have become a well-known source of information for the comedy-going public. During the Edinburgh Festival, numerous other reviewing sites become live and contribute to the reviews of performing acts, including, significantly, *Fest* magazine, which was established in 2002 (where Friedman, alongside his work as an academic, has acted as publisher).

Friedman found, in interpreting his research findings collected via a method of surveys and follow-up interviews, that despite the increased legitimacy of comedy critics, it was impossible to link the reading of reviews to behaviour:

While these findings certainly indicate that comedy criticism is important to consumers, it doesn't explain the influence of criticism on audience judgement. It couldn't elucidate the impact of comedy reviews. (2014: 130)

Friedman discovered that audiences may seek out reviews and generally find the information helpful, but they may not act on that information. This is possibly due to the way comedy is such a subjective art form and many of the most critically and commercially successful comics may well not appeal to certain senses of humour.

In addition to his consideration of the role of critics, Friedman shadowed comedy scouts, who he refers to as 'hidden tastemakers' during the 2012 Edinburgh Festival. This is a particularly significant aspect of his work, in that he was investigating the way the comedy industry decides who breaks through to wider audiences via mediatized forms. Friedman attended performances with comedy scouts to observe their behaviour, before subsequently conducting interviews about their role in finding the next breakthrough acts. He identified that during the month of August at the Edinburgh Festival many people, who are occupied in other professions for the rest of the year, perform this temporary function for venues, broadcasters and agents.

Whilst Friedman's gatekeeper participants were gender balanced, strikingly they all had similar backgrounds and experiences:

In line with cultural intermediaries in other fields (Negus, 1999; Kuipers, 2012), eight of my nine respondents were from privileged backgrounds, with at least one parent who was, or had been, in a professional or managerial employment. All nine scouts were also graduates, with six holding humanities degrees in aesthetic subjects such as English literature, theatre studies, history of art and film studies. And eight of the nine lived in London. (2014: 148)

It is unsurprising to find that there is a certain type of person afforded this role as a tastemaker or a 'homogenous class habitus of comedy scouts' (Friedman 2014: 160). Simply having more women comedy scouts will not solve the issue of why women do not break through into the mainstream. Women are just as capable of upholding a patriarchal system due to internalized gender bias or misogyny, and so simply swapping men with women still potentially replicates racial and class biases. This is especially likely if *all* other identity traits, other than gender, remain the same. The ethnicity of the particular scouts Friedman followed is not explicitly mentioned in the text of the research, but it is currently evident (and as would have been the case when Friedman was writing) that in Britain, Black and minority ethnic (BME) people disproportionately exist in lower socio-economic categories that would be defined as working class, as outlined in the Runnymede Trust's *Minority Report: Race and Class in Post-Brexit Britain* (Khan and Shaheen 2017). Those identifying as Black or from an ethnic minority in the UK (who may actually be from an ethnic majority in a global sense) are less likely to be 'privileged' in the way Friedman describes his cohort of participating scouts, as a result of structural barriers. This homogenous pool of scouts is an impediment to inclusion as Friedman, drawing on the work of Giselinde Kuipers (2012), identified that much of the brokering selections were 'based on "imagined audiences", on "gut" instinct about the fit between types of culture and types of audiences (Kuipers, 2012)' (Friedman 2014: 146). Therefore, we can see a very clear link between the identities of those performing this scouting function and the maintaining of ideas about what audiences want to see.

Without any concrete understanding about audience tastes, a key question is whose gut instinct decides which women comedians make it? Friedman also identifies that comedy scouts relied heavily on informal networks and the judgements of people they know and trust to advise them. We can see that when these informal networks are at play, across many art forms, class and gender privilege is involved and maintains a barrier to those attempting to engage (Brook, O'Brien and Taylor 2018).

Notably scouts working in the sub-field of mass comedy (as opposed to those scouting specifically for an alternative comedy setting)

[W]ere guided not by aesthetic preferences but by an instrumental occupational imperative to reduce economic uncertainty. This compelled them towards the safe and inoffensive, the 'T-shirt comic', who fits into existing markets or repeats a successful formula. (Friedman 2014: 159)

Friedman defines the T-Shirt comic as one that fits the description of a 'young, white, attractive male' (2014: 152), and the comedy industry continues to overwhelmingly reflect this (even now nearly ten years after his writing) both in the live and broadcast environments.

Where talent scouts might be considered a hidden part of the industrial functions of the festival, critics and reviewers, who publicly articulate an opinion on the comedy they observe, are conversely often starkly visible as a mechanism of taste-making. As part of my discussions with my interviewees, the subject of reviews and the impact they can have on performers were considered. Allyson June Smith, a Canadian comedian who has been performing since 2000 and living and working in the UK since 2011, discussed with me how performing as a 'version of herself' on stage, as opposed to in role, impacts on the way reviews are received. She recalled the following example in relation to her own work:

> Stand-up is really personal, again if it's done from that traditional, not character place. Because it is you. It is you. It wasn't until I actually came to the UK that I actually had a review done on me because in Canada, we have no celebrity system [. . .]. Nobody really reviews comics [. . .] it's not like here. Where you go to Edinburgh and everyone gives you reviews. And I received like my very first review here and it was awful. It was very nasty [. . .] he was not a fan of mine, we'll say that. [. . .] So it can be personal. [. . .] I only read it once [. . .] because I was just like there's no point dwelling in the negativity. But the vibe generally was just [. . .] [they] thought I was a shrill, brash North American woman, who was crude. [. . .] A lot of it came down to I think this person decided they didn't like the type of comic that I was. And I feel had a pretty early decision about how they were going to watch the actual jokes and the material.

Reviews can very easily be interpreted as a personal attack, especially for comedy performed without the 'buffer' of a character, as the comic persona is based on the identity of the performer. We can see in this particular review, which Smith did not identify directly but was very easy to locate online, that Steve Bennett from Chortle spends much of the word count (40 per cent) being critical of Smith (Bennett 2013). He also uses the term 'spouting' which arguably plays into the stereotype of women being incessant talkers. Where he describes Smith's material as unimaginative and bland, he then goes on to describe her male colleague's observational material as 'none of the material is classic, but it's funny enough'. This reads very much like the bar is lower for the male comic than Smith.

Recently there has been increased pressure from feminist performers and campaigners on reviewers across all art forms to consider their tone when reviewing women. Where Smith understandably takes issue with the gendered language on display in her review related to her tone/personality, there have been several high-profile instances of the reviewing of women's bodies rather than their performances which have been widely reported. Actor Nicola Coughlan's fight back against *The British Theatre Guide*, who referred to her as 'an overweight little girl' as part of a review of the Donmar Warehouse's *The Prime of Miss Jean Brodie*, provides an example here (Siddique 2018).

Sophie Willan recalled a similar experience in relation to reviews she received for her first solo show, *Novice Detective*, which she performed at the Edinburgh Festival in 2014:

> I don't know if I'm just being 'oh it's sexist' or whatever but I definitely felt as a female comic, going up to Edinburgh saying this is a comedy show, doesn't matter that audiences have booked it out, I sell it out or that I'm getting rounds of applause throughout, the critics were not up for me. [. . .] I mean one man started by saying 'she's a lot smarter than she first appears', I don't actually know what that means, how do I first appear? Is it the Bolton accent? What is it that first appears stupid to you? Because there's nothing in the show where I say 'oh I'm a bit daft' or I don't play a character who's ditsy or anything, so it was interesting.

Here Willan identified that one of her reviews that year included a comment that referenced class and possibly gender-based assumptions about her. Irrespective of the initial mixed reviews of her early work she has gone on to great success. Willan was nominated in 2017 for the Edinburgh Festival Best Show Award, for her solo show *Branded*, and more recently has won a British Academy of Film and Television Award (BAFTA) for screenwriting the pilot of her autobiographical BBC sitcom *Alma's Not Normal* in 2021 and another BAFTA for Best Female Performance in a Comedy Programme in 2022 for her performance in the show. What is evident through the interviews collected as part of my research is that performers bump up against these stereotypes about women and comedy in the reviews of their work fairly frequently and often very early on in their careers.

Friedman's findings make it apparent that gatekeepers play a significant role in maintaining the current comedy industry and the white male dominance within it. This has not gone unnoticed by large broadcasters who have in recent years attempted to address their lack of diversity in several ways. I will focus here on the BBC as the UK's public broadcaster and the biggest commissioner of radio and television comedy in the UK. The BBC's announcements and public agendas that started to materialize around 2014 relating to diversifying TV comedy form a key part of the contemporary comedy context in the UK. It was with the following BBC public agendas and initiatives in mind that I spoke to those interviewed as part of this research.

In early 2014, the BBC Trust publicly acknowledged the need to increase gender parity across the corporation's comedy output, especially panel shows (Kanter and Delgado, 2013). The then Director of Television Danny Cohen responded to publicity surrounding the Trust's comment, pledging to ensure at least one woman on every panel show. Speaking to *The Observer*, Cohen made the statement, '[w]e're not going to have panel shows on any more with no women on them. You can't do that. It's not acceptable' (Cooke 2014a). Although the thought behind increasing women's presence on panel shows was broadly welcomed, the decision to make such an announcement public met with equal amounts of praise and scorn. It also resulted in much discussion of the complexities of such a generic announcement. Questions such as 'How many women on a comedy line-up is too many?' and 'Does tokenism help or hinder the progress of women in comedy?' were widely discussed online and in newspapers. Many high-profile comedians, such as Jason Manford, made the point that by making the announcement public it 'undermined' women on panel shows (Plunkett 2015).

On 10 February 2014, the BBC current affairs programme *Newsnight* (1980 to present) brought together a panel to discuss women in comedy. The panel, made up of stand-up comedian Lucy Porter, comic impressionist Jan Ravens and actor Maureen Lipman, spoke to Jeremy Paxman about the recent announcement by Cohen. Paxman patronizingly introduced his guests as an 'entirely testicle-free panel'. This panel on its flagship current affairs programme evidences an attempt by the BBC to demonstrate that it takes issues of diversity seriously – though not seriously enough to fully consider other aspects of intersectional identity such as age, race or class when selecting the panel. Various radio producers came forward to highlight that radio comedy continued to have better gender parity than the televised equivalents. Ed Morrish, producer of BBC Radio 4 comedy panel show *Dilemma* (2011 to 2015), hosted by Sue Perkins, responded directly to the announcement in a blog post squarely aimed at television producers. Within his post, which was subsequently re-printed in the *New Statesman*, Morrish highlighted how there were many women comics he had managed to find and book and could vouch for (Morrish 2014). He argues that he has always attempted to have more than one woman on each of his radio shows (he produced *The News Quiz* [1977 to present] for several years) as this enables a wider range of perspectives to contribute to debate, resulting in a better show. This article highlighted just how little effort had gone in to diversifying television comedy panellists, especially in terms of gender, prior to this point, as radio seemed to be a lot more open to involving a variety of voices. The overwhelming whiteness of the list is still notable, however, which again evidences the additional challenges for women of colour attempting to break through at this time.

The way in which this new, more inclusive, programming policy was handled unsurprisingly came up repeatedly in my interviews. Lynne Parker, who has extensive experience in PR, did not think that the corporation had managed it well:

> I think they should have done it but not make a big hoo-ha about it. I think they should have just done it. I don't know who, which stupid person in their PR department, said 'Oh I know what we'll do, I'll put a press release out about it!'.

For Parker the way the announcement was made undermined the positives of the initiative. She continued:

> And that was where it's wrong. I think it's good, I think quotas are always a good thing, I hate to say it, I know people disagree with me, but you know, I think particularly in terms of politics and that and public life we do have to have quotas. However, I don't think that means you just put any old woman on the panel or whatever, they've got to hold their own. But I think what it's done, it's made the BBC actually think about, instead of just putting token women on, you now, soap stars or what have you [. . .] they've got to look, they've got to put Zoe Lyons on, or Katherine Ryan, or Kerry Godliman, or Holly Walsh or Ellie Taylor, or you know, we could go through a list of women who are doing really well on panel shows, who were always going to do well on the panel shows. But now they have to book them, so that's a good thing, you know. But they were always there.

Subsequent to interviewing Parker, all of the comedians she mentioned (all of whom are white) have indeed had increased presence on BBC content. However, they continue to often work in isolation on panel shows. Allyson June Smith had also picked up on the fact that panel shows had tended to field women panellists who were not from comic backgrounds, a phenomenon still observable in television comedy content produced in 2022:

> [T]hat's my biggest thing lately, panel shows, they're like 'oh we are going to have more women on panel shows'. But you know who they are putting on, models and presenters. They're not putting female comedians on. You might get a few, you get a few, a Katherine Ryan, a Holly Walsh, yes you get female comedians, but there is a hell of a lot of us out there, that you know don't. But yet we have presenters being the female comedic voice on a panel show.

Smith, echoing Morrish's argument, identifies that variety is key, not only across gendered lines but in every possible combination due to the variety of comic tastes and possible audiences for televised comedy. The inclusion of women on panel shows who are not equipped to contribute to the humour of the show (models, presenters, actors) reinforces the idea that women are less funny than men or are incapable of being funny. It is programming decisions like these, which are influenced by scouts as tastemakers, that help perpetuate the stereotypes about comedy being naturally associated with men.

The phrasing of these kinds of policies also came under scrutiny from many comedians I spoke with, as Sophie Willan commented, when comparing live comedy line-ups to television panel shows on all broadcasters:

> [I]t's the same with panel shows, which are trying to balance out now. But I find it annoying now that they have been saying 'you should have at least one woman on a panel show' because it's still the same problem. Because at the end of the day, [. . .] if she's the only female there then you can't help but physically notice. So instead of just being aware of her as a human being, because there's three women and three men, and it's an equal, balanced bill or panel show or whatever, all you're thinking is 'oh god, woman'.

Thus, even when TV bookers do include women comedians, rather than simply any women who can fill the space up, there is additional pressure to represent the whole of their gender. The added pressure placed on a single comedian that identifies as a woman, amongst a line-up of men in the live comedy context is something that will be considered further later in this chapter. What is essential to consider here, however, is that the BBC's reductive language did not acknowledge the intersectional aspects of identity in 2014, and this has arguably been reflected in the resulting outcomes of their policy. Many of the women comedians who now do make it onto panel shows are still overwhelmingly from privileged backgrounds. Replacing white men with white women does not achieve enough in terms of unpicking the structures that continue oppression. Often the programming decisions mean that white, attractive and often young women are now the go-to guests – note how similar this description is to the T-Shirt comic of Friedman's findings. There are still very few women of colour making it on to these shows, and this continuing disparity, I would argue, was baked into the policy from the start.

Even when women do start to integrate into such industries, the voices of middle-class white women are the first to be allowed into the space. The focus of this book as well as the underlying research is not to argue that nothing has changed or that progress has not been made regarding gender equality in comedy. Rather it is an opportunity to reflect on specific issues faced by those who identify as women on the current circuit, to consider where there is still progress to be made, and how this might be achieved.

Barriers identified through performer and promoter interviews

When interviewing promoters and performers as part of this research I was keen to capture individual understandings about whether the industry has improved for women. The issues raised during the interviews form useful contextual information about why women-only nights still exist in the contemporary environment. The interviewees had worked within the industry for differing lengths of time, and so their perspectives on this topic varied. Some had been promoting comedy nights since the 1990s and others had commenced performing as stand-up comics in the early 2010s. Nonetheless, the overwhelming consensus was that, although things are getting better in terms of gender parity on the comedy circuit, sexism still exists. Lynne Parker, director of Funny Women, commented:

> I think it still exists and I think you are always going to get a level of sexism in something that is predominantly a bit of [...] a boy's club. But I think we just become a bit more, immune's the wrong word, we've learnt to deal with it a bit better. [...] We get less upset by it. Because there is more publicity about it and you know you've got organisations like Everyday Sexism and people waving the flag for women generally, so I think we, as women feel empowered and a bit stronger. So, we are less affected by sexism. That's my opinion. [...] And I just think there's just more of us out there championing women in comedy.

Parker believes that although some of the attitudes and behaviours women encounter have not changed significantly since the early 2000s, the way women deal with these attitudes and behaviours has changed. Parker's comment is pertinent to this research in that it attributes the changes to the circuit to women, the minority group trying to infiltrate the sector, rather than those in existing positions of power. It is women who have done the adapting in her view, more so than the industry itself.

Hazel O'Keefe of Laughing Cows and the founder of the UK Women in Comedy Festival responded in a similar way when asked if things had changed for women on the comedy circuit:

> Yeah, I think it's definitely changed. [...] I do still think we live in a misogynistic world and we haven't got true equality yet, but things have got a lot, lot better. [...] I think things still need to be improved upon but we are certainly getting there. People are paving the way and producing comedy nights that do embrace diversity, whether it be gender or race or age or ability, people are actually valuing that a lot more nowadays.

Here O'Keefe comments on the way that genuine diversity of the circuit relies on more than just gender, and this was a central part of her conversation with me. She believes that there is more of a value placed on diverse voices within comedy nights than there has been in the past. As Parker and O'Keefe both run women-centred comedy organizations, it is worth considering the way comedians, who work across multiple nights, venues and festivals, feel about the current circuit. Throughout my conversations with comedians, several key issues affecting performers who identify as women were discussed. We also discussed many positive aspects of the circuit, so this should not be seen as a list to put women off participating, but simply a realistic look at current barriers. The themes can be summarized as: being understood to represent all women, sexist audience reactions, poor introductions, sexism from industry professionals, badly advertised women-only nights, economic disparities and aesthetic pressures.

Understood as representing 'all women'

The way in which women comics exist in the minority on mixed-gender line-ups means that, by default, they are positioned as providing the 'female perspective' on behalf of all women. It is impossible for one woman to represent all women. However, in these instances, audiences are provided with only one woman's perspective. Therefore, that comedian, whether they want to or not, performs the role of 'the woman'. Allyson June Smith commented in 2014:

> I challenge anyone to look at the listings of comedy clubs and you see the numbers. And you tell me that women are fairly represented in this industry. It's changing, but so slow. And I would say even coming over here [to the UK] I felt it even more. Even more than I did over there [Canada].

On the current UK circuit women still, despite slow positive changes since I spoke with Smith, disproportionately work in isolation on mixed-gendered line-ups, very rarely having the opportunity to work with other women. Lara A. King, an experienced performer who often works in both mainstream and alternative spaces across Britain, responded in the following way when asked about her experiences of what would be termed an average or typical comedy night:

> When you say you're obviously used to working with men and women on an average comedy night, on an average comedy night I wouldn't be working with men and women, I'd be working with men. Because I'd be the woman.

This sentiment was echoed by feminist comedian and activist Kate Smurthwaite:

> Like the average comedy night, people talk about one woman on the bill, but the reality is the average number of women on the bill is less than one. The average number of women on the bill is there aren't any.

For many performers, the progress being made to build a more inclusive industry is painfully slow. Comedian Kiri Pritchard-McLean observed how freeing the experience of working with other women can be, as it can release women performers from feeling the pressure of having to be the 'voice of all women'. Speaking in 2014, she commented:

> We're still a novelty act, which is why I prefer it when there is a female compère, because when you come on you're just another comedian then. Especially if they are good, I mean if they're bad they're a bit like 'is she's going to be shit as well?'. But they would never think that with a male comic. It's never like, if a male comic's shit, it's 'cause he's shit, but if a female comic is shit, it's because female comics are shit. But yeah if [you're working with] a female comic and she's good when you come on it's brilliant, it's so liberating because they are like 'oh what have you got to say?' and you're like 'oh wow this is what it's like to be a guy'! And it's a really nice feeling. Lucky fuckers.

Pritchard-McLean's point here is of particular relevance when we consider the way that stand-up comedy as a form has been defined. Double argues:

> Stand-up comedy is an individual talking to a community. A lot of it is about defining who the individual is, who the community is and how one relates to the other. (2014: 239)

This definition may well be true for white cisgender male comedians where there is no assumption that they are there representing a unified group, as all men are considered complex and unique. However, numerous women comics I spoke to as part of this research commented on the way that women are often read by audiences as there to represent a whole gender. Therefore, the way in which many of my participants discussed working in isolation as a woman results in the perception that *a community* is talking to *a community*. As faulty as this thinking is, since women are of course not a homogenous group, there is very little room in stand-up comedy for notions of the individual or nuance without more than one woman performer on a line-up.

Sexist audience reactions

All my interviewees were acutely aware that their own experiences could not necessarily represent the experiences of all women (as noted); nevertheless, almost all had experienced a negative reaction from audiences to their inclusion in a line-up. Many comedians had stories that involved potentially well-meaning audience members approaching them after a gig to say how much they had enjoyed their performance, despite the performer being a woman (of all things!). Soula Notos discussed the reactions she had received when starting out in the Netherlands, where she established comedy night Comedy Kitchen in order to address the under-representation of women in the industry:

> When I started out people came up to me and were like 'I usually don't like female comedy or comedians but I kind of liked you' so I'm like 'Gee wiz thank you for the compliment I think?'. Like even women said that. Like you don't like your own gender? So, you're actually saying you don't have a sense of humour yourself?

This is a very popular anecdote, with most of my interviewees having experienced this kind of poorly phrased audience interaction. Pritchard-McLean highlighted the way that women performers can often sense a subtle negative reaction from the audience when they arrive on stage.

> [S]ome rooms you can just feel the air change when you go on stage. Other than Laughing Cows, [a women-only night] when they know what they are in for. Generally, The Frog [The Frog and Bucket Manchester], I love it and it's been very supportive of me [. . .] as an individual, [but] something about the room or the people that come or whatever it is [. . .] there's literally a change in the air.

Pritchard-McLean continued to explain how she had arrived at this conclusion:

> I thought it was in my head for ages, but then once when I was doing a Thursday there [The Frog and Bucket], [. . .] because you always just think, oh this stuff is in my head. [. . .] Then I came off stage and someone I know was watching, a comic, and he said 'I can't believe that'[. . .]. And he'd heard two people go 'oh bloody hell it's a woman'. And I was just like, that's all the stuff we don't hear as well. So, like you think it's in your head and you never want to say it out loud because it feels like you are making an excuse.

What I find particularly pertinent in this response is that even though the performer's instincts were consistently telling her that the reaction she received was gendered, she doubted herself. It was not until a male friend informed her she was right, providing tangible evidence of her feared responses, that Pritchard-McLean had any confidence in her own experience. Women are often, in all industries, made to doubt their own experiences of sexism and racism, gaslighted into thinking that they are overreacting or imagining things (Abramson 2014). Pritchard-McLean's experience of being concerned that to acknowledge the issue would make her seem weak, or as if she was making excuses, is one that will no doubt resonate with women in other industries too.

Poor introductions

Reactions from audiences for comedy are heavily guided by the compère. Jason Rutter in his research into the role of comedy compères outlines their role in the following way:

> Compères are more than just announcers who bring on the act. They provide continuity between acts who often have varying reputations, divergent styles and or different performance skills; perform routines between acts using their own material; pass comment on the performers; share details of the evening's itinerary. (2000: 464)

Compères function as a vital glue that binds the individual performances from comedians into a coherent event. They achieve this through encouraging and controlling audience participation in the form of clapping, cheering and general welcoming of comedians to the stage. Rutter identifies the following recurring elements found within compère introductions: contextualization, framing of response (attempting to instil a specific attitude in the audience, e.g. excitement and intrigue), evaluation of the comedian, request for action (e.g. 'put your hands together') and an introduction in the form of the comic's name (2000: 465). It is through the contextualization, evaluation and introduction aspects of this role that compères can make a huge difference to how women comedians are received by their audiences.

Poor introductions or introductions that foreground the gender or appearance of the comic have been commonplace for women comics. O'Keefe gave a particularly striking example whilst acknowledging that as a promoter she has not been on the receiving end of these kinds of introductions.

> [as a promoter] I don't know what it's like to be introduced by an MC in an inappropriate manner, which happens all the time. 'And now we have a woman, let's hope she doesn't get her flange out' was how Maureen Younger got introduced once, which is frankly disgusting.

Overt sexism in introductions, as with the example above, is now increasingly objected to and frowned upon. However, there are more subtle behaviours at play that feed into the continued 'othering' of women comedians, for example, the use of gendered language. Comedian Kerry Leigh, who performs the role of compère for the Laughing Cows nights in Manchester, understands her role in framing audience reactions to comedians on stage. When discussing how compères operate on mixed-gender line-ups she commented:

> I've heard lots of horror stories, of [puts on voice] 'it's a woman'. I've never had anyone introduce me in a really awful way but there's just little things like they'll refer to your looks when introducing you. Whereas that doesn't really happen I don't think when men are introduced. So, 'the gorgeous Kerry Leigh' or whatever. It isn't a massive issue. [. . .] I think in recent times I've had nice introductions by respectful people who just say 'she's on next, she's fabulous'.

Leigh's response highlights, through her example of 'she's on next', that even when the word 'woman' is not used by a compère as part of an introduction, the use of the pronoun 'she' is potentially equally as challenging. The use of 'she' will ensure awareness of the gender of the performer before they make it to the microphone. This clearly links back to the discussion of stereotype threat in the previous chapter where both the audience and performer are acutely aware of gender stereotypes before the start of a set. As a result of the awareness that a poor introduction can have negative consequences, many comedians have strategies to avoid this. As part of our conversation, Allyson June Smith highlighted her own approach to handling this situation:

> Sometimes I'll tell a compère, if it's the first time I'm working with them and I feel like brave enough to actually bring it up to them. I say 'when you are getting ready to introduce me, please use words like, 'this next comic', 'your next performer', save my name to the very last minute. Because if you say 'you're gonna love this next lady', 'I've worked with her', 'she is', it gives them that thirty more seconds to already choose whether or not they are gonna zone in. So that to me is a sign of a very

good compère, someone who makes it totally irrelevant the gender of the next performer. Communicating directly with the compère so as to ensure that gender is obscured until the last possible opportunity is not something that male comedians, operating from society's default position, need to concern themselves with. The second that the gender of the performer is articulated, the control the compère has over the response the incoming comic will receive from the audience is significantly undermined. Even when a compère makes an active choice to obscure the gender of the performer by saving their name until last, there are other aspects of language that can trigger the audience's, and possibly the performer's own, awareness of gender stereotypes. The success of a compères 'call for action' to welcome the comic to the stage, which always occurs just before they leave the space and hand over to the act, with the applause covering the awkwardness of the handover, can still be negatively impacted by gender stereotypes beyond their control.

Sexism from industry professionals

In addition to the complex relationship between comedians and compères, there were several examples, explored during the interviews, of women comics being undermined publicly by other comics, promoters or journalists. As part of our conversation, Sophie Willan discussed a recent awkward moment she had experienced on stage. I had been in the audience for this particular comedy night and also noticed the reaction from the audience that she observed.[2] She recalled:

> I do also feel sometimes that there's this macho thing between the male comic world, that I really don't connect to. I mean I'm quite a competitive person, but I don't have that. [. . .] There was a male comedian, where I was hosting a gig recently, quite a big gig. This male comic came on after me and said 'yeah alright yeah, you've had your moment'. [. . .] And I thought that was a real. I mean I thought it was

funny and it was fine, but it wasn't funny actually because a few people in the audience went 'oooo', and he completely undermined me as the host. [. . .] Because I'm more 'new' you know, he came on stage and he just completely undermined me with my audience. And I've got to carry them for the night. So I thought that was an interesting move for him [. . .] As far as he saw it this is a new and female, girl getting up flouncing about the stage, with loads of people, 'having my moment' as he called it [. . .], he wasn't working with me was he?

When the male comedian made the aforementioned quip when arriving on stage it broke the concept of unity. As Rutter observed, the role of the compère is to create an event out of smaller performances, to facilitate a cohesive narrative across disparate approaches. In this moment the male comic attempted to increase his status by making Willan the butt of a joke.

To make clear that it is not always men, or indeed comedians, that help maintain barriers for women entering the live comedy circuit the following example is pertinent. When asked about negative onstage experiences, Kiri Pritchard-McLean drew upon an experience she had when starting out in 2010:

I did a new act competition when I was about a year in [to my career], the final of which was judged by and I will name them [leans in and enunciates directly into audio recorder] Greg and Marissa and someone else from The Lass [The Lass O'Gowrie pub in Manchester]. There were like ten of us in the final and I went up, and the judges gave you feedback after your set. [. . .] And then [. . .] I went on and didn't have a great one, I didn't die but didn't do brilliantly. [. . .] In the feedback afterwards he just said 'great tits'. And then he kind of went 'Marissa?' and she went 'Yeah great tits'. And I was like thanks sister! And I have never been so humiliated in all my life. Just stood there after having not a great gig and have professional comics [say that], when you are new as well, and a room full of people just talk about your tits, and that was all that he said. [. . .] They stood there and humiliated me for their own laugh. And it was a man who did it and then a woman who laughed along with him.

What strikes me about this recollection is that such sentences would not seem out of place in a description of the 1960s working men's club hostility towards women. To have encountered this level of sexism, facilitated by both panellists and relatively recently, would be shocking to many. This instance, experienced as part of entering a new act competition, could easily have put Pritchard-McLean off continuing in comedy. It is clear that hostility towards women, in sexist comments or micro-aggressions from those within the industry, is not as few and far between as most would like to think.

Badly advertized women-only nights

A key part of the discussions with all my participants was the role women-only comedy nights and events play in the wider circuit. Many highlighted to me how women-only nights were seen, by promoters and other comedians, as somehow less challenging than mixed-gendered nights. Pritchard-McLean highlighted that the general feeling towards them, on the mainstream circuit, is overwhelmingly negative:

> I hate that [. . .] people call them 'oh they are like the Paralympics of comedy nights', that's what they get called in the industry. Yeah like 'why do you get to gig at The Frog just because you've got a fanny?', because there are plenty of places I don't get gigs because I've got a fanny'.

She continued to reflect on where she thought this negative attitude to the development of women-only spaces would lead:

> It's weird because [. . .] the zeitgeist at the moment, it's definitely going to go back, and it already is. Everybody wants to be seen to be addressing [it] and be engaged in the idea of gender equality. Yet stand-up is one of the last places where you can go 'oh no ladies can't do this job, because they are ladies' and it's weird that they are allowed to say that out loud [laughs]. Because you can't and wouldn't

say that about anything else, like 'I'm not having a female lawyer, because what if she's on her period when the trial's on, there'll be no talking to her?'.

Here Pritchard-McLean is referencing the way Manchester's Laughing Cows' nights across the 2010s ran at The Frog and Bucket, a club that has an element of prestige, since it has been a starting point for many of the North West's most successful comics. It seems that comedians who are not able to get a spot on a night in this venue are promoting the idea that women who take the opportunity to perform as part of women-only nights do not deserve their spot on the stage. It is the same thought process that occurs around quotas in all industries and across multiple aspects of identity. The implication is that if you achieve success through affirmative action then it is undeserved in some way. This of course obscures the way that white male privilege is undeserved and has been enjoyed by men for most of human history.

The comedians I interviewed had all participated in women-only line-ups and overwhelmingly thought they were a useful and necessary part of the industry. Kate Smurthwaite, whose comment is indicative of the overall feelings of my participants, argued:

> I think that female-only comedy nights are necessary and vital because the rest of the comedy circuit is for the most part male-only.

Even though the consensus was positive, the participants picked up on a developing trend in badly advertised women-only comedy nights. These nights reframe this positive space for women performers as something that reinforces outdated gender stereotypes. Daphna Baram, a London-based Israeli-born comic and journalist, highlighted how a badly marketed gig can hinder women performers and the public perception of comedy by women:

> [R]ecently I was at a night [. . .] a little festival in Margate in Kent and the guy who was running it, really with all the good intentions, was running this female night, a female line-up. And he said to me, he titled it 'Something for the Ladies' and I said I'm not doing this

night unless you are changing it to 'Something from the Ladies'. So at least it will be clear that it is a female line-up but this is not just for ladies.

The title of an event, the colour choices for publicity (pink) and the use of specific wording on a flyer can help to build up the idea that comedy by women is automatically *for* women. Smurthwaite also observed a postfeminist reinforcing of gender binary in some poorly conceived nights:

> [Y]ou do also sometimes do this horrible thing of marketing a female comedy night, and I mean Laughing Cows would never do it, but marketing an all-female comedy night like it's sort of [puts on a voice] 'ladies night'. And you get like half-price Lambrusco, and it's sort of like they'll put on the big match on the big-screen in the back room for the lads. [. . .] Or I've done one where, they're on like military bases while the boys are away in Afghanistan or whatever and you're like 'this is quite odd'.

The phrase 'ladies night' was roundly dismissed as being negative. The Women in Comedy Festival, a detailed consideration of which will form the next chapter, purposely stayed away from colours or terminology that might alienate anyone (be they male, LGBTQ+, Black or from an ethnic minority), and its focus was always on integration, not segregation. Nights, or even comedy solo shows, that are publicized in this postfeminist or retro-sexist way are damaging the progress made by women who wish to be seen as equal to their male contemporaries. My interviewees saw women-only nights as a means to an end, and as a tool for achieving equality, through equalizing the opportunities to perform, and not the endgame in and of itself. O'Keefe also referenced the way in which Laughing Cows was evolving and how, in the long term, she looked forward to putting on mixed-gendered nights that reflected the diversity of the industry across multiple identity characteristics. O'Keefe's focus seems to remain very much on making change in the wider industry, rather than simply creating a market for comedy by women in specific spaces.

Economic disparities

A further theme identified unexpectedly from the interviews was the economic disparities enacted on the circuit and how these disadvantaged women. I initially asked O'Keefe about barriers to women entering the industry when she established Laughing Cows in 1998:

> At the time those venues [bigger comedy clubs] weren't valuing that some females would bring those people in [large enough audience numbers] and would justify the costs. And even when you did have females they generally weren't headliner or opening, they were in the middle, probably on unpaid open spots, or even if they were on paid spots it was ten, fifteen, twenty quid, it was pennies. So how can a woman then actually make a true career out of comedy, because you can't justify it, you can't justify the cost of it. You're going to a gig and you're losing money even with your underground fare. You know you're just not getting anything back for it. So, I just think [. . .] at that time, it was certainly a bit more difficult for females.

In the 1990s and early 2000s, women rarely headlined gigs on the mainstream comedy circuit. Often women operated in the opening or middle spots on a line-up where the pay (if there was any) was not as good, women would also be offered unpaid spots as an opportunity to develop their skills. Unpaid spots, as with all forms of unpaid labour (such as internships), are certainly barriers to the participation of anyone who is not economically secure. A counterargument would be that all comics have to start somewhere, and unpaid spots can be an invaluable way of finding a voice and developing craft. However, when women had developed enough skills and confidence to perform a paid set, the opportunities to do so were few and far between. This, combined with women often only being booked on their own, meant that there were simply numerically fewer opportunities to advance. Whilst bookers are getting better at not only booking one woman, some of these practices are still present on the current circuit. As O'Keefe observed regarding the inclusion of women comedians on the circuit of the mid-2010s:

> I don't think all of a sudden promoters started thinking 'Oh I know I can make money out of female comics'. I see that happening now though and that irritates the hell out of me. It really really does. [. . .] Or I think people were challenged. [. . .] If you're challenged then you have no choice but to then start booking in a fairer way and then you go 'oh actually!', your eyes are opened, your blinkers are taken off and so you start going 'actually that woman's fantastic and this really added something to the showcase'. [. . .] And then if you get a better product, you get financial benefits surely. I think there's also a risk as well, (the cynic in me), that people are booking females for a cheap option. That's even more disgusting than not booking women, it's more of an insult. You know yeah 'I'll throw in a token woman here, I'll offer people 5-minute open spots and I won't pay them a penny' it's worse! Just don't give them the gig, do you know what I mean? Let them go to actual clubs that value them and actually pay them to have proper slots. [. . .] I think that's something that is not being raised in the comedy circuit. [. . .] But to actually book a male and pay a male more, than you would pay a female is illegal. Not just discrimination, and that needs to be challenged, well I suppose through legislation. It needs to be enforced, that's the issue, because how do you enforce it, how do you prove it? But that's the reality of what's going on now.

O'Keefe believes that there were two motivating factors that affected the industry during this time in terms of inclusion. First, showcases and comedy nights that were women-only proved to be successful and demonstrated to other promoters and producers that a market did exist. These pioneering organizations evidenced that an opportunity was available and that the needs of a specific audience were not met elsewhere. This then inspired other promoters to adopt similar approaches to (potentially cynically) capitalize on a market they did very little to help develop. Second, people were openly challenging the booking practices that did not include women. Organizations like Laughing Cows and Funny Women have spent a significant amount of time advocating for changes to booking practices and highlighting the range of untapped female talent that exists in the UK. Organizations are better placed to challenge questionable practices than individual comedians. Comics have to be at a certain stage in their careers in order to challenge booking practices and unethical decision-making, as making a stand comes with an element of risk – such as no longer being booked, getting a bad reputation and so on which can be career-ending for an up-and-coming comedian. Over the last ten years, and in the contemporary context, an increasing number of women comics have managed to build successful careers in comedy. This means that there are now more people than ever in a position to make a stand and challenge gender inequality on the circuit without fear of repercussions.

In terms of O'Keefe's final point (regarding women being routinely paid less for performing), she was not the only person to highlight this concern. Pritchard-McLean made a similar point:

> [A]lso speaking candidly the pay is a lot worse on female comedy bills. So it feels like another thing 'oh we get paid less for doing this? [. . .] some others [promoters] they take the 'we are so supportive of women and comedy' position but are just not willing to pay you the going rate.

Here Pritchard-Mclean is highlighting that even women-only nights can enact unequal practices around pay. If women are not being booked as regularly as male comics (evidenced by women still being in the minority on mixed-gendered line-ups), and so have to travel further to access spots and opportunities (which itself has economic consequences) and *even then* are still paid less (either on mixed or women-only bills), it is a wonder how any women manage to achieve a sustainable or viable career in the industry. This issue is particularly acute in the context of the 2020s in the UK. The global Covid-19 pandemic produced gendered (and racialized) economic consequences for women. First, additional care responsibilities were disproportionately experienced by women (especially women of colour), limiting opportunities for work outside the home (Power 2020), and second in relation to live comedy, the pandemic resulted in the closure of many smaller hospitality venues where the majority of women's opportunities to perform exist. The UK's ongoing cost-of-living crisis (2022) will also almost certainly again shift the burden of further care work on to women who already are over-represented in lower-paid professions (Oppenheim 2022). These contextual factors will result in fewer women (who are not independently wealthy and therefore do not need to work), attempting to make a sustainable career in comedy as the economic realities they face will further restrict their choices and opportunities.

Aesthetic pressures

In addition to the practical and economic issues, Janice Connolly, who performs as the character Barbara Nice and runs the organization Women and Theatre, expressed concerns about the circuit of the 2010s in the following way:

> Now there's more female comedy about, [there is this] kind of movement where if a young woman's good looking, sexy, whatever that means, in a mainstream kind of way, then they're really pushed by the agencies, so they're like little bred ponies really. And the kind of more unusual, like a Jo Brand kind of character, I don't see much evidence of them higher up. They have to be kind of quite good looking to progress now. Whereas Jo kind of came in back when that didn't kind of matter. I think there's kind of a beauty pageant thing going on around female comedians now, in terms of mainstream comedy, not, you know, not grassroots comedy.

Some felt this pressure more than others and age will, of course, be a factor since the broadcast industries tend not to take women over the age of forty seriously, often erasing them from our screens. Dana Alexander, a Canadian comedian who has been working in the UK since 2011, completely rejected the idea that she was pressured to look a specific way:

> I stay away from generalisations, they're not helping any of us. I dress pretty boring. I'm in sneakers and a mismatched outfit. It's all different some guys dress to the nines you know, some girls dress down because they feel that they'll be objectified, so they'll actually you know, dress

> down on purpose. It's so individual. It depends on where you are, what club you're in, what country you're in. [. . .] I don't read my reviews. I don't care. [. . .] I have bills to pay. [. . .] Yeah nobody really bugs me about my clothes.

Being clear that this is not something that she has ever personally felt the need to consider, Alexander does acknowledge that other women may well be aware of experiencing objectification and so dress accordingly. When I interviewed comedian and compère for Manchester's Laughing Cows Comedy nights, Kerry Leigh, she highlighted that the performer's choice of clothing can make a big difference to the way they feel on stage.

> When I first started out those first few years, it would always be jeans and a t-shirt or jeans and a top. I don't really know why that was, I didn't analyse it. But I remember thinking I would feel uncomfortable doing this in a dress. Vulnerable I think is probably the right word. I do remember thinking that, and then as I have grown more confident and got into my persona, I really like playing with what I am wearing on stage [. . .] I want to be eye-catching now, whereas I used to be 'I don't want anyone to think about what I am wearing', because that used to worry me.

I followed up by asking Leigh why she had chosen the word vulnerable to describe her early experiences of selecting costumes. She commented in the following way:

> I think it was because, and I don't want to make something up here because I can't really remember, but I do remember having that feeling. And this is where you are doing open mic gigs where there is more opportunity for people to heckle, and I have you know gone on to a wolf whistle before. I've had a guy shout out, this is years ago, you know 'get your tits out' or 'take your pants off' was one of them, which was quite funny. So I think I just felt safer if there wasn't the opportunity for them to see like leg or [gestures at her chest] breasts. Yeah I didn't want anyone checking me out I suppose, I wanted it to be more about the comedy, but I don't care now. That's because I'm comfortable.

Leigh acknowledges that as she has evolved as a more confident performer throughout her career, her attitude has changed. The thought process behind Leigh's decisions, for her early performances, highlights how the responsibility in this specific situation is placed on the comedian to make changes to their appearance, to self-police their appearance, in order to defuse a potentially confrontational situation. This responsibility is not placed on the comedy clubs or nights themselves to better educate or police their audience to stop them objectifying, insulting or disrespecting the comedian. The heckles Leigh recounts, which in the context of this research I have found to be far from unique, are popular catcalls or heckles women receive on the streets. Even the costume choices of a female performer can relate directly to wider cultural attitudes towards women. Leigh does not explicitly make this connection herself but remembers a feeling of vulnerability born of an expectation that she would be objectified. This thought process, and Leigh's explanation of feeling vulnerable, is arguably symptomatic of a society that still places responsibility on the victims of misogyny and sexism. Often, in cases of sexual violence and rape, the victim's clothing is discussed as if in some way a woman's clothing invites, or somehow excuses, acts of violence against her as she was 'asking for it'.

Notably, Janice Connolly also felt this pressure to look a specific way impacted on male comics too in the contemporary context:

> I think that's true of the boys as well actually. [. . .] When you think about the kind of classic, skinny jeaned, floppy haired boy that's going on, and actually traditionally comics were all shapes and sizes and odd-looking people often. [. . .] Proper comedians in my opinion were kind of funny looking buggers actually, and now they've all got to be fanciable, sexy rather than funny. And I think funny is the best thing about comedy really, I think we often forget to be funny, we try to be clever or smart, I think we've maybe forgotten what funny is.

Here Connolly is clearly describing the 'T-Shirt comic' discussed previously. It is apparent that in the current mediatized context, irrespective of gender identity, the need to look a specific way has increased in importance since the alternative movement of the 1980s. This imperative impacts on everyone participating in television comedy (be that a recording of a live set or a panel show) but results in specific challenges for women who are held to a different level of beauty standards than their male colleagues.

This chapter has set out the barriers identified by women working within the contemporary UK live comedy industry and some of the difficulties in attracting a wider audience through mediatized forms. The next chapter will consider the role of women-only nights from the perspective of the audience and whether as a tool for addressing these barriers, women-only comedy nights can be effective in changing attitudes to comedy by women.

3

Women-only comedy spaces
Addressing inequality on the UK comedy circuit

The role that the audience plays in the co-construction of live comic performance has long been of concern to researchers; however, due to the complexities of working with live audiences, many studies that consider the way audiences understand comic material have often taken recorded or screen comedy as their starting point. The work of sociologist Giselinde Kuipers (2006) provides a notable example of research into audiences for various forms of television comedy and how this links to taste cultures. The central questions of Kuipers' research are whether television audiences for comedy construct taste hierarchies about high and lowbrow comedy and how this may be linked to the age and education of the individuals. Her research concluded that those with more education had more general knowledge of television comedy and therefore felt they were in a position to offer a taste judgement, in instances where many participants with less education did not. It was found that highbrow comedy (one of four categorizations Kuipers used within her research, which also included 'lowbrow', 'celebrities' and 'old-timers' comedy categories) was mostly unknown to less-educated participants. This means that rather than having a negative attitude towards highbrow comedy these participants were simply indifferent due to a lack of awareness.

Critically Kuipers comments that in order for tastes to be forged into taste cultures, first an awareness of the forms under discussion must be present. 'Knowledge always precedes appreciation: you have to be aware of something in order to like, hate or be indifferent to it' (Kuipers

2006: 360). Whilst I am not contending that comedy by women is a specific taste, as comedy performed by women comes from a variety of comedy genres, this point is relevant. Audiences for creative content in any form (theatre, television, film) are built; they do not just occur spontaneously. Comedy by women is not a genre in and of itself; however, as discussed in the previous chapters, a lot of the stereotypes surrounding comedy performed by women make the assumption that all women, and more specifically all women comedians, are the same; one can easily be substituted for another and, therefore, only one is required on a line-up. This attitude often originates from a *lack of awareness* of the range of comic material being performed. This chapter will consider the role that women-only comedy nights and events play in developing knowledge and nurturing audiences for comedy created and performed by women.[1]

In terms of generally understanding the motivations of audiences to attend live comedy events, in the light of the continued proliferation of recorded versions of stand-up performance on television (e.g. *Live at the Apollo* [2004 to present], *Michael McIntyre's Comedy Roadshow* [2009–11]), Sharon Lockyer and Lynn Myers' mixed-methods study provides valuable insight. '"It's About Expecting the Unexpected": Live Stand-up Comedy from the Audience's Perspective' (Lockyer and Myers 2011) highlighted the interactional aspects of the form as key factors in motivating audiences to see live comedy. Their study used a two-stage approach. First, an online questionnaire about comedy attendance was used, and completed by 277 people, to ascertain information about how regularly people go out to see live comedy, as well as capturing a variety of participant-characteristics data. Subsequently, follow-up interviews with eleven participants were conducted to further explore attitudes and opinions expressed during the first stage. This provided important quantitative and qualitative information about UK audience experiences of live comedy. The findings of their research noted that respect for the stand-up comedian's skill in performing live, the unexpected and interactional nature of stand-up performance, the intimacy of the event and the sharing of a collective experience with others were all key motivations to attend live comedy.

In relation to the interactional motivation to attend live comedy, Joanne Gilbert (2017) acknowledges the shifts in the America comedy context due to increased engagement with comedy on the internet. With this in mind she argues that stand-up comedy

> is a fundamentally different experience, one that involves membership of a community of laughers. Because the genre of stand-up comedy is inherently interactive, and because humor is the only discourse that requires an audience to be legitimized through laughter (Gilbert, 2004), this community is vital to the very existence of live comedy, a unique medium that continues to be a viable and popular form of entertainment, interaction, and thus, social engagement and reflection. (Gilbert 2017: 65)

Therefore, even within a contemporary context where audiences have ample access to a variety of comic forms, stand-up comedy continues to hold a unique position and therefore is worthy of further detailed consideration. This chapter will explore the motivations of audiences to attend women-only nights specifically and the opinions about women stand-ups held by audiences for these events.

To set the scene it is useful to start by considering how the industry presents itself in relation to inclusion. In 2014 Ticketmaster, a large event ticketing company, conducted research into the UK comedy industry, creating *The State of Play Report*. This report was authored by three Ticketmaster employees, Tina Mermiri, director of research and analytics, research analyst Sophia Rawcliffe and business intelligence analyst Thomas Rea. The report also included an introduction by Bruce Dessau, an influential and well-known comedy critic who runs the comedy website *Beyond a Joke*. This research was widely reported in the media, used as a sign that things were economically healthy for the circuit and that women were on the rise across the industry. This argument was made by a wide range of media outlets including various BBC online and broadcast formats, the *Radio Times* and *The*

Independent newspaper (see Daly 2014 and Sherwin 2014). However, it was apparent to me, even right at the start of my research process, that there were several key flaws in this data in terms of considering gender equality on the circuit. These can be summarized as follows:

1) *The data set*: The transactional data used to form the basis of the report is flawed in that it originates with Ticketmaster and TicketWeb and so is exclusively from events that they ticketed. There is nothing categorically wrong about the origins of the data, but claims that this data is representative of a whole industry are problematic when the data comes from a specific source. As a result, the report does not capture any information about events that other organizations ticketed, or indeed for any comedy events that were *not formally ticketed at all* (which of course includes many at the grassroots end of the industry). Thus, the performance spaces where the majority of women comics operate are not represented in this data.

2) *Recruitment of participants*: The report does not make clear in its interpretation of the data where respondents originated (e.g. was the survey promoted to only Ticketmaster customers or more widely?). It does, however, indicate that the survey was designed, set up and facilitated in-house. Recruitment of participants for any kind of research impacts on the data set. In this case if the respondents are limited to Ticketmaster customers only, then their comic experiences may be limited to bigger (formally ticketed) events. This means that they cannot be considered representative of the entire comedy-going public, as the data would not be inclusive of those who only see comedy in less formally ticketed contexts.

3) *Participant selection criteria*: In order to qualify as a member of the comedy-going public and thus be able to complete the online survey, participants had to have attended at least one comedy event in the last three years. This is an incredibly low bar for inclusion in the survey. This raises questions about why those

conducting the survey allowed such a long timeframe and how reliable the responses are.

4) *Need to source additional data*: Data from TicketWeb was sourced by Ticketmaster to provide information for smaller venues and 'female comedy events' (2014: 35). The methodology and the fact that this additional sourcing of information was necessary are only mentioned in the appendices (the final page of the report). It is not highlighted within the text. This results in a misleading picture of greater inclusion than is the case. If Ticketmaster, the largest of the comedy ticketing companies, had to take additional steps to include data on women comics, then that in itself is worthy of note. The report diminishes this fact by obscuring it in a footnote. The report was often used to make claims for the success of women in the industry, so to not foreground that women still disproportionately work outside the profitable (and formally ticketed) contexts within the main report is a distortion of reality.

In addition to the flaws in communicating the methodology, the report's presentation is a masterclass in the postfeminist reinstatement of a gender binary.

5) *Use of language*: The text of the report makes repeated reference to the way in which women artists are breaking through (Sarah Millican and Miranda Hart are used as examples). It uses the terms 'comedienne' and 'female comedian' throughout the text, both of which prioritize the gender of the performers above all else, reinforcing gender difference.

6) *Presentation style*: Whenever a woman comic is mentioned, or gender is an index of measurement on a graph, the information is accompanied by a small pink 'women' sign. The symbol was presumably envisioned as a way of flagging up to the reader how inclusive the sector has become. However, the use of the symbol achieves the effect of highlighting just how un-inclusive the industry is. First, because of the stereotypical use of pink which

reasserts difference (visually supporting the language differences examined earlier), and second, because of how rarely the symbol is featured. Thus, the gatekeepers and beneficiaries of the comedy industry, when making use of the report, make grotesquely misleading public announcements about how inclusive the industry is becoming, whilst simultaneously reasserting a gender binary that foregrounds women's gender and continues to other them.

Further to these issues, the ethnicity of the survey respondents is not made clear as part of the data, although gender and age are foregrounded, so no conclusions or information about the ethnicity of the comedy-going public have been shared. Depressingly, of the fifteen directly named comics within the report only two are women and every single one is white.[2] Where the text attempts to frame steps towards inclusion as positive, the actual data (and the way it is presented) when scrutinized paints a more pessimistic picture. This was the context in which I commenced my work with the Women in Comedy Festival.

The UK Women in Comedy Festival

To understand more about the purpose and role of women-only comedy nights, I undertook research with attendees to the 2014 Women in Comedy Festival in Manchester, where I was a researcher in residence annually until 2018. By happy coincidence my audience research was conducted the same year the Ticketmaster *State of Play* report was published in the UK which, as discussed earlier, explored audience attendance to comedy events.

Whilst I am aware of other women-only comedy organizations – Funny Women (UK wide) and What the Frock (Bristol) are two obvious examples – my research was conducted with the support of Laughing Cows and the UK Women in Comedy Festival in Manchester.

The UK Women in Comedy Festival ran its first event in October 2013, which I attended. It was put together at short notice when Hazel O'Keefe, who had by this point been running Laughing Cows (a women-only stand-up organization) for fifteen years, decided that she wanted to build a bigger platform for women comedians trying to gain exposure. O'Keefe set the festival up to try and create a space that addressed some of the problems explored in the previous chapter (such as being the only woman, poor introductions and industry sexism). The Edinburgh Festival of 2013 had highlighted the potential of women comics to make it to the top of their field, with Bridget Christie then becoming only the third woman to win the Best Comedy Show prize, but getting booked on mixed-gendered line-ups remained difficult for many. O'Keefe felt that establishing an annual festival had potential to showcase the range of talent on offer to audiences, and, by inviting promoters and bookers to attend for free, could give women performers the boost they needed to get into mainstream spaces. The festival, in its first five iterations (2013–18) did not have core funding of any kind. It was not until the Covid-19 pandemic and the festival's move to be organized by the venue The Frog and Bucket did it benefit from Arts Council England's Culture Recovery Fund in 2021 (when comedy finally became a 'fundable activity' due to the decimation of the entire arts and cultural sectors during repeated lockdowns). The team that made the festival possible whilst I was embedded as a researcher in residence was made up of volunteers. As O'Keefe commented at the time:

> [Y]ou have communities that grow, the Women in Comedy Festival Crew is a perfect example of that. [. . .] I think we have got about thirty people, in and out, and I think out of that crew anybody would do anything to help and it's very, very genuine. And that was evident in year one when, you know, I'd created this massive project, I'd just created chaos basically, and the crew just came in and picked it all up and just filled in all the little gaps and dotted all the i's and the t's. And that's from a genuine desire for progression and equality.

The volunteers across the years have come from a wide range of backgrounds, including bank managers, students, IT specialists, teachers and social workers. All the volunteers were brought together through a shared passion for live comedy and a desire to see more diversity across the form. The spirit of the venture was feminist in its truest sense (working collectively for equality for all), but this does not mean that all volunteers shared the same idea of the meaning of feminism. The volunteer team, of which I was part as a participant-observer since early 2014, were from across the gender spectrum and contributed in a range of ways. From liaising with artists to book and programme the festival, marketing, front of house work and technical assistance (including lighting and sound for some performers), the volunteer team were involved at all stages of the process, overseen by the professional expertise of O'Keefe as the festival's director.

As a participant-observer I sat in on, and contributed to, a significant number of meetings across a four-year period which enabled me to understand how decisions were made and the rationale behind them. It was clear from the start that inclusion was front and centre of all that the festival was trying to achieve. Although the event's focus was on gender equality, this focus was never positioned in opposition to marginalized characteristics such as ethnicity or sexuality. The festival's team, led by O'Keefe, had a nuanced understanding of how women from minority ethnic groups, or with disabilities, experience additional barriers to inclusion within live comedy. The festival took steps to make clear in materials (print and online) that it was trans inclusive and wanted to engage with *all women*. It was seen at the time as especially important to assert this (that the festival understood trans women were women), and this was discussed in meetings, as contemporaneously there was an increase in the UK in the levels of publicity around Trans Exclusionary Radical Feminists (TERFs) or Gender Critical (GC) ideologies and accompanying trans hostility. The transphobia inherent in certain kinds of exclusionary feminism in the UK and internationally was already in the media at the time the festival was established, and, as a result, an explicit distancing from that kind of ideology felt necessary to the group.

The festival also wanted to set itself apart from other poorly publicized events to ensure it avoided reinforcing stereotypes. The website and publicity intentionally stayed away from stereotypical imagery or colours. Pink was featured but did not dominate as the environment the team wanted to create needed to be inclusive of, and appeal to, women with varying connections to stereotypical femininity (Figure 2).

The festival was always an LGBTQ+-inclusive space and many high-profile comedians who identify as LGBTQ+, such as Zoe Lyons, Jen Brister, Suzi Ruffell, Bethany Black, Kate McCabe, Susan Calman and The Short and Girlie Show, were quick to support the venture. It is

Figure 2 Image of UK Women in Comedy Festival Poster from 2017, designed by the author.

important to recognize here the clear connection between equality for women and the fight for LGBTQ+ rights – at no point were these seen as contradictory. O'Keefe is a well-known and influential figure in the LGBTQ+ community in Manchester, and the festival was supported by friends and volunteers she met through this scene too. Trans women not only performed as part of the line-ups but supported as volunteers and technicians too.

The remaining part of this chapter will consider my findings from research conducted with audiences during the 2014 festival. The data was collected early on in my relationship with the festival as the opportunity for the festival to run year to year was always tenuous due to a lack of access to funding. In total, 336 people completed an initial survey, 334 in-person and 2 online. I then conducted fourteen follow-up interviews with participants, who were sampled to reflect the make-up of my overall cohort. The identity characteristics of the full group of surveyed participants are illustrated in Tables 1–6.

Table 1 Gender Identity of Survey Respondents

Gender identity	($n = 336$)
Female	72.92%
Male	24.70%
Prefer not to say	0.60%
Other	0.30%
N/R	1.49%
Total	100.00%

Table 2 Sexuality of Survey Respondents

Sexuality	($n = 336$)
Yes LGBT	39.58%
No LGBT	55.06%
Prefer not to say	2.98%
N/R	2.38%
Total	100.00%

Table 3 Age of Survey Respondents

Age (years)	(*n* = 336)
16–20	5.95%
21–30	27.98%
31–40	20.54%
41–50	28.87%
51–60	10.71%
61–70	2.98%
Over 70	0.60%
Prefer not to say	0.60%
N/R	1.79%
Total	100.00%

Table 4 Disability of Survey Respondents

Disability	(*n* = 336)
Yes disability	4.17%
No disability	91.96%
Prefer not to say	2.98%
N/R	0.60%
Void	0.30%
Total	100.00%

Throughout the remainder of this chapter, percentages will be rounded up or down to whole numbers.

Of the 336 respondents, 73 per cent (*n* = 245) identified as female. This is broadly reflective of the gender breakdown of many of the audiences for the shows performed as part of the festival, which tended to have more women than men as audience members (although no exact figures for the festival's audiences exist due to the un-ticketed and ad hoc nature of some of the performances).

Nearly 40 per cent (*n* = 134) of the respondents identified as LGBTQ+.

This can be interpreted in relation to a number of factors, for example, Manchester's significant LGBTQ+ population, general LGBTQ+ openness (several performances took place in venues in, or near, Manchester's Gay Village), O'Keefe's connection to the LGBTQ+

Table 5 Ethnicity of Survey Respondents

Ethnicity	(n = 336)
Black British	0.89%
White British	83.33%
White Irish	2.68%
White European	4.46%
Asian British	0.30%
Indian	0.00%
Black African	0.00%
Black Caribbean	0.30%
White and Black African	0.00%
White and Black Caribbean	0.60%
White and Asian	0.00%
Chinese	0.30%
Other	3.57%
Prefer not to say	1.79%
No response	0.89%
Void	0.89%
Total	100.00%

community and the programming of several high-profile lesbian comics on the bill.

The majority of audiences, 92 per cent ($n = 309$), did not identify as having a disability, and the age range of participants was spread across all the age categories. An overwhelming number of my respondents were white, with 88 per cent ($n = 296$) identifying as either white British or white European.

In comparison to Lockyer and Myers respondents (for their research into motivations to attend live comedy generally), the ages of my respondents overall were higher, with 29 per cent falling in the 41–50 category, as opposed to Lockyer and Myers' 14 per cent. This could be due to the online format of Lockyer and Myers' survey stage, which may have attracted a younger demographic of participants.

11% ($n = 37$) of the respondents were students.
This reflects Manchester's large student population, with four universities serving undergraduates and postgraduates very close

Table 6 Professional Area of Survey Respondents

Employment	(n = 336)
Student	11.90%
Homemaker	1.19%
Construction	1.19%
Science	1.79%
Education	8.04%
Civil servant	3.87%
Healthcare	12.80%
Finance	2.98%
Retail	7.74%
Arts	4.17%
Charity	5.06%
Hotel/Food	2.68%
IT	5.95%
Legal services	1.79%
Retired	1.79%
Unemployed	2.38%
Other	18.15%
Prefer not to say	1.49%
N/R	1.79%
Void	3.27%
Total	100.00%

to the venues: University of Manchester, Manchester Metropolitan University, University of Salford and Royal Northern College of Music.

The average number of times respondents attended live comedy was four times a year.

In line with Lockyer and Myers' findings, my respondents predominantly attended with other people: 49 per cent (*n* = 165) with friends and 30 per cent (*n* = 101) with their partners.

The average number of women-only comedy events/nights respondent attended in a year was two.

A high number of my survey respondents, 57 per cent in total, attended very little women-only comedy. In total, 19 per cent (*n* = 64) of my respondents said that they see no women-only comedy nights a year, and 38 per cent (*n* = 128) indicated one. As the purpose of the festival was to enable comedians to reach new audiences with their work, this is encouraging, as a significant number of respondents were not regular attendees of women-only line-ups.

54 per cent ($n = 183$) normally saw live comedy in small comedy clubs.

46 per cent ($n = 155$) normally saw live comedy in small arenas/theatres.

44 per cent ($n = 148$) normally saw live comedy in small rooms in pubs. (Note that for this question respondents were able to select multiple responses.)

When asked about preferred venues for comedy the responses for these top-three venues remained consistently in their first, second and third position. This differs slightly from Lockyer and Myers' findings in that their study found small arenas/theatres to be the most popular venue, with small comedy clubs in the second place and small rooms in pubs the least visited venue.

Large arenas were the least visited venue for comedy, at 16 per cent ($n = 53$), and when asked about preferred venues to see live comedy, large arenas dropped even further to 6 per cent ($n = 21$).

This may reflect the tastes of the particular audience for my study and the fact that I was facilitating the survey in person at an event which took place predominantly in small venues (whereas Lockyer and Myers conducted their survey online). Women-only line-ups take place more often in small venues (Laughing Cows' monthly women-only comedy nights occur in The Frog and Bucket which could be considered a small to medium sized comedy club) and women performers are still disproportionately found on bills in these smaller venues. Therefore, if the audiences were motivated to attend the festival to see women comics it is not a surprise that their other comedy-going experiences occur in smaller venues where they are more likely to see women performers across the year (Figure 3).

A majority of respondents, 65 per cent ($n = 218$), stated that the gender of the performer was not a factor when deciding to see live comedy in general (agreeing or strongly agreeing with this statement).

Figure 3 Image of publicity for Manchester Arenas comedy offer, as seen in public spaces across Manchester in 2018. Photograph by the author.

However, 279 of the respondents then completed the free text box when asked about their motivations to attend a women-only comedy event and 44 per cent ($n = 122$) of responses explicitly foregrounded gender. Comments in this section unequivocally mentioned respondents' support of women comics, a positive decision to seek out comedy by women and a desire to engage with a sense of humour they could connect to. So, whilst gender may not play a part when attending mainstream events, it is, somewhat unsurprisingly, a key motivator for women-only comedy event attendance.

Comments that fell into this category (all from women) included statements such as the following:

'To support women comedians. I also relate to their humour.'
'I am a feminist and I like to laugh.'

'Enjoy watching female comedy and socialising with other women.'
'I can relate to the humour of women-only comedy.'
'I love listening to and talking about women.'
'Because most line-ups never have a female act. If there wasn't any women-only shows I'd never see a female performance.'
'Because women are funny, but I can't see that on my TV.'

For the people responding in this way, it was clear that the gender of the performer was relevant and a motivating factor to attend the festival. This was articulated in the free text response box either in terms of participants wanting to support women to develop further in the industry, or that they wanted to hear a kind of comedy they related to more.

In contrast to those who stated that gender was a motivating factor to attend women-only comedy, 9 per cent ($n = 25$) of respondents, both men and women as indicated in the following, used this text box to reiterate the point that the gender of the comedian is irrelevant to their choice of comedy night. Comments included the following:

'I don't particularly attend women only comedy nights – it would usually be because someone I like is part of the show or because of the theme – I view all comedians as equal and watch them on their own merit how funny I find them.' (woman)
'I don't! I don't selectively attend women-only comedy – I watch what I want and judge by the quality not the gender.' (woman)
'No particular reason. If I like comedy the performers gender [sic] bears no issue.' (woman)
'Don't make a choice based on gender, just quality.' (man)
'I don't target women's comedy specifically. I just like comedy.' (man)
'I attend many comedies [sic], I don't base it on gender.' (man)

These comments are reflective of wider attitudes to inclusion and diversity, in that they tended to foreground terms such as 'quality' or 'merit' over the gender of the performer. These are, arguably, evidence of how, in the wider social context, initiatives such as positive action to address gender or racial disparities, or quotas, are undermined, as explored by Reni Eddo-Lodge (2017), Anamik Saha (2018) and Sara Ahmed (2012). The assumption is often made that addressing an inequality will result in a lowering of standards and that quality alone is how (white) male comics (businessmen, politicians, academics etc.) attained their success, rather than a result of structural barriers to wider inclusion. Whilst we cannot assume this was the motivation for all the comments in this survey, acknowledgement of these attitudes provides contextual information about the society in which the data was captured.

In contrast to those who stated gender was not a factor, the comments in this section also evidenced a perception that the comedy that respondents would encounter in this environment would be qualitatively different in some way to mainstream comedy (Tomsett 2022). In total, 8 per cent ($n = 21$) of the comments highlighted the participants' desire to avoid certain aspects of previous mainstream comedy experiences. Comments (all from women) included:

'Less risk of sexism/general awfulness.'

'No sexist rubbish.'

'Less dick jokes.'

'Because I'm sick of hearing shit comedians telling shit jokes about their mums and their girlfriends' vaginas. Oh??!! Women are nuts? Get a life you sad case! Also poo, there are more topics than poo.'

'I'm a feminist and appreciate comedy that's less likely to be sexist/ discriminatory.'

'To avoid misogyny, sexism, stereotypes. Hate "cock jokes" and "blokey" sense of humour.'

'I can feel intimidated and uncomfortable in a mixed setting even though the material is just as 'raunchy'. I feel safer.'

'Because most comedy is male-dominated and unfortunately much of it is misogynist.'

'Because most line-ups never have a female act. If there wasn't any women-only shows, I'd never see a female performance.'

'Enjoy women's comedy and gives me more to connect with than endless male perspectives.'

'Good non-threatening atmosphere.'

In a similar way that the alternative comedy of the 1980s was framed as a reaction against the working men's club environment of the 1960s, for some audience members at least, women-only spaces are providing an alternative experience to that encountered in contemporary live mainstream, and televised, comedy (Tomsett, 2022).

Interview stage

Following on from the survey I sampled participants for follow-up interviews. Ninety-eight people volunteered to participate in the interview stage and I selected participants based on their identity characteristics so as to be representative, as much as possible, of the wider pool of survey respondents. Due to the overwhelming number of white attendees, it was not possible to select along ethnicity lines. All interview participants were white British or white European. The identity characteristics of those interviewed can be seen in Table 7, and exact ages, when provided, are included. The final column of Table 7 states whether they intentionally attended the Women in Comedy Festival.

The interviews conducted were semi-structured conversations where participants' responses to the survey, and their experiences of comedy and motivations for attending a women-only event were discussed. In the conversations, I also explored with participants some of my own views about the topic, when relevant. This was to ensure the interaction was collaborative and mutually beneficial, rather than a one-way 'data-mining' exercise. The conversational tone of the interviews was to put participants at ease, and whilst my attitudes were occasionally discussed,

Table 7 Characteristics of Sampled Participants for the Interview Stage of Audience Study (exact ages, when provided, are included)

Number	Age	Gender	LGBT+	Profession	Intentional attendance
309	(41–50)	Female	Yes	IT	Yes
318	53	Female	Yes	Charity	Taken by friend
266	(21–30)	Male	Pref not to say	Finance	Taken by friend
247	18	Male	No	Student	Taken by friend
31	34	Female	Yes	Education	Taken by friend
71	(21–30)	Female	Yes	Education	Yes
201	39	Male	No	Healthcare	Yes
81	58	Female	No	Other	Yes
155	42	Female	Yes	Healthcare	Yes
250	19	Female	Yes	Student	Taken by friend
237	41	Female	No	Arts	Yes
296	30	Female	No	Media	No
295	31	Male	Yes	Media	No
46	31	Female	No	Education	Yes

questions were designed to not unnecessarily lead the participants to specific conclusions.

The interviews enabled me to explore further some of the attitudes tested as part of the survey. The survey contained a Likert scale section that enabled respondents to decide whether they agreed or disagreed with certain statements. These statements related to attitudes about comedy performed by women and women-only comedy spaces and the interviews provided a chance to really get to the bottom of where these attitudes had arisen from.

Audience attitudes regarding women comics

In total, 76 per cent ($n = 255$) of survey respondents agreed or strongly agreed with the statement that there are fewer female comedians than male comedians on the UK circuit. Even though those surveyed were physically at a women-only comedy event when completing the survey, 10 per cent ($n = 34$) of respondents thought that all women comics talk about the same topics and 9 per cent ($n = 30$, broken down as eighteen women and twelve men) believed those topics to only be relevant to other women. Whilst this could be seen as quite shocking internalized misogyny from the women responding in this way, the fact that these respondents would be exposed to women comics, who could change their minds on this topic at the festival, provides room for optimism. Holding these views and never seeing any women performers is different from at least being open to attending events such as this or watching women comics.

During the interviews, several participants hypothesized why this attitude might still exist: Participant 46 (heterosexual woman, early 30s) stated the following:

> [I]f you watch TV or you watch panel shows and stuff it's always one female comedian and I suppose people see 'the' female comedian and kind of think that they are all the same. But if you go to an event like that [a women-only comedy event] there is absolutely no way that you could ever say that they are all the same. [. . .] I thought that that was one of the really good things about the event really.

When asked whether women comedians were better at representing respondents' experiences, opinions on politics and opinions on relationships, the most popular selected response (an average of 44 per cent across the three questions) indicated that they neither agreed nor disagreed with these statements. This highlights how gender alone cannot be the only point of connection between the performer and the audience but that other aspects of intersectional identity are also at play. Participant 31 (homosexual woman, mid-30s) noted that the sexual identity, along with the gender of the performer, made a difference to how much they could relate to the material. She articulated how other identity characteristics make a difference to how audiences relate to performers:

I kind of felt more of an affinity with some of the comedians who [. . .] outed themselves and they talked about being in a same sex relationship that kind of thing. So, I felt more strongly affirmed with those comedians but there were some of the kind of things, issues that the women were talking about generally [. . .] where it kind of relates. [. . .] So, it might be like class, or rather than gender, it might be class or ethnicity or something like that. They might kind of feel drawn to a comedian. So, I think it's more individual and possibly based on prior experiences and the way people identify things that are important to them. But their identity will be important in shaping how they relate to a comedian.

The sexuality of the comedian has potential to play a role in forming a connection with lesbian audience members; this could also be said about other identity characteristics. This was a sentiment replicated in discussion with participants 71 and 155 too. It is important not to be reductive but, for the LGBTQ+ members of the audience, exploration within stand-up comedy of the sexuality of the performer potentially provides an opportunity to have their identities validated, in ways other art forms do not achieve.

The interview with Participant 296 (heterosexual woman, early 30s) evidenced by far the most conservative and stereotypical views regarding women and comedy. What is particularly interesting about this interview is that at the time this participant worked for a major television broadcaster, which she referenced throughout our discussion. She did not intentionally attend a women-only comedy event but was simply given a flyer whilst in a bar with a friend and decided to give it a go. When asked what she expected from a women-only comedy night, she commented:

> There's going to be a few lesbian jokes in there definitely. There's probably going to be a bit of men-hating, which there was, I think, if I can remember correctly.

The phrasing here is reminiscent of criticisms levelled at the feminist movement and women-only spaces in general. The idea that feminists hate men is a mainstay of criticisms of feminism. When asked about whether the sexuality of a comedian would impact on her ability to relate to them, she commented:

> No, because they'll end up just talking about a relationship and if they are talking about relationships, they'll talk about how a couple are. And I think most couples are quite similar in the sense of what they are going to be arguing or laughing about, so no, not really.

Whilst of course comedy that explores relationships between individuals will contain material that can be understood by all who have engaged in relationships with others, there are aspects of lesbian identity that are specific, not least the lack of representation and othering that lesbians encounter in mainstream media, and homophobia. Sexuality may well not impact on heterosexual audience members' ability to connect but for lesbian women, who encounter positive representations of themselves less frequently, live comedy is an important form for exploring sexual identities. In UK culture more broadly heterosexual perspectives are framed as the norm from which everything else deviates, whether articulated by a male or female performer, and so straight identity can easily find validation elsewhere.

Perceptions of women-only comedy spaces

During the interviews I was able to ask what participants thought they would get from attending a women-only comedy event. Many respondents stated that they felt it would be different from the mainstream circuit, in terms of both content and atmosphere. Participant 46 (heterosexual woman, early 30s), when asked what she expected from a women-only comedy night, commented:

> [W]hen I was an undergrad I'd been to a few nights at The Comedy Store and stuff, and they were quite laddy [. . .] not intimidating but laddy and it was mostly men in the audience and like girlfriends [laughs] of

the men, and it was mostly men on stage. [. . .] I kind of just thought it'd [the women-only comedy night] be different, that the vibe would be a bit different than that. Like not necessarily that it would be any less raucous or any less people having a good time. [. . .] But I suppose I just thought it might be a bit more chilled and a bit more sort of just, I don't know I want to say inclusive but I don't know, I don't think I really mean that [. . .] just less sort of laddy [*laughs*]. I know that's an obvious thing to say but um [. . .] I don't know how else to describe it. [. . .] I really do think that the festival was absolutely brilliant, because as I've said for someone who had been to the Comedy Store and thought well yeah it was great and everything, but perhaps I felt it wasn't really my thing, to then go and see something where I felt it really was my thing.

This sentiment was echoed by a comment made by Participant 71 (homosexual woman, 21–30 age bracket):

I've been to a lot of women-only spaces, and I know the audience was mixed, so my expectation was that it would be really inclusive, it would be almost a different type of comedy to kind of like your mainstream kind of white male things that they talk about. So, for example my expectation of a women's comedy night would be along the lines of the subject matter they talk about and the attitudes and values which they show through their set. So, for example when I listen to male stand-ups the way they talk about women, it may not be sexist or derogatory per se, I think it's the gender roles things and the stereotypes that inadvertently male stand-ups still have within their set.

In addition to the kind of comedy found in these environments the idea that the audiences contribute to creating a different atmosphere was commented upon. Participant 309 (homosexual woman, 40s age bracket) regularly attended women-only comedy nights and stated:

The heckling is always less aggressive. [. . .] And less sexual. I find a lot of when there's men the whole sort of sexual aggressiveness it disturbs me, even if it's kind of meant to be in fun. Because I can't quite tell sometimes, when [there are] those levels of sexual aggressiveness between strangers. As in [when] somebody on stage and somebody in the audience is actually meant to be a joke. It feels threatening to me.

I include these statements here not to make the case that women-only nights are some kind of utopia of inclusion but that several of my participants as audience members for comedy sought out an experience that was different from the mainstream. The sexism still found in mainstream male-dominated clubs clearly impacts on some audiences' decisions to seek out an alternative experience.

As part of the attitude statements section, respondents were asked whether they agreed that all comedy nights *should* have equal numbers of men and women. This statement was designed to assess attitudes towards the implementation of quotas. In total 40 per cent ($n = 134$) of respondents stated that they did agree that this should be the case. 24 per cent ($n = 81$) of respondents did not agree with the statement, and the remaining 36 per cent ($n = 121$) did not indicate an attitude either way. During the interview stage, participants felt that whilst line-ups should be more representative of the population, quotas would not be productive.

Participant 81 (heterosexual woman, late 50s) made a point similar to the general attitudes picked up in the free text boxes of the wider survey:

> I'll go to wherever the person makes me laugh and their gender or their sexual orientation is kind of, well is totally irrelevant if they are funny.

Hence we arrive back at this idea that, if comedians are funny then participants would go and see them and that gender was irrelevant. It was clear that in these instances respondents did not realize that their access to the work of comedians is influenced by industry decision-making, that is in itself heavily gendered. This seeming lack of recognition that quality does not guarantee exposure is a key finding and evidences why engagement with audiences should play an increasingly significant role in comedy research. Interestingly, this lack of awareness of power structures is not limited to audiences, and this attitude was also evidenced by BBC comedy executive Steve Canny on a discussion panel at Mixed Bill's Comedy and Power Conference at Sheffield Hallam University in November 2018. Canny repeatedly denied the existence of structural barriers to inclusion within UK broadcast comedy. He stated that 'the power' to get comedy made and exposed to a wider audience rested solely with the performer, much to the evident incredulity of the audience and other panel members.

Further to this idea of a meritocracy, in the interviews participants shed light on their attendance habits and how these are often formed by wider exposure to comedians on TV. Participant 295 (homosexual man, early 30s) also worked in television and commented that the way he selects shows to go and see is based on knowledge of at least one of the line-ups.

> [I]t's knowing, that for example I've seen Barbara Nice before and I know that if she's on the billing then there's an element of familiarity and I'm more likely to go and try other new comedians too. Or if it's so and so who's a familiar comedian or knowing that it's someone who has performed in a show that I like before, again I'm more likely to go and see that person and then inevitably other people through seeing that person.

Participant 201's (heterosexual man, late 30s) attendance habits were notably similar:

> So yeah, I don't have too many blind, blind comedic nights that I can think of. I might have the odd one but most of them I'd know at least one of the line-up.

These comments illustrate perfectly the double bind facing women performers. How do you know a comedian is funny until you have been exposed to their work? If audiences only go to see people they are aware of already, they will mostly be seeing men who have dominated the wider platforms. Knowing at least one of the line-ups is an important part of motivating people to attend live comedy. This foregrounds the need for women to be included in mixed-gendered line-ups as well as women-only spaces. This is because well-known comics have historically been male, due to their monopoly on television and recorded forms, and so using their status to expose audiences to a more diverse range of comedy is a key way to make long-term change to the industry. Crucially, for the festival 59 per cent ($n = 198$) of respondents agreed that they were more likely to see women comedians again now they had seen them perform live. This is a very positive statistic as the focus of the festival was to develop an audience for comedy, both in general but more specifically by performers who identify as women.

Unsurprisingly, due to the news coverage in the UK at the time regarding the BBC's new policy on panel show gender parity, 75 per cent ($n = 252$) of respondents agreed with the statement that there were not enough women on TV panel shows. Regarding the question about why participants thought there were fewer female than male comedians, many referenced television as the key factor in how they had arrived at this conclusion.

Participant 247 (heterosexual man, late teens) highlighted that what he sees on TV has led him to believe there are fewer women in comedy than men.

> I think it's the sort of media I'm exposed to because as I'm a teen, a young adult, I watch shows like *Mock the Week* and *Live at the Apollo* and you see from those shows there are very very few female comedians who perform and the ones who do are always the big-name comedians. So, there's Jo Caulfield will always be on *Mock the Week*, Sarah Millican will be on *Live at the Apollo*. So I think it's the way I formulated the belief; my belief that there are fewer female comics is because they get less exposure.

Many of the participants were aware of the wider context surrounding inclusion on panel shows. Participant 250 (bisexual woman, late teens) commented:

> I am aware that the BBC have now made it mandatory to have at least one woman on every panel show, which I agree with because it's linked to what I said before about representation, it's important. But also, I think that it's slightly bizarre that all we ever do seem to see on some programmes is men and the women that you do see are the same women every week. It's Miranda Hart for example or Shappi Khorsandi and it's not really necessarily the most diverse group of people, whereas you know the number of male comedians that seem to get the chance to go on these panel shows and to get themselves a better reputation and things like that. [. . .] For me it's not really about say tokenism for example but it's about the idea that in order to perhaps to push more people to do something, they need role models. So, if you know you're a little girl and you're interested in comedy, but you never see any women being funny, you might think women aren't funny. I think it's important that live events try to be as diverse as possible and have as many voices as possible speak because, again partially for representational purposes but also because I think you are more likely to get diverse, different kinds of humour, from diverse kinds of people.

Whereas the youngest interview participants (250 and 247) were aware of wider debates around representation and the media, what stood out from the interview with Participant 296, a woman who works within the television industry, was the openly hostile attitude towards positive action. When discussing how they had arrived at the understanding that there were fewer female comedians than male comedians they said:

> I'd say yeah there are fewer women, is that because they are less funny? I don't know, that's a question I'm asking myself. And then I try and think well actually they are [there], I mean there is always generally at least one on a show. I just I don't know, I'm not fussed by that. It just doesn't bother me that there's less women.

This participant was clearly unconcerned that women were in the minority within the content of television comedy. When I followed up by asking whether they felt the current system was a meritocracy and that comedians were simply booked because they were the funniest, she replied:

> Because they are the funniest, not because they are male or female. I can't stand positive discrimination.

It is not possible in this context for an answer to these interview questions to be 'wrong'; however, there is a discrepancy here between the data that exists regarding the exclusive nature of the cultural industries and this respondent's perception. Their answer is in many ways indicative of a wider unwillingness to acknowledge privilege in all its forms. A reticence to appreciate structural advantages (be they gendered, racial or in relation to additional identity characteristics) is often because to do so forces us to reconcile with our own forms of privilege and the ways in which we as individuals benefit from systems that oppress or obstruct others (Eddo-Lodge, 2017). This can often, especially when discussing racial privilege, make people defensive and uncomfortable. By acknowledging that there is no meritocracy in the TV comedy booking procedure, this participant would have also had to reflect on some of the obvious diversity issues and structural barriers within television production (in which she worked) too. She also evidenced a postfeminist attitude in response to further questions. An attitude that implied that somehow women have gone too far, and now men are in the position of being oppressed in some way. She made the argument that male comics now have a harder job of poking fun at the opposite sex, in a way that women do not experience.

> I think if you've got a woman saying a funny joke about a man she could say anything really small and we'd be like 'oh yeah, so true' but if men start saying just little things about women, I personally think women start getting uppity about it. Whereas if you've got to go so much further and take it much further. Women comedians can take it really, really far about men. I think men it's a very hard line that they have to sometimes tread to be able to go that far to make the same sort of jokes that we are talking about.

The views expressed in this particular interview are indicative of the attitude, explored in the previous chapters, that women, especially those who subscribe to a feminist ideology, are killjoys. The use of the word 'uppity' also has connotations of women getting 'above their station' and is eerily reminiscent of comedian Harry Enfield 'Women Know Your Place!' sketches of the 1990s, yet without the satirical undertones. This evidences that this attitude is still very much alive and well (and in the case of this respondent, working within the television industry).

Overall both the performers I consulted and the audience members who participated in this mixed-methods research believed the Women in Comedy Festival and women-only comedy events to be positive for inclusion. Audiences spoke of these spaces both in terms of the meeting of specific audience needs, women-only spaces have often provided safe spaces for lesbian and feminist groups for example, and also as a means to an end, to engage with an event that makes an impact on the representation across the wider comedy circuit.

The original organization of the Women in Comedy Festival clearly adheres to Sara Ahmed's description of feminist organizing. Ahmed writes of the discipline of women's studies and the desire within this field to transform the academy in the following way:

> [The discipline of women's studies] is to build in an environment that needs to be transformed by women's studies; the point is to transform the very ground on which we build. We want to shatter the foundations. It is not surprising that if we try to shatter the foundations upon which we build something, what we build is fragile. (2017: 176)

This description rings true of the way the Women in Comedy Festival had been put together prior to being more formally established within a venue (The Frog and Bucket) in 2020. It is an event that will only be thought of as truly successful when it is no longer necessary, something of which O'Keefe, the festival's founder, was acutely aware. It was an event created by the force of will of like-minded people, without core funding, beholden to no one, and without profit for the organizers. In my four years as researcher in residence, it was never possible for the group to submit a bid for Arts Council England (ACE) funding, regardless of the fact that such a bid would have been unlikely to be accepted, due to ACE's attitude towards comedy at the time (which I explore further in the conclusion of this volume). This was due to volunteers having insufficient time to apply for funding. The events themselves took place in the very spaces where male-dominated comedy also occurs. Thus, as with women's studies, the festival attempted (and continues to attempt) to fundamentally alter the system within which it builds itself. This way of working of course results in instability, or fragility to use Ahmed's term, as is the way of all feminist organizing. O'Keefe is a comedy industry professional but all the volunteers, upon which the event relied, were not. Arguably the Women in Comedy Festival illustrates that a feminism of another era is still alive and well, having more in common with the consciousness-raising initiatives of the late 1960s and 1970s than current binary-reasserting postfeminist organizations. The LGBTQ+ inclusiveness at the very heart of the organization, led by O'Keefe (a self-described butch lesbian), has enabled the festival to present a huge range of images of women and womanhood rather than attempting to align itself with a contemporary ideal of femininity.

This identifiably feminist organizing practice is distinctly different from, say, Funny Women, an organization that has always managed to achieve a good level of sponsorship, possibly because of the way it has historically reasserted a male/female binary as part of its publicity (although it has been making notable progress away from this in recent years). Parker, Funny Women's founder, talks of the organization as a brand; it is a professional outfit and it has been a very successful one, clearly contributing significantly to the progression of many contemporary comedians. However, previous sponsors of Funny Women include cosmetics brand Benefit, skincare brand Nivea and alcoholic drink brand Babysham, all of which are aligned with a certain kind of female experience and femininity and have used gendered stereotypes as part of advertising. The use of pink in Funny Women's branding combined with slogans such as 'laughter is the best cosmetic' present a postfeminist reassertion of women's difference. There is nothing inherently wrong in this approach. Parker is an experienced public relations professional who knows the benefit of financial backing, and it has enabled her to lead the organization into a well-known position in the industry. However, the observation that I wish to make here is that, despite the similar aims, the structure of these two organizations is very different. This has not, however, stopped collaboration between Funny Women and the UK Women in Comedy Festival, united by their shared goal to improve conditions for women on the live circuit. The existence of both organizations is evidence of the way widely divergent approaches to feminism, and to tackling ongoing inequality on the circuit, currently exist side by side. The following chapter will consider how, now that women have infiltrated these physical comedy spaces, and often with the help of the aforementioned organizations, social media facilitates, but also hinders, this process.

A clear finding from the audience interviews was that these women-only events contribute an enjoyable and necessary alternative space, and experience, for audiences. Many respondents discussed the way they had had negative (and gendered) experiences of mainstream spaces (sometimes years before) and therefore felt that they wanted an alternative to this experience. Mainstream comedy spaces, where white cisgender male comedians still dominate, are clearly still not perceived as inviting or inclusive *to everyone*. Women-only spaces therefore contribute an alternative space for audiences who feel more included in these environments.

Consulted audience members felt they took away something positive and different from these spaces, although it is worth noting that these feelings may also be contingent on stereotypes (e.g. the idea that women's spaces are more inviting or less aggressive, which is not always the case and is arguably based on stereotypical views of femininity). When audiences were asked if there should be a Women in Comedy

Festival, all interviewed participants agreed that the event should continue and the contribution was positive. This research contributes additional information to existing audience studies (such as that conducted by Lockyer and Myers [2011]) about motivations to attend women-only comedy nights and how these events are interpreted as an alternative to mainstream experiences.

4

Online to IRL

The impact of social media on stand-up comedy by women

The key focus of this book is live stand-up comedy performed by women and the spaces within which these performances occur. However, it is impossible to ignore the impact that both the internet and, more precisely, social media have had upon these physical performance spaces. The stand-up comedy performed by women in the contemporary UK context occurs in a highly mediatized environment where technology has profoundly influenced and altered relationships between people. Contemporary feminisms have also been impacted by these technological developments due to the potential they hold for gender liberation, as explored by the collective Laboria Cuboniks in their Xenofeminist Manifesto (2018). Fourth-wave feminism is notably connected to online spaces and the social media activism evidenced in campaigns such as #MeToo and #TimesUp (Boyle 2019). This chapter considers the way that online environments, specifically social media platforms, both challenge and maintain the current barriers facing women within the UK comedy industry.

The internet plays a vital role in circulating information about contemporary comedians; for example, extracts of their work, reviews of their shows, information about their career and when they have attained a certain level of success, gossip about their personal relationships. Social media furthers and embeds this role by creating an environment of unprecedented interaction between a comic and their live audiences. This was evident in comedy practice before the Covid-19 pandemic of

2020 and became increasingly significant during the global response to controlling the virus. In this chapter, I will argue that social media, focusing on the Twitter platform, plays a meaningful role in changing the relationship between stand-up comics and their live audience. In particular, I will consider the impact this evolving digital landscape has on women comedians. Comedy and comic personas developed and perpetuated online in digital spaces have direct and significant implications for the current context of live comedy performance.

A significant aspect of the current digital context is the availability and access to American comedy facilitated by the internet. This is true of both American stand-up shows, recorded 'specials' or clips of live performances, and televised comedy, such as sitcom and sketch genres, for example, *Saturday Night Live* (*SNL*) (1975 to present). Extracts of longer-form broadcast comedy can easily be repackaged and edited into short social media-friendly clips for circulation on YouTube. Furthermore, streaming services have provided new opportunities for stand-up comics on both sides of the Atlantic (i.e. those working in the English language), to record and distribute their live shows across online, rather than televised, platforms too. Netflix, which promotes 'stand-up specials', provides an outlet for the solo shows of many British and American women comics. For example, the shows made available via Netflix over the last seven years include Bridget Christie's *Stand-up for Her* (2017), Hannah Gadsby's *Nanette* (2018), Katherine Ryan's *In Trouble* (2017) and *Glitter Room* (2019), Maria Bamford's *Old Baby* (2017), Ali Wong's *Baby Cobra* (2016) and *Don Wong* (2022) and London Hughes' *To Catch a Dick* (2020). The opportunity to distribute a solo show in this way is welcome; however, the decision to release a recording of a full show means that the included comic material cannot be delivered (fully) in a live environment again. This opportunity to showcase full shows is therefore more relevant to established comics who have already significantly toured with the material before recording it.

The distinctions between US and UK television have been eroded as a result of streaming services such as Netflix, Amazon Prime and Hulu.

The process of watching comedy content from America has become almost indistinguishable from the process of watching UK television, possibly differing only in the use of different services or sites which hold the rights to the content. Due to this heightened awareness of both the products and discourse of the American comedy industry, it is often apparent that the UK lags behind in gender and racial diversity in relation to comedy output. The career of Black British comic Gina Yashere provides just one of many examples here (see Mahdawi 2017). There is a sense that 'the grass is greener' in the United States due to the increased profile of women writers and performers in and on US television comedy. The access we in the UK now have to comedy content via the online environment and the way this has impacted on fan cultures have provoked increased interest from academia. Examples here include Alex Symons' (2017) consideration of 'podcast comedy' and outsider status, Jillian Belanger's (2015) exploration of the impact new media has on stand-up production and Rebecca Krefting and Rebecca Baruc's (2015) insightful discussion of social media and American comedy, all of which focus on US contexts. Inger-Lise Kalviknes Bore's book *Screen Comedy and Online Audiences* (2017) considers comedy fan cultures and the ways in which audiences judge and debate comedy content across Tumblr, Twitter, Reddit and the wider internet. Kalviknes Bore's work discusses US, UK and transnational screen comedy and foregrounds the access audiences now have to a wide range of this comedy content.

The proliferation of sketch comedy on American network television offers a clear and well-trodden pathway between live stand-up or sketch performance and moving into narrative television formats such as sitcom (as was the case with Amy Poehler, Aidy Bryant and Tina Fey, *SNL*'s first female head writer) or Hollywood comedy films (evidenced by Kristen Wiig, Lesley Jones, Maya Rudolph and Kate McKinnon). Whilst this format has been significant for performers of all genders, as the alumni are very well known, the reach and scale of *SNL* is such that it has been key to launching the careers of a substantial number of women comedians, at a time when a comparable UK equivalent format does not exist – despite many attempts to launch similar UK versions. Alongside the circulation of content from broadcast formats, clips of women comics presenting or hosting events often circulate on Twitter. Examples of this include Amy Poehler and Tina Fey's speeches when hosting the Golden Globe Awards (2013–15) and more recently comedian Michelle Wolf's turn as 'Roastmaster' for the 2018 White House Correspondents' Association Dinner, which attracted huge amounts of gendered criticism, both of which were circulated across the world within hours of broadcast (Smith 2018).

In tandem with Britain's wider access to American comedy, we are also seeing increased amounts of user-generated content (UGC) online from both established comedians, those with ambitions to become comedians, and the wider general public. Comic short films and sketches are created for online platforms such as YouTube, and more recently Instagram and TikTok, and then circulated on Facebook and Twitter to gain a wider audience, occasionally going viral and attracting thousands or even millions of viewers.

In 'Is Vlogging the New Stand-up Comedy? A Compare/Contrast of Traditional and Online Models of Comedic Content Distribution', Matthew McKeague (2018) considers the differences and similarities between creating online comedy content and that of live stand-up comedy form. He summarizes his findings in relation to the following four areas: 'starting one's career, dealing with opposition, honing the craft and landing the big break that drastically increases popularity' (2018: 85). McKeague's research mainly focuses on those identifying as male and is created from literature reviews and quotes from interviews conducted by others. He does include considerations of a female married couple's online comic content, and the work of stand-up Maria Bamford in relation to 'dealing with opposition'; however, the gendered nature of both online and live spaces and how opposition encountered by those belonging to groups considered minorities is different to more general 'heckling' is not the focus. Although McKeague's attention is on the American context, and examines a male-heavy set of examples, it is clear that, in terms of starting a career, online content creation provides a new opportunity for those wanting to break into the comedy industry. This can be said both of those whose long-term goal is to move into screen comedy and those wishing to perform comedy in a live environment.

Alongside the use of social media and the internet for the dissemination of comic content, we are also living at a time where these online tools are used in an unprecedented manner for political means. A significant amount of political commentary, debate and opinion is delivered to the public via social media channels. These channels can be facilitated by individual politicians, political parties (the official Conservative Party and Labour Party social media sites, for example) or the online presence of broadcast news or the national press (*Channel Four News*, *The Guardian*, or *Huffington Post* for example). At the time of writing, the 2022 Russian invasion of Ukraine and the resulting humanitarian and political crises are disseminated around the world via the social media feeds of the general public and political/media organizations alike. This includes the Ukrainian prime minister Volodymyr Zelenskyy, who notably, prior to ascending to office, completed a law degree before working as a comedian and actor. Throughout his term in office (2017–21) American president Donald Trump's controversial use of Twitter as a way of speaking (uncensored) directly to the public, both those whom he governed and the wider world, as well as the world's political leaders, exemplifies a wider awareness and use of tools such as Twitter in recent years. Trump was removed from Twitter after the January 2021 Capitol riots and moved his online rants to other (even) less-moderated online spaces (before being reinstated by Elon Musk in 2022). There was widespread reporting of Trump's various Twitter furores in the mainstream news at the time. In addition to the Trumpian approach to social media, which is perhaps terrifying rather than comic, we also have politicians making use of humour to convey serious points. Kate Fox (2017) highlights that we have entered a new political climate, aided by the changes to the digital landscape, that combines comedy and seriousness. Fox posits the term 'humitas' to describe 'discourse which enjoys incongruity and paradox and doesn't draw a clear line between satire and sincerity' (Fox 2017). Social media provides a particularly effective space for this kind of comic political discourse as comic and serious messages sit side by side so boundaries are often blurred.

The focus of my discussion in this chapter is the platform Twitter, which operates as a public-facing tool. Twitter places emphasis on the ability to 'follow' high-profile individuals whose work or opinions may be of interest. This is dissimilar to Facebook, which functions, in line with the platform's original objectives, for the most part in relation to existing interpersonal relationships. It is of course useful to remember the gendered origins of Facebook, however, as it provides insight into the way social media spaces and platforms are developed with recourse to gender stereotypes. Susan Watkins reminds us that as a result of Facebook's (now called Meta) dominance, 'culture has been transformed by a means of communication premised on an Ivy League "hot or not" game' (Watkins 2018: 8) and thus it is hardly surprising that so many digital spaces reflect existing gender disparities. This more recently includes the development of Virtual Reality (VR) social spaces, which also create an opportunity for the continuation of physical and spatial harassment in new, digitally facilitated, ways (Blackwell et al. 2019). Even with the increased availability of multiple well-known social platforms, Twitter as a public platform has become a key way for comedians to maintain connections with and provide information to their audiences.

Impact on comic practice

The online context of contemporary comedy, social media use by comics and the impact that all these have had on the comedy industry was a topic of my conversation with comedian David Schneider in 2014.[1] Schneider, a comedy writer, performer and director, also founded the digital media company *That Lot*. Schneider's wide-ranging and long-running career, as well as his social media expertise, made him an ideal person with whom to critically discuss the changes observed in the industry since starting his career in the 1980s. Schneider's career, developed from his live comedy work initially as a student at Oxford University, has seen him perform as part of the cast of *The Day Today* (1994) and *I'm Alan Partridge* (1997), direct BBC3 sitcom *Josh* (2014–17) and co-write the feature film *The Death of Stalin* (2017) alongside the long-term collaborator Armando Iannucci. Schneider has (at the time of writing) 538.2k Twitter followers and is well known online for his left-leaning satirical humour.

During our conversation Schneider acknowledged immediately that his engagement with Twitter had both positive and negative impacts on his own comic practice:

> It's been transformational for me in many ways. [. . .] It's given me the ability to, err [. . .] [laughs] to polish my tools, to sharpen up. I've got better and better at writing one-liners. That wasn't necessarily a forte of mine beforehand, so it's helped me be more confident, it's helped me get better as a writer. It's had negative effects on my longer form writing, in as much that it is so obsessive and addictive.

Schneider believes Twitter has provided him with a place to hone a craft (in line with McKeague's findings in 2018), specifically short one-line jokes. He went on to suggest that the use of Twitter will depend upon the stage people are at in their careers:

> People who are already professional comedians it's allowed them to have a promotional tool and to also hone their techniques. To see maybe if this joke will work, maybe that joke, has it got several retweets, has it got lots of retweets, so it's a testing ground.

Not only can Twitter help to develop a skill then, it can also prompt some degree of formative feedback from a potential audience: this allows for a testing of the water for a specific joke construction or theme for further writing. In addition to being used to explore comic wording or joke construction, Twitter can also be used by comedians as a promotional tool, to give potential bookers, producers and audiences access to, and a flavour of, the style of comedy one that they would perform in a live environment or find evident in their written work.

More recently comedians have developed material for use on stage directly related to their online presence and interactions on social media (including Twitter and Instagram). A recent example is Birmingham comic Joe Lycett's 2022 UK Tour *More More More. How Do You Lycett, How Do You Lycett?*, which took many online interactions with the public and celebrity figures as the basis of material performed live (including his online parody of the Sue Gray report into #Partygate, the investigation into Downing Street parties during the Covid-19 lockdown periods) (Figure 4).

Figure 4 Image of author and friends with comedian Joe Lycett (L-R Poppy Wilde, Marverine Duffy, Ellie Tomsett, Joe Lycett) after a work-in-progress show of More, More, More, How Do You Lycett? How Do You Lycett? at Midlands Arts Centre March 2022. This image was shared on social media to encourage friends to see the show when on tour. Photograph by Poppy Wilde.

Space for development

Schneider also drew on his awareness of up-and-coming comics to consider how Twitter can assist in establishing a presence in the industry:

> I think it also has given confidence to a lot of people who would have never have tried stand up to try it. A lot of people who feel 'I'm not a comedian', 'Am I a comedian?', and might want to be a comedian, they can test out whether their jokes are funny which allows a bridge between that thing you have in your head, 'I think I might be funny', and standing up and saying jokes in front of people, which is a terrifying thing to do for the first time, or anytime. So social media allows a sort of confidence bridge, a bridge made out of confidence that helps people get to that step of actually standing up and doing live work.

In this way social media provides a space between having a potentially funny idea and getting up on stage for the first time. Whilst this process cannot replace the improvement of performance or delivery skills, such as comic-timing, which can only be developed in a live environment, the practice can give new performers a degree of confidence in their material. Clearly there is a difference between being labelled the funniest person in a social group, where the creation of humour may well be contingent on existing social relationships or knowledge of the joke-teller, and tweeting out a joke which enables access to a new audience with no social or affiliative stake in finding the joke funny. Nevertheless, due to the limited responses available to people on Twitter (such as 'favouriting' a tweet or re-tweeting, with or without further comment), it can be hard to tell exactly what kind of response people are indicating. A one-liner compressed into Twitter's 280 (initially 140) characters may receive the same response (the same number of 'favourites', re-tweets etc.) as a political comment, personal insult or call to action. Whilst the analytic information can indicate a quantitative interest from an audience, the appeal of tweets that go viral, or have a high number of re-tweets, could also be read as comprehension of the basis of the joke and indicate a fruitful topic for comic material. However, it is less common for someone to re-tweet or reply to a humorous tweet simply by saying, 'I found this funny' or using an emoji to express this response, thus providing more qualitative information to the joke-teller and, even if they did, it would still be hard to ascertain exactly how or why amusement was arrived at. The exchange of energy between performer and audience in a live context, where comedians can make constant judgements about the reception of their performance based on, amongst other things, the kind, duration and volume of laughter, is not easily replicated online due to the limited kinds of responses available.

If Twitter jokes do provoke a response via the reply function, it often turns into an act of participatory humour, where respondents attempt to add or further the joke in some way, although this again can indicate that a concept is ripe for further exploration. Irrespective of the multiple ways one could interpret online engagement with a one-line tweet, the interaction other Twitter users have with the tweet is providing basic information to a potential comedian before they arrive in another environment, be that a writing room or a performance space. As Schneider suggested in our conversation, this relatively new online space may be a step towards getting on stage and has the potential to broaden the pool of those who have the confidence to get up and try live comedy in the first place, possibly removing for women some of the stereotype threat that exists in a live environment.

Schneider stated that he personally knew several people who had started to perform live and acquired roles as writers after successfully establishing a following for their humour on Twitter or social media sites. When I spoke with Schneider he had recently worked with Jenny Bede, a former musical-theatre performer. Bede, who at the time of my discussion with Schneider, was very new to the comedy industry, is now known for her comedy work on BBC3, having built up a following on YouTube by posting parody music videos and sketches.[2] With a performance background, Bede was no stranger to the live environment, but YouTube provided a space to experiment with comedy and to build up a following for her material.

Musical and sketch comedy seem to be particularly effective forms for this movement between YouTube, and more recently TikTok, and other recorded comedy forms. This is due to the way short musical comedy videos exploit the specifics of the recorded forms themselves, satirizing the form and content of other screen media (such as music video formats or vlogging's direct address to the camera). The work of Munya Chawawa (@munyachawawa) provides an example of someone who has built up a significant following online through his creation of short sketches and musical parodies – especially during the Covid-19 lockdowns in the UK. Both Rosie Holt (@RosieisaHolt) and Eleanor Morton (@EleanorMorton) provide non-musical examples of comics finding success via Twitter. Holt subverts and satirizes the broadcast media's engagement with politicians by inserting videos of her fictional Conservative MP character into existing pre-packaged clips of interview footage. Morton performs a variety of characters that directly address a fictional live audience – for example, her various 'tour guides who don't give a fuck' videos, satirize unenthusiastic tourism and hospitality staff and prove particularly popular. The way in which short comedy videos are also integrated seamlessly into the existing content of the online platforms means that they sit alongside unironic music videos and interviews, and this contextualizes the well-observed parody.

Online, geographic barriers are broken down and so a niche audience can be found more easily and nurtured in order to create a potential audience for live work. Michael Spicer (@MrMichaelSpicer) transported his 'Room Next Door' character, a long-suffering PR adviser feeding lines via earpiece to various politicians, to a live environment as part of his *Room Next Door Tour* in 2021. This opportunity to convert online audiences into live attendees may be more significant for the UK context due to the way America is a larger geographic area. In the United States, online awareness does not as easily translate into attendance at a live event due to the greater physical distances involved.

Accessing information about comic labour

Twitter also creates a space that potentially enables audiences to understand the mechanics behind the comedy they encounter. A significant number of producers, writers and directors of screen comedy also have a Twitter presence and so it provides a source of information about the labour that goes into broadcast comedy. Examples here include writer and producer Saima Ferdows (@SaimaFerdows), *Derry Girls* (2018–22) writer Lisa McGee (@LisaMMcGee) and sketch writer-performer Gemma Arrowsmith (@mmaarrow). Similarly live comedy promoters and comedy nights also create a presence for themselves on social media and this sheds light on the process of bringing something to the stage. An example of this is the Twitter presence of Kiri Pritchard-McLean, which gives followers a wider understanding of the range of work she undertakes as a comic. She not only performs as a stand-up comedian but writes for and directs sketch troupe *Gein's Family Giftshop*, runs comedy nights *Suspiciously Cheap Comedy* and *Amusical* (with Jayde Adams and Dave Cribb), co-hosts a podcast *All Killa No Filla* (2014 to present) with Rachel Fairburn, and during the Covid-19 pandemic co-founded and hosted online comedy nights under the banner of *The Covid Arms*. Her Twitter feed explores all these differing comic roles and provides a wider understanding of the labour that goes into producing and promoting a live night, researching and creating a podcast or writing for radio or broadcast television. It exposes a process that previous generations of comics had been able to keep hidden from public view.

Silencing women online

Online spaces, particularly those facilitated by social media which encourages responses and interaction between users, hold particular challenges for women. This is an even more potentially complex space to negotiate for women of colour, as explored by Francesca Sobande, who notes, 'Overall, different digital spaces may enable Black women's public documentation of encountering oppression, profiling, and abuse, but can also be a source of such experiences' (2020: 85).

The abuse and trolling, online behaviour designed to provoke a negative or emotional response, that women receive when expressing opinions online was a key concern whilst conducting interviews as part of this research. Just as the physical spaces for comedy and public oratory have historically been resistant to the inclusion of women's voices, so too is the digital space of social media. Across the internet in general, but especially on Twitter, we can see widespread attempts at a systematic silencing of women in positions of power through trolling and abuse – although conversely, we can also see examples of very powerful and privileged women using social media to target minorities too. Again, there is an additional barrier here for Black women who are, according to a 2018 Amnesty International report, '84% more likely than white women to be mentioned in abusive Twitter comments' (Sobande 2020: 86). This is played out in a context where insufficient safeguards are in place online to prevent or tackle rape threats, calls to violence, or sexist, racist, homophobic and transphobic insults.

Comedian Kate Smurthwaite, who has herself been the victim of such threats, put forward her thoughts on this matter in the following way:

> I actually in a weird way don't think it's bad that we get all this abuse on the Internet. I mean obviously it's horrible that it happens. But however long it was ago, several decades ago Germaine Greer said, 'women have very little idea how much men hate them.' Well guess what, the Internet, thank you for letting us know. [. . .] Now we all know.

There are almost too many high-profile examples of women experiencing online abuse to consider this in detail here and existing scholarship on social media trolling exists elsewhere (e.g. Lumsden and Morgan, 2017). However, two examples have particular resonance with this research. I have selected these illustrative examples as the first (Mary

Beard) was referred to by some of my interviewees as a high-profile case of trolling and the second (Leslie Jones) illustrates the additional barriers for women of colour in online spaces in relation to comedy.

First, the Twitter trolling of classicist Professor Mary Beard provides a clear example of attempted silencing. Beard, who regularly appears on British TV and Radio to provide expert information about historical civilizations, was targeted following an appearance on BBC *Question Time* (1979 to present) on 17 January 2013. Beard is in a position of power, both within the academy and in the sense that she is able to express opinions on her specialism to the wider public. This seems to have been interpreted by many as an opportunity, an invitation almost, to publicly criticize her (Dowell 2013). The abuse faced by Beard predominantly focused, across intersectional lines, around her gender and age. As Beard notes, regarding online abuse, in her 2017 work *Women and Power: A Manifesto*:

> It's not what you say that prompts it, it's simply the fact that you're saying it. And that matches the detail of the threats themselves. They include a fairly predictable menu of rape, bombing, murder and so forth [. . .]. But a significant subsection is directed at silencing the women. 'Shut up you bitch' is a fairly common refrain. [. . .] In its crude, aggressive way, this is about keeping, or getting, women out of man's talk. (37)

Whilst Beard was more than qualified to express her opinions in public, the mere fact that she was a woman, and one who did not adhere to feminized ideas of beauty, and was intervening into the traditionally male sphere of public oratory, was enough to enrage some users of Twitter into a campaign against her. It is Beard's use of the term 'predictable' which is particularly depressing as we are now in a situation where many who write or speak publicly expect, or at least are not surprised to encounter, abusive reactions online. Comedy, as with all public oratory, has historically been considered 'man's talk'. Beard's experience provides an example obviously laden with misogyny, the abuse arriving seemingly with the motivation to use fear to prevent her from speaking out further. This reflects in many ways the abuse women receive in real-world environments. As Laurie Penny observed in an article for *The Independent* newspaper in 2011, 'an opinion, it seems, is the short skirt of the Internet' (Penny 2011). Many of the comedians I spoke to as part of my research were aware of, and referred to Beard's Twitter ordeal. Beard's more recent uses of social media have however fallen into the trap of white feminism by displaying a lack of awareness of the issues facing women of colour when trying to get their voices heard. She has also been criticized for mobilizing emotive imagery and language to prioritize white women's comfort over the right of minorities to call out racism in all its forms, casual or otherwise (Ramaswarmy 2018).

Second, a more recent and comedy-specific example of the hostile online environment faced by women is the backlash encountered by African American comic and actor Leslie Jones. Jones was targeted when appearing in the 2016 re-boot of the *Ghostbusters* franchise, directed by Paul Feig. Similar to Beard's argument about an online backlash being provoked to keep women out of men's business, in this instance the male-dominated fanbase of the original film appeared to see the female re-boot as a threat to the very core of their existence and identities. The online commentary around a female *Ghostbusters* repeatedly reflected on how a new version would ruin the childhood memories of men who loved the original film, whilst simultaneously dismissing the childhood memories of the young audiences, perhaps specifically girls, who would see the 2016 version and also be inspired or empowered by it. As Kalviknes Bore identified when discussing the Twitter response to the director's announcement of a female-led *Ghostbusters*, 'the aggression in some of these responses suggested a greater anxiety about what Feig's film might mean for fans' gendered identities' (2017: 45).

The racist misogyny Jones encountered for being in a comedy film was a wake-up call to many who naively thought that society was becoming more inclusive or accepting of more diverse depictions of women of colour on screen. This example highlights the way that trolling on Twitter is now often a gateway to more widespread and aggressive forms of online abuse, such as hacking, doxing (releasing personal information such as home addresses publicly without consent) and pictorial retaliation in the style of revenge porn. There also exist online cultures where groups collectively act to target those they want to be silenced. This can also relate to the more extreme ideologies proliferated in the sites under discussion in the work of Angela Nagel (2017), such as 'incel' culture. This way of perceiving the world centres on the idea that men are now being denied sexual intercourse by women and as such have become 'involuntarily celibate' (which has been contracted to the term 'incels'). This kind of misogyny is much more prevalent online than has been widely known. The term only became part of public debate due to a shooting in Canada by a man who professed to hold these beliefs (Tait 2018).

The abuse received by the women discussed earlier related to opinions expressed in written or televised forms or their inclusion within screen comedy. Therefore arguably, the hostility faced by women online mitigates against some of the identified positives, for example, the chance to develop a following or fanbase. The opposition encountered by women on social media is an additional barrier to those trying to develop a following online when starting a comedy career. For example, stand-up comedian Dotty Winters discussed with me her own experience of writing for the online magazine *Standard Issue* and the level of criticism and abuse she received as a result for this.

> I'm not sure people understand what happens in the online arena. [...] There are lots of things that are the same for all people, but there is something different that happens to women, in all jobs, but in comedy it's quite acute, if you are female and you express opinions publicly. And I don't know any male comics who regularly get death threats or rape threats on Twitter but that is standard practice if you are a female comedian expressing an opinion. I write for a magazine, as you know, [...] and there would be no point in writing articles and not expressing your opinion that would be a really bad article, but even knowing what was coming I am sometimes surprised by the response [...] that that

gets. And particularly the direct messages that you get on Twitter that are just vile and even though [. . .] you know where that's coming from and you know logically not to worry about it, it does affect you. Part of me just thinks [. . .] I don't think my male colleagues are sitting thinking 'shall I open my messages today on Twitter' or do I just not want to deal with that shit because I've got other stuff to do and that's going to bring my day down?

Whilst Winters is clearly not claiming that online abuse is unique to women, in her own experience she feels that cisgender male comics do not receive the aggressive response that women expressing comic viewpoints in public encounter. For every potential woman comic thinking of making use of social media to develop a following or a profile, the awareness of the gendered abuse experienced by many on Twitter will impact on whether they feel confident to express ideas online. The 'confidence bridge', to use Schneider's phrase, for women, still has a toll. This is additionally problematized by the racism present on social media that functions as an additional barrier to women of colour looking to use online platforms to develop a comic career. Women sharing comedy publicly still requires confidence, perhaps just a different type when compared to stand-up in a live environment. At least in the live environment hecklers do not have anonymity and are (for the most part) held accountable for their behaviour.

Kate Smurthwaite makes the additional argument that this online abuse, of which she has also regularly been the target, highlights the attitudes about women that often social structures keep hidden and thus could be positive in terms of exposing existing misogyny. She makes the case that just because we have not heard these attitudes articulated so bluntly previously does not mean they were not there bubbling away. Maybe, she argues, we just were not as aware of them before, as there was no anonymous way of sharing those views with the world.

> Like these attitudes didn't not exist before the Internet? These attitudes were out there and we sensed that they existed because you know, we noticed that we didn't get jobs and we noticed that policies seemed

to discriminate against us, and when we were applying for things we weren't listened to, and when we were asking for stuff we were ignored, and our needs were prioritized last, and the things that women did were not valid in the way that the things that men did were and dot dot dot. And now like, there is no, 'oooh no one's quite sure what's going on', it's really obvious, I can print it out and show it to you like, I've got folders full of it at home. [. . .] So I think that Internet trolling is a very useful way of telling us [. . .] what attitudes are really out there. And not to say that everybody feels that way but you know those attitudes haven't just emerged all of a sudden they've been there all along.

It is certainly true that, as with relief theories of humour that foreground the comic arena as an opportunity for exploring taboos, the relative anonymity of the online environment makes people feel they can say and express views that would otherwise be repressed. Therefore, as Smurthwaite argues, we could read in these views expressed online the historically hidden aspects of toxic masculinity (Salter and Blodgett 2017). So whilst the digital space can be democratizing for comedy, it is also clear that some aspects of these spaces are openly hostile to those who identify as women.

Building a following and highlighting connections

Following a comedian's Twitter timeline can provide basic insight into the kind of material they produce and their style of humour before seeing them in a live environment. This change is especially relevant to women comics as, as discussed in the introductory chapters of this book, it is still harder for them to infiltrate live comedy line-ups with the same regularity as their male contemporaries, and this makes it hard to build up a following of people familiar with their style. Additionally, the challenges women have faced when trying to progress from live into broadcast forms mean that it is unlikely that potential audiences will see them showcase their talent on television either. In this way, public-facing social media platforms such as Twitter can be seen as bridging a gap and enabling potential audiences access to information about what they will see in a live environment.

Comedians also regularly tweet about where they are playing, who they will be working alongside and new material or shows they have developed. Access to this logistical information was, as a comedy fan, my own initial motivation for joining Twitter. If I had just turned up at my local comedy clubs each week hoping to see women comics, this research would have taken significantly longer. Information shared via social media has made it easier for comedy fans to access the work of comics of interest. Historically with mixed bill line-ups or open mic nights, it was difficult or even impossible to know who would be on stage in advance. The information about where a comic is playing also often arrives with a useful element of contextual additional information. As Twitter functions as a social network it is easy to see connections between comedians who regularly promote the work of their collaborators and friends. If you enjoy the work of, for example, David O'Doherty (@phlaimeaux), you will often be informed about the work of fellow comedians working on the Irish circuit, such as Aisling Bea (@WeeMissBea) or Alison Spittle (@AlisonSpittle). This tendency creates an Amazon-style recommendation system where connections exist between comics with similar senses of humour (e.g. if you like X, why not try Y?). This results in well-known comedians taking on the role of social influencers, to some extent replacing or complementing the work done by traditional gatekeepers such as the critics, talent scouts or producers. By following those mentioned in tweets by comedians of interest, a Twitter user can expand their reach and broaden their awareness of new comedians. Thus, endorsements from comedians themselves, alongside reviews of shows, undertaken both by professionals, bloggers or simply enthusiastic members of the public, assist in building up a picture of the performers' work for the comedy fan before attending a live show, in a way that was simply not achievable prior to mainstream uptake of social media.

Participatory online humour

The connections between comedians become particularly obvious when large public events occur that provoke a comic reaction. Whilst some comics are very forthcoming about their political positions on Twitter, others are more interested in using the social media site to showcase their sense of humour, rewarding their fanbase for following them. As part of our conversation, Schneider suggested the example of the collaborative response to *The Eurovision Song Contest* (1956 to present), which provides an example of collaboration between comedians, comedy writers and producers, as well as members of the public.

> It definitely, obviously gives access to comics. It's that classic thing of watching *Eurovision* on Twitter is just sublime, because all the comics and all of the funny people just know that here's the time to be funny, and we didn't have that 10 years ago. It's a whole different performance thing [. . .] there's a performance on *Eurovision* night, you know you book your ticket for Twitter. That's what you want to see.

In instances such as this, Twitter users are responding humorously to a social or cultural occurrence. One comic may start a joke that another picks up, builds on or takes in another direction. The shared understanding required for humour to occur is based upon something all users are engaging with (be that something of national or international importance, like *Eurovision*, the EU referendum campaigns, a Royal wedding or something more local or niche such as a sports game or lesser-known TV show – the extensive online reaction to the 2018 BBC documentary *Bros: When The Screaming Stops* provides an example here). Often the more successful Twitter jokes merge together several topics of national importance; for example, many of the most popular tweets from the #Eurovision2018 feed referenced both Brexit and the song contest – drawing parallels between how unpopular the UK has become in Europe both politically and musically.

Twitter enables real-time feedback between users, and re-tweeted content can spread far beyond an initial group of followers. The labelling of tweets with a hashtag (e.g. #Eurovision2018) enables those following that topic to see content from every Twitter user labelled in this way and therefore is a very effective way of becoming exposed to new comedians and their comic approach. Twitter can provide advanced knowledge of a comic's humour, their performance schedule and an awareness of their social context within the industry, and this empowers audiences. Now, more than ever, audiences have the opportunity to make informed choices about who they see live and this benefits women comedians who lack exposure through other forms.

Interaction with comedians

The opportunity for individual audience members to interact with comics through social networking sites is one of the most significant changes to the comedy landscape. This change was further entrenched during the significant industrial changes occurring during the UK's Covid-19 lockdowns, when live comedy was forced to move online for a prolonged period (Tomsett et al. 2021).

The experience of watching a comic perform live was historically a time-limited experience, which perhaps would contain an element of audience interaction. However, on social media, the opportunities for interpersonal communication are a key part of following a comic on Twitter. This interaction can occur before seeing a performer live, either through the participation in a collective expression of humour (as with the aforementioned examples) or through direct questions in the forms of tweets to a particular performer, achieved by adding their Twitter handle to the post. For example, questions regarding the content of the shows and appropriate age levels can be asked in advance. Occasionally logistical information is requested from a performer too (e.g. 'when will the show finish so I can book a train?' Or 'will there be any tickets sold on the door?'). These kinds of questions appear on the surface very mundane. However, for the first time, the existence of the comedian external to the space and time of a performance is really present in the mind of an audience member before attending a show.

Not only can these interactions precede live performances but they can also form a crucial part of the relationship between performer and audience. Certain comedians use Twitter to highlight the often not-so-glamorous mechanics of being a stand-up on tour, affording their followers a look behind the scenes of life on the road. For example, Al Murray (@almurray) when touring engages in a long-running game of 'sink vs kettle' where he posts images to his followers of the complex and occasionally impossible tea-making facilities his hotel rooms present him with. Sarah Millican (@sarahmillican75) posts images on her Twitter feed of the snacks she consumes during the interval when on tour. These kinds of tweets show the audience some of the context of the performances and provide insight into the comedians' lives (in these cases as snack-eating or frustrated tea-making rounded people). These kinds of tweets can be seen as reinforcing their stage persona (as with Millican) or as helping them maintain a difference between their onstage and real-life selves (as with Murray).

After seeing a performance the audience now have a way to communicate their thoughts directly to a performer. This can be positive, in the sense that those who have enjoyed the performance can express their enjoyment and encourage others to see the shows too via social media (as was the use of Figure 4). Alternatively, this communication can be negative, with criticism being levelled at a comic for being offensive, using bad language or expressing specific opinions. The opportunity to voice judgements about a comedian's show, directly to the comedian, can occasionally form part of the hostile environment discussed in relation to women's online presence. Whereas any disruptive or threatening audience members can be ejected from the comedy club by security (silencing them), the online space is not as tightly policed, and occasionally audience members use this platform to retaliate when they feel slighted. Irrespective of the reaction evoked by the performance, Twitter gives the performer access to some of the audience's responses to their material, and for the audience, Twitter humanizes the performer highlighting the difference between their onstage and off-stage personas.

This opportunity for interaction can be used by comedians to nurture a sense of community in their fanbase or audiences. Luisa Omielan, a comic discussed in detail later in this book, provides a useful example of a comedian creating a sense of cohesion between her fans using Facebook and Twitter. Omielan's sharing of personal information and interactions with her fans creates a sense of shared values and interests around topics and experiences such as heartbreak, being single and bereavement. In this way we can see Omielan managing her online profile as a kind of brand, developing what Khamis, Ang and Welling (2017) outline as a micro-celebrity status.

In contrast to comics taking control of their own online presence, there are some comedians who have completely eschewed this kind of interaction. Stewart Lee and Daniel Kitson (as well as Bridget Christie who engages very sporadically with Twitter) are examples of high-profile UK comics refusing to participate in this kind of online profile building. Each nurtures their fanbase by using mailing lists for those who have signed up – a much more one-way approach to communication. It is telling to note, however, that these three comedians have been present within the industry for a significant period of time, pre-dating the mainstream use of social media. They have each built up a fanbase by performing live for a long time or showcasing their skills in broadcast forms (as was the case with Lee's TV work in the 1990s). Perhaps, therefore, these comedians have had the option to not engage with social media in a way newer up-and-upcoming comedians do not. Symons' (2017) discussion of outsider comedians in an American context provides examples of those who make use of social media and online platforms to maintain their 'outsider' status proving that it is possible to find a middle ground between protecting an alternative persona and engaging with fans via new technologies.

Schneider commented back in 2014 on how a presence on Twitter now forms part of the audiences' expectations of a comedian and can pose a problem for certain performers who do not wish to engage with the public in a social media space:

> [T]hat old fashioned thing of 'here's the performance' then 'I am a shy person and I want to go away', that's harder now. It is much harder to do as a performer.

The ability of a comic to walk away from a performance and conduct their own analysis of it is now replaced by access to audience feedback and opinion on an unprecedented scale. This may result in comedians leaving social media once they have reached a certain level of success of celebrity, as the pros of exposure no longer outweigh to cons of constant criticism – we can certainly see this is the case in the current context, several years after Schneider made this observation. He also considered how exposing the process or personality behind a comic performance challenges audience perceptions of performers:

> Sometimes Twitter can be, you know, 'pay no attention to the man behind the curtain'. We want to see the Wizard of Oz, we don't want to see the man sort of doing all the levers, the old geezer. So, some of the magic in that way has sort of gone, but that's all about, you know, the advantages outweigh the disadvantages because there's the proximity to the performer.

Therefore, whilst audiences may have gained a 'proximity to the performer' as Schneider terms it online, audiences also encounter information about the background to a performance that they may not want to see, or it could, in fact, actively detract from the collective enjoyment of the performance. Arguably managing a social media profile is a different kind of performance, and this is labour that some are unwilling to do, or do not have the time to engage in. Management of an online presence is time-consuming (non-paying) work that those with multiple part-time jobs or caring responsibilities may simply be unable to undertake. Whilst self-presentation strategies affect the way all social media users present themselves online across multiple platforms (the work of Ellison, Heino and Gibbs (2006) provides some insight into how impression management plays out in an online dating context), this kind of impression management is also relevant to the way comedians manage their online presence to attract potential audiences, rather than romantic or sexual partners.

To consider Schneider's 'Wizard of Oz' comment further, the management of a social media presence will be different for those who perform as a more pronounced character on stage rather than a heightened version of themselves. Those comics who perform character comedy acts may not wish to draw attention to the illusory or performed elements of their onstage persona, although for some this awareness is vital to understanding a performance.

A shift in performer/audience relationships

It is clear that a fundamental shift has occurred in relation to the possible interactions between stand-up comedians and their audiences in very recent years and that this has specific implications for women performers. These changes have been exacerbated because of the huge increase in the use of online platforms during the Covid-19 pandemic. Social media sites give audiences an unprecedented level of access to, and awareness of, a comedian's work and career. This information has the capacity to impact on whether audiences make the effort to see a performer live and also whether they choose to interact with a performer after an event. The information about a performer, accessible through social media, is contextualized within an awareness of what other comedians and audiences think about the comic and indications about their political leanings and comedy collaborators. Consequently, the information which is gleaned from this discourse is more powerful and convincing than simply informative text or imagery on a website. Comedians can make use of the tools of social media to refine their short-form joke-writing skills, test new material, engage in showcasing their topical humour through collaborative activities and foster a sense of connection with their current and potential audiences. For women starting out in UK comedy, the digital space of social media provides opportunities to develop comic material and personas on a scale currently unmatched by those found on the live circuit.

Whilst we can see many of the applications of social media as positive for performers and audiences, it is important to highlight that this digital space is often reflective of the wider societal context and thus contains specific gendered (and in the case of women of colour, racialized) hostility towards women. As Sobande highlights, 'the digital lives of Black women in Britain, and, around the world, continue to be marred by the prospect and reality of encountering disturbing content that depicts and communicates violence' (2020: 86). In relation to comedy, this hostility can be seen as a reflection of that found within the physical environments of comic performance. In the following chapter, therefore, I will turn to a consideration of how the current social context, facilitated by digital and online culture, impacts on the presentation of women's bodies within stand-up comedy performances by women in the live environment.

5

Bodies on stage

Feminisms on the comedy circuit post-2013

This chapter will explore the complexities of women using self-deprecatory and, conversely, body-positive humour within stand-up routines over the last ten years in the UK. I will consider the evolving and contradictory uses of self-deprecatory comedy, how this is related to the context of contemporary feminisms and the direct rejection of this approach by comics operating from a feminist and postfeminist position.[1]

Self-deprecation is a form of satirical humour that, as the term implies, targets the speaker or writer. Danielle Russell in her 2002 article 'Self-deprecatory Humour and the Female Comic: Self-destruction or Comedic Construction?' comments that self-deprecation occurs when 'satire is directed towards the self rather than confronting external targets. In a sense it is a form of accommodation – accommodating the perceptions of others' (Russell 2002). Self-deprecation can depreciate the perceived cultural value of the performer by lowering their status in relation to their audience and is a complex feature of comic work produced by those considered to be from minority groups.

Russell concluded from her content analysis of 150 American comedians, 37 of them being women, working in the 1970s, 1980s and 1990s that '[S]elf-deprecatory humour is neither restricted to, nor the staple of, female comics. It is, however, more prevalent in their stand-up routines than in those of their male counterparts' (Russell 2002). She highlights that self-deprecation is often seen as a key aspect of stand-up performances by women, as the need to 'recognize (and neutralize) audience resistance to her mere presence further complicates the issue of building a quick and positive rapport with her listeners' (Russell 2002).

In the two decades since Russell's article, and her articulation of her definition, it is reasonable to expect that the perceptions being 'accommodated' by those self-deprecating in comic performance, as well as the ways self-deprecation is used, will have changed. In the years since the alternative comedy movement of the 1980s, women in the UK have had increased opportunity to present themselves through comedy, taking control of their own comic representation. So where does self-deprecation fit within the post-alternative movement comedy industry?

The current approach evident in the UK circuit of using self-deprecation can be seen as *both* liberating and undercutting the power afforded to women when taking control of a comic situation (Tomsett 2018). This chapter will briefly outline where engagement with self-deprecation sits within a contemporary context in relation to feminisms that foreground empowerment narratives (Banet-Weiser 2018), before considering examples of comic practice that directly rejects this self-deprecatory mode of address so prevalent in previous eras.

Changes to feminist contexts of self-deprecation

The UK cultural backdrop against which the performances considered in this book occur (2013–23) is a place where the language and imagery of women's empowerment are commonplace, even if we accept that, in many instances, these terms have just been co-opted to sell us things, lifestyles, diets, deodorant and so on (Banet-Wiser 2018). Manufacturers of razors, sanitary products and other items designed to tame the unruly nature of women's bodies continue to make use of empowering neoliberal language in their campaigns, aligning the purchase of their product to some kind of feminist act. This current situation makes self-deprecation in stand-up comedy *more noticeable* than in previous generations as these utterances go against the prevailing tide of progressive yet depoliticized messages about women. This aligns with what Shani Orgad and Rosalind Gill describe as 'confidence culture' where, despite a context where 'gender, racial and class inequalities deepen, women are increasingly called on to *believe in themselves*' (Orgad and Gill 2022: 1) as if wider social issues have no impact on an individual's ability to succeed.

Alongside, and inherently interlinked with the 'empowerment' advertising trend and its connection to a new form of policing of women's bodies (comic or otherwise), celebrity feminisms have risen in popularity and this contributes to a commodification of this language of empowerment. In many cases, celebrities and those in the public eye who identify as feminists (e.g. Beyoncé and Taylor Swift but also former UK prime minster Theresa May) foreground the 'neoliberal discourse of meritocracy, which asserts that hard work is a universal equalizer' (Chatman 2015: 930). This then makes a failure to meet expectations of womanhood the individual's failure alone and often results in the homogenizing of the differing discriminations faced by women of colour, disabled women, trans women, gay women and so on. Celebrity feminisms often place the onus back on the individual to improve themselves, to make themselves worthy of success, without considering the myriad of structural inequalities that prevent this.

Often feminist considerations of humour originating prior to the rise of postfeminism and fourth-wave feminisms have focused on the problematic nature of self-deprecation by women. When considering the social role of humour for women, Regina Barreca contends that women have tended to laugh along with humour that demeans them, rather than challenge this form of joking. This is due, she argues, to the cultural programming of women to produce correct responses, even against their own interests. Self-deprecation has therefore provided a way for women to assume, or collude with, the demeaning and submissive position within which they are placed by wider society. Barreca furthers this argument by claiming that faking a laugh is the same as faking an orgasm and that 'laughing at something that isn't funny is just another version of "putting out". You're concerned with appearing to produce the right response' (2013: 117). Self-deprecation can be used to ingratiate oneself with the majority group and has often been interpreted as simply normalizing hetero-patriarchal attitudes to women.

Sara Ahmed writes extensively in her work *The Promise of Happiness* (2010) about the concept of feminist killjoys. Her observations resonate in relation to how not laughing or accommodating others is read as a transgression of a social contract. She comments:

> To create awkwardness is to be read as being awkward. Maintaining public comfort requires that certain bodies 'go along with it'. To refuse to go along with it, to refuse the place in which you are placed, is to be seen as trouble, as causing discomfort for others. (2010: 69)

Here Ahmed is discussing the experiences of Black women who felt the need to prevent awkwardness created by the presence of their bodies, their very presence being read as a disruption to the comfort of (white) others. Ahmed's comments have far-reaching implications for understanding pleasure responses in women.

This culturally instilled need for women to avoid creating awkwardness clearly links to what Ahmed describes as 'the rather uneasy dynamics of conditional happiness' (2010: 57). Women, Ahmed argues, are socially conditioned to derive pleasure from other people's happiness, irrespective of whether the object of the other's pleasure harms women in some way, and this is especially acute for women of colour. She articulates the dilemma thus, 'I am made happy by your happiness, but I am not made happy by what makes you happy' (2010: 57). This makes clear that we cannot assume that women signalling pleasure through laughter or smiling (socially, or in the context of a comic audience) is anything other than accommodating the needs or happiness of others. This is potentially the case for self-deprecation where denigrating the self enables the pleasure of others and is used as an accommodation to address gendered power dynamics.

With the live context, more so than recorded comic forms, performances require the cooperation and willingness of audiences to accept the premise of any self-satire by a comedian. The joking contract between the performer, audience and target of the joke is made more complex when all the parties performing these crucial joking functions are spatially together. When the butt or target of the joke is physically present before an audience, this will have an impact on the responses. When we consider self-deprecation, the element of spatial and possibly emotional detachment from the subject of a joke, experienced when watching a recorded form of comedy, is not comparable to the live environment. In a live comedy context, the person you are *laughing at* can see and hear your response, as with interpersonal social uses of humour. This inevitably impacts on the way live audiences will respond to self-satire and will differ from that of the audience for a recording. The live audience's reaction is heard and, due to the lack of fourth wall, acknowledged by the performer.

With the inevitable presence of a physical body within stand-up comedy performance, the cultural taboos around the women's bodies, such as the projection of overt female sexuality and divergences from 'feminine' behaviour, impact on the inclusion of self-deprecatory humour. Cisgender male performers, whilst still performing in a society that places value on body conformity, operate with fewer parameters in this regard. This may go some way towards explaining why Danielle Russell, back in the early 2000s, observed a higher percentage of women self-satirizing than men in her sample. Subsequent to Russell's writing, with the increased access to visual culture via new technologies and the internet, women arguably have an even higher number of criteria that they can fail against, compared to their male contemporaries. This is why, although self-deprecation is not unique to comic performances by women, it endures as an approach, especially within the live comedy arena where bodies are very literally on display. This relates to what Angela McRobbie terms 'visual media governmentality', which describes the increasingly significant relationship between women's understandings of their lives, experiences and bodies (especially in relation to femininity and maternity within the context of work) and the visual depictions to which they are exposed. McRobbie notes that the 'landscape of power is intensified and made more complex in the age of digital and social media' (2020: 35) and, as a result, the governance/self-governance of women in Western society through mediated representations has become normalized. It is within the social context of an abundance of emancipatory and neoliberal messages that the instances of self-deprecatory comedy by women performers are now situated. There are so many more images against which women can compare themselves in comparison to previous decades.

The exploration of women's bodies that is evidenced on the UK stand-up circuit of the last ten years directly considers aspects of women's lived experience that are kept hidden and silenced. Mikhail Bakhtin's influential discussion of the grotesque in his work *Rabelais and His World* (1984) remains a touchstone for those discussing women's bodies in comedy. Central to Bakhtin's argument is that the grotesque figure in comedy is fundamentally linked to nature and the world around it.

> [T]he grotesque body is not separated from the rest of the world. It is not a closed, completed unit: it is unfinished, outgrows itself, transgresses its own limits. The stress is laid on those parts of the body that are open to the outside world, that is, the parts through which the world enters the body or emerges from it, or through which the body itself goes out to meet the world. (1984: 26)

For Bakhtin, a grotesque figure marks and protrudes into the world and therefore grotesque depictions focus on the aspects of the body that enable this, including 'the open mouth, the genital organs, the breasts, the phallus, the potbelly, the nose' (1984: 26). The unavoidable way in which women's bodies engage with the world can be considered grotesque. Very clearly, through the lens of Bakhtin, we can see that the vagina is both the way the world enters the body and also a literal conduit for people entering the world. With this in mind, there are many ways cisgender women's bodies secrete into and mark the world, unlike their cisgender male counterparts: menstruation and lactation provide examples. When performers discuss these topics within their comedy, it is often within the parameters of self-deprecation.

For example, in her 2014 solo show, Shaparak Khorsandi described undergoing a cervical smear test. The test, which checks the health of a cervix, is described: the insertion of a speculum into her vagina and so on. The humour is not only derived from the casualness with which Khorsandi evokes the imagery of the scene, a process that is rarely discussed so openly and graphically, and the awkwardness of the situation, but also through the self-deprecatory punchline of the joke – that the doctor got further with her than her ex-boyfriend did – evidence of her romantic dysfunction.

Whilst acknowledging Bakhtin's undeniable contribution to the understanding of the grotesque body, Kathleen Rowe Karlyn argues, in *The Unruly Woman: Gender and the Genres of Laughter* (2011), that his analysis was focused on class rather than gender.

> He does not depart significantly from traditional representations of the feminine. His idealization of the women as the 'incarnation' of the 'lower bodily stratum' falls into one of the most enduring and misogynist of philosophical traditions, that of relegating the feminine to matter and the masculine to spirit, and then privileging the latter. (2011: 34)

Rowe Karlyn sets about exploring what she terms 'the unruly woman', which has links to Bakhtin's concept of the grotesque, but moves beyond the concept to interrogate how women use laughter to break out of social conventions. Rowe pushes further than the silent and embodied aspects of comic monstrosity, to consider the way that comic women's bodies also facilitate a challenge to the conceptions and conventions of 'femaleness' through speech acts. Women for Rowe Karlyn are never just about matter and the body. She argues, '[A]s women we cannot simply reject these conventions and invent new "untainted" ones in their place, we must learn the languages we inherit, with their inescapable contradictions, before transforming and redirecting them towards our own ends' (2011: 4).

Women comedians have inherited the language of their male predecessors in terms of comic performance traditions, as well as the language (verbal and visual) used to describe their own bodies. Therefore, for Rowe Karlyn, it is imperative that women comedians must acknowledge how these languages are used as part of their oppression in order to subvert them through comedy for their own ends. Self-deprecation in relation to the body can be read as one of these subversions, as these jokes draw upon the existing conventions which place women as the butt of the joke or object of humour, but has the potential to carry with it a critique of the stereotypes it draws upon.

To this end, self-deprecation can be seen as a positive part of comic performance in that it gives the performer control over the way an audience reacts to her body. Anne Hole argues, in her exploration of the work of Dawn French, for the empowering nature of the fat female body as it destabilizes notions of gender:

> The fat female body, then, is a figure embodying gender ambiguity and instability. Its threshold position and refusal/inability to perform a consistent gender identity makes it a representation of female mobility and mutability, of the move away from traditional feminine pursuits, expectations, and behaviours and into the male-structured world. (Hole 2003: 319)

For Hole, the fat female body in comedy is playing with the 'threshold position' it occupies, exploring aspects of female identity and femininity that are not societal norms. Women comedians can be revolutionary, then, when embodying these characteristics, through breaking down expectations about both gender and body norms by ridiculing society's attempts to control their bodies.

In a practical sense, within stand-up comedy, self-deprecation that focuses on women's bodies often features as short introductory comments at the start of the routine. Examples here include Annette Fagon's comments when reaching the microphone that the dress she is wearing used to be a lot less tight in her routine in 2013/14, or Lara A. King saying that she is getting in shape, and the shape she has chosen is 'round', in her 2015 club set. Alternatively, self-deprecation can form the foundation for whole sequences, such as Angela Barnes' set in 2016, where she discussed having a knee injury and being sent to a sports physiotherapist, only to find her body shape was not consistent with the others (sportspeople) in the waiting room. The resolution for this joking narrative was that others must have assumed her to be a darts player – darts players traditionally being very large-framed men who drank beer as they played, as opposed to their fitter comparators in other sports. Irrespective of how self-deprecation is included, due to the enduring nature of stereotypes about women's bodies, it is still very much a part of live comic performance, even now in the early 2020s.

Given that many of the uses of empowering language, the word feminism and seemingly pro-women imagery are nothing more than a marketing strategy, it is vital to remember that it is against this backdrop that self-deprecation in comedy is now taking place. When so many apparently positive messages about women abound, the self-deprecatory utterances stand out even more than they have done in previous social and historical contexts, as they run contrary to the discourses of empowerment and what Orgad and Gill describe as 'confidence culture' (2022). As these discourses of empowerment in many instances *reinforce* the pressures placed on women, self-deprecation provides a necessary space for critique of these pressures, especially in relation to women's bodies. Self-deprecation by women is thus inherently linked to wider gender politics, contemporary feminisms and cultural body norms.

Beyond self-deprecation on the UK circuit

In direct contrast to the self-deprecatory humour, a move towards overt body positivity is apparent in comedy performed by women on the UK circuit post-2013. Many comedians are finding themselves explicitly addressing notions of empowerment, especially in relation to embodied issues, within their work. To provide evidence of this I will now critically consider several examples of women actively using stand-up comedy to explore readings of their own bodies and to challenge societal control of women's bodies more widely. I am specifically concerned here with performances that occur within a UK context.

Adrienne Truscott

The work of Adrienne Truscott provides us with a clear example of this strategy in action. Truscott is an American performer and comedian and one-half of the New York-based cabaret and burlesque duo *The Wau Wau Sisters*. Her solo show *Adrienne Truscott's Asking for It: A One-Lady Rape about Comedy, Starring Her Pussy and Little Else* had a very successful run at the Edinburgh Fringe Festival in 2013, winning the Foster's Comedy Award Panel Prize. The show can be considered body-positive due to its clear examination of women's right to reclaim ownership of their bodies and to fight back against the way women's bodies, and violations against them such as rape, are presented in comedy (by predominantly cisgender men).

Truscott's show merged audio clips, music, character-based direct address and circus-style performance to explore the topic of rape jokes. Throughout the show she performed naked from the waist down and frequently moved amongst the audience, shattering any opportunity to disassociate her exposed body from her words. The character she presented was playful but ditzy, commenting early on in the performance that 'I've been brushing up on the rules of rape and comedy, because I'm new to comedy'. The contrived naivety of the character provided a vehicle for Truscott to make some highly political and challenging statements whilst keeping the tone of the show light and humorous. She reminded her audience, through an artfully constructed understatement, that irrespective of their political leanings, social background or gender identity, 'if there is one thing across the board that we can agree on, it is that rape is rude'.

On stage Truscott drank cans of beer and handed out a rape-whistle to the audience, reminding them that they were free to leave at any time, with the caveat that the rest of the audience would think them a rapist for doing so. Her rationale for this last statement was that only rapists should find her material offensive, as it is them that she was targeting. By making this comment early on in the performance she made clear that whilst acknowledging that the material could indeed be triggering for survivors of rape and sexual violence and that she had previously had people walk out during performances, she was not making light of rape itself, only those inconsiderate enough to take it as the basis for a joke.

The premise of the show was, as Truscott's website outlines, to ask, 'Can you make jokes about rape? She plans to, all night long. Even if you tell her to stop'.[2] The way in which the content and presentation of her material would make her audience uncomfortable was part of the experience of understanding violation, coercion and vulnerability. Although performance art has always included and explored the naked form and the limitations of the body, often containing extreme examples of self-objectification and body modification (such as piercing and cutting in the work of artists ORLAN or Marina Abramović), comedy, where the desired outcome is laugher, has drawn less on these techniques. In no way was *Asking for It* a traditional comedy solo show.

The majority of the performance was delivered through direct communication with the audience where Truscott explored victim-blaming practices and the patriarchy's instinctive defence of accused men – for example, 'I know you guys are still like "not Bill Cosby" and I'm like "yes Bill Cosby" – it's normally someone you know and trust'.

In between the direct addresses to the audience, Truscott would repeatedly perform a headstand on a chair and project a face on her upturned body whilst playing audio of male comedians making rape jokes. On stage, throughout the performance, sat a collection of framed photos of male comedians famed for telling rape jokes. This included an image of one of Britain's most popular comedians, Jimmy Carr, who is well known for actively positioning himself as controversial within his live work (see Gold 2012). The implication was that her vagina provided the vehicle through which the words of these men arrived in the performance space.

At no point was the tone self-deprecatory: Truscott's body was used to make a political rather than solely personal point. The show and Truscott's use of her body challenged assumptions about the vulnerability of women's bodies and exposed stereotypes around victim blaming. Truscott's work can be considered body- and sex-positive in a way that makes a conscious break with the self-deprecatory mode. This show presents women as multidimensional sexual subjects and seeks to challenge systems and instances of negativity directed at women's bodies, including objectification as a gateway to violence against women. By putting herself in a vulnerable position, by exposing her body in front of an audience, Truscott was able to adopt a politically critical position from which to examine the way society perpetuates the idea that 'women make themselves vulnerable' through their choices. This enabled her to invert this notion of vulnerability and exposure, as she had the power in this situation, and the fully clothed audience members were rendered vulnerable and exposed through her actions.

Throughout *Asking for It* the point repeatedly returned to, and being constantly made by the presence of Truscott's body in the space, reinforced by the title of the show itself, was that irrespective of how few clothes a woman is wearing, and no matter how much she drinks and swears or moves completely naked amongst others, her body is hers, and rape is a fundamental violation of body autonomy. Even when she (in this case Truscott) is moving totally naked amongst strangers a woman is never 'asking for it'. Truscott's nakedness clearly made the audience uncomfortable, with many not knowing where to look during the performance I witnessed. This state of discomfort with Truscott's nakedness was compounded by the content of the show, which was cleverly manipulated to continually destabilize the audience.

In many ways, the show's subtitle, 'a one-lady rape about comedy', was an appropriate metaphor, as the jokes and performance style were used to violate the audiences' space, make audiences uncomfortable and provoke a complex reaction that went beyond straightforward humour. By linking the more traditionally comic moments of direct communication to verbatim quotations from American lawmakers and judicial system professionals, as well as male comics from the United States and United Kingdom, Truscott managed to contextualize how rape jokes could be seen as part of the wider system of rape culture in Western society.

It is worthy of note that one of Truscott's examples within the show was Louis C.K., a highly respected stand-up comic at the time and producer and writer at the top of his powers. C.K. had attracted criticism for seemingly attempting to reconcile his version of feminism with his use of rape jokes within his routines. In 2017, several years after Truscott's performances, in the wake of the high-profile sexual assault scandals across the entertainment industries in both the US and UK, initiated by rape allegations against Hollywood producer Harvey Weinstein, revelations about C.K.'s abuses of power emerged. This was of seemingly little surprise to many within the industry. The accusations from women comedians were subsequently publicly confirmed by C.K. as true in a 'Trumpian' statement of apology (where emphasis was placed on the respect these women had for his talent, rather than the harm he had caused them) (C.K. 2017). In this example, we can see a very clear discrepancy between claims to feminism or feminist beliefs, and actions, especially in relation to behaviour within the industry that reinforces patriarchy and rape culture.

These events highlight again how power and status within any industry are what help maintain silence around rape and sexual violence towards women. These issues exist within the comedy industry (as will be explored in Chapter 7) and so it is notable how comedy can also be used as a tool to challenge and call out this behaviour too. Whilst not all comedians who make rape jokes are rapists, the inability of some to see rape jokes as offensive arguably stems from the same inability to see why sexualized behaviour towards women without their consent may also be seen as offensive. The attempt to argue that rape jokes themselves, and problematic sexual behaviour towards women, are done 'in fun' and that women are 'overreacting' is, without doubt, part of what maintains the silence of women within rape culture. The way often the perpetrators of abuse have power and a voice where their accusers do not is arguably echoed in the relationship between comics on stage making rape jokes and any offended audience members.

Even though Truscott is an American comedian, with the content of her show heavily referencing American culture and celebrities, the success of her show at the 2013 Edinburgh Fringe Festival, and its subsequent run at Soho Theatre in London, highlights the relevance of her work to UK audiences too. Several of the high-profile US examples that Truscott touched upon had been reported in the UK media, reigniting debates about rape jokes. Daniel Tosh's use of a rape threat to silence a woman in his audience who had challenged his proclamation that 'rape is always funny' provides an example of something widely reported in the UK press (Holpuch 2012). As the UK's own politicians and legal systems have also been found to hold problematic and discriminatory attitudes towards female rape victims, the examples used were close enough to be recognizable to a British audience. Truscott's achievements in the UK evidence that, in 2013/14, live performances by women who adopted a more body-positive and political tone were both critically and commercially successful.

Gráinne Maguire

Irish comedian Gráinne Maguire's work can also be seen as a comparable example of someone developing comic material to challenge state control of women's bodies.

> I'm one of those immigrants you've been hearing so much about on the news. [. . .] I'm a proud Irish woman. I didn't come all the way over from Dublin to steal your benefits. I specifically came here to scrounge your abortion rights. (Maguire 2016)

In the wake of the successes of women comics in 2013/14, Maguire, who has always dealt in political material, likewise explored issues relating to the control of women's bodies by those in positions of power. In Maguire's case, the focus was women's right to choose to terminate unwanted pregnancies (Maguire 2015). Maguire's handling of this topic can be considered body-positive in the sense that it rejects state and religious interference, in both cases predominantly male interference, in women's right to make decisions about their own bodies. These rights are something that in England, Wales and Scotland (though notably not currently Northern Ireland) are often taken for granted, forgetting the long feminist struggle and agitation for autonomy which resulted in the 1967 Abortion Act and abortion being made available via the National Health Service (NHS). However, this ability to access abortion easily and safely was not the case in Ireland (prior to a referendum in 2018). In 2015 Maguire made use of her social media profile on Twitter to send Irish Taoiseach Enda Kenny detailed information about her menstrual cycle. She did this in order to make a political point about state control of abortion: the graphic descriptions of her menstrual cycle were framed in a comic way so as to make the point that the state should not have control of women's bodies. Calling for others to follow her lead and tweet their cycles to the government, Maguire made full use of Twitter's hashtag function to encourage others to highlight the intrusiveness of Ireland's laws relating to female bodies.

Maguire's actions formed part of her public support for *Repeal the Eighth* (#repealthe8th) – a pro-choice campaign which politically agitated for abortion rights in Ireland before and during the 2018 referendum. She engaged with this topic within the content of her live material too, including her 2016 solo show *Great People Making Great Choices*. Menstrual or 'period' humour has traditionally made use of a self-deprecatory tone, being one of the many taboos surrounding women's bodies and appropriate behaviour in public (as explored earlier). Maguire dragged the traditionally private information about women's menstrual cycles into the public to highlight both the restrictiveness of the laws around abortion and the ridiculous wider societal squeamishness regarding periods. To summarize her comic argument: if the state wants to control women's reproductive systems, it also has to deal with all the bloody detail.

In Maguire's instance period humour was not self-deprecatory; she did not make her body the subject of ridicule or make herself a grotesque figure. Rather she turned the functions of her own body into a tool for political change in line with the embodied politics of third-wave feminism. Maguire used the unifying effect that humour can have in order to galvanize a response to a pro-choice campaign, with her comedy thus containing a call to action. Her humour on this topic, evidenced both online and in her live work, focused on behaviour change, first asking women to join in with tweeting the Taoiseach and second, to follow up this action by protesting against state control of abortion and voting to overturn the law. The jokes went beyond simply highlighting the problem, by demonstrating a way to challenge the norms at play too. Even though this reflected a law specific to Ireland (and despite Northern Ireland continuing to have a complex relationship with pro-choice laws), there was a very strong link to the material for UK audiences, as often the women of Ireland who wanted to terminate a pregnancy flew to mainland Britain to undergo the procedure. Maguire's comedy around this subject evidences how period humour has evolved to be more political, rather than self-deprecatory in this fourth-wave feminist context. Body positivity in current comedy output can take many forms. Maguire's work demonstrates that information about the biological functions of one's own body can be used not only for comic effect, which has been a long-standing application of bodily functions, but also to be reframed as a shared experience, to provoke political thought and change.

Lolly Adefope

A third example of comedy from this period that operates from a more self-assured position is found in the work of comedian and actor Lolly Adefope. Adefope's show *Lolly 2* (2016) directly responded to the way critics of her first solo show disproportionately focused on her identity as a Black woman, criticizing her in reviews for not discussing her race. *Lolly 2* explores how Adefope was acutely aware that she would be criticized for drawing too much attention to her identity had she chosen in her debut show to do so, and so could not win. Adefope performs sketch comedy and switches between many different characters during her live performances, showcasing her skill of capturing characters with accents and gestures. She has recently put these skills to use across various mediated comedy performances, including *Ghosts* (2019 to present) and *Shrill* (2019–21).

In *Lolly 2*, Adefope successfully highlighted the double bind that Black women experience in relation to having to acknowledge and explore their intersectional differences from the majority group (white cisgender men), whilst also having to try to not make their work 'about' their identity: a Catch 22 scenario. When existing in a marginalized position within the comedy industry, there is arguably an *expectation* that this difference will be addressed in some way by the material. Although many comedians create work explicitly exploring their racial identity (Shazia Mirza, Shaparak Khorsandi and Fatiha El-Ghorri provide examples here), this expectation results in a situation where the comic can be both criticized for being too political, by making comedy about their marginalized position, and also concurrently criticized for not addressing their unique viewpoint too. As Joanne Gilbert comments:

> Marginalized individuals are often afforded a freedom unique to their insider/outsider position; in the context of stand-up comedy, women who perform their marginality may offer a potentially subversive critique of hegemonic culture while simultaneously eliciting laughter and earning a living. (2004: 3)

However, there is arguably a problematic societal *expectation* that women, and Black women especially, will use the freedom of comedy to explore their political and social position in relation to their gender and racial identities. Arguably then, this freedom to assume an outside position is not in fact a freedom at all, but just another form of constraint.

If you include women, ethnic minorities, LGBTQ+ performers and/or disabled people into the comedy industry, but only on the condition that they discuss their marginality or difference from the societal norm, another form of control exerts itself. This expectation reinforces notions of difference rather than affording performers in marginal identity positions a genuine choice of material (the choice available to white cisgender male comedians). Is this expectation not just another form of discrimination that once again reinforces a white male universality against which all must be positioned? This is what Adefope's show artfully considered, whilst also provoking laughter.

In terms of exploring and, in some ways neutralizing, visually evident differences from the majority group, we find that, as explored earlier, self-deprecation has often served a precise purpose. However, Adefope's show is unapologetically political rather than self-deprecatory. By referring to and projecting reviews of her first show on a screen behind her whilst performing her sketch comedy, Adefope is able to critique the uncomfortable relationship society has with race and gender. The show displayed her character comedy skills and simultaneously made the broader point about the expectations placed on Black women to somehow speak on behalf of an identity. Several cultural reference points were used, including the discussion of the casting of a Black actor (Norma Dumezweni) to play, as Adefope terms it, 'Black Hermione', in the stage show *Harry Potter and the Cursed Child*, and the high-profile publicity around the racial inequality of the Academy Awards system and the #OscarsSoWhite campaign (see Cox 2016).

Many of the sketches in *Lolly 2* directly considered the reactions of people to the presence of Black women's bodies and highlighted the continued marginalization specific to the ways race and gender (amongst other characteristics) intersect. As Reni Eddo-Lodge comments in her work, *Why I'm No Longer Talking to White People about Race*:

> Whiteness positions itself as the norm. It refuses to recognise itself for what it is. Its so-called 'objectivity' and 'reason' is its most potent and insidious tool for maintaining power. (2017: 169)

Whilst it is crucial to understand that Black women and women of colour experience distinct forms of oppression to those benefitting from a system of white privilege, and thus the perspective they articulate in their comedy will be different, so too is it important not to force women of colour to take responsibility for the educating of white people on racism. Criticism of Adefope's debut show can be considered an example of this racial and gendered expectation placed on Black women. *Lolly 2* rejects this responsibility, reasserting that Adefope's comedy is above all else comedy, whilst not denying her unique viewpoint and managing to highlight many of the ways structural racism still plays out in Western society.

Each of these examples highlights how, running concurrent to comedy that continues to use self-deprecation to critique or lampoon gender stereotypes, women comics are also choosing to tackle the stereotypes head-on, abandoning the self-deprecatory approach in favour of a more self-assured and body-/sex-positive position aligned to current feminist thought. There is evidently a wide range of approaches to body positivity within the performances discussed earlier. Truscott's use of her naked body within the performance space provides a critique of rape culture that simultaneously demonstrates positive attitudes towards her own body through her refusal to be policed. Maguire discloses information about her own body, specifically her menstrual cycle, a subject that society still sees as taboo. Her comedy challenges women to see their bodies as positive tools for change, speaking up for women's rights through highlighting the similarities in our experiences and the way shame is often used to keep all women silent. Last, Adefope's work directly addresses the additional silencing and discrimination faced by women of colour by laying bare racialized criticism of her work. She uses her body to reaffirm her identity and her refusal to be made responsible for educating others of her experience as a Black woman. Her work subverts criticism into positivity by proclaiming her right to self-define and be creative in any way she sees fit. To summarize, Truscott uses her naked body within the space of the performance, Maguire discloses graphic historically taboo information about her body to her audience and Adefope addresses criticism of the use of her body as a Black woman, with each comedian promoting positive self-determination rather than self-critique.

Further to this brief overview of the body-positive material evidenced on the current circuit, I will now focus in detail on the work of Bridget Christie and Luisa Omielan as I posit that these comics provide illustrative examples of the multiple and sometimes contradictory feminist comedy on the current circuit. My case studies seek to demonstrate how, as women, these comedians face gendered challenges to making work in the UK context, developing an audience and progressing to the higher levels of the industry. The analysis of Christie and Omielan's comic material and performances also explores how body positivity is evident in both feminist and postfeminist comedy in the current UK context and is a direct rejection of previous tendencies towards self-deprecation.

Feminist comedy: Bridget Christie

Bridget Christie provides an example of a comedian producing stand-up comedy, from an overtly feminist standpoint.[3] In 2013, Christie became only the third woman to win the Best Comedy Show Prize at the Edinburgh Fringe Festival, catapulting her from relative obscurity into one of (if not) the best-known 'feminist comedians' in the UK.

It is relevant to note at the start of this section that Christie is a comedian, rather than a 'female comedian' or a 'feminist comedian' – the point I made in my 2017 article on her work (Tomsett 2017). Although I am here considering her work in relation to feminism and will therefore reference her gender identity, her right to define as a comic without further caveat is an important foundational consideration. The right to be considered a comedian (rather than a 'female comedian') is central to current debates around women and comedy and this point is always worth restating. Gender should not be considered a genre (as outlined extensively in the introductory chapters of this book).

One of the ways that Christie was different from her contemporaries in 2013, when being considered for Best Show, was the overtly feminist content of her material. Barreca, writing about the strategic use of women's humour, points out, 'The writer Kate Clinton has come up with a compact word for feminist humourists – "Fumerist" – because it captures being funny and wanting to burn the house down all at once' (2013: 178). Christie can be considered a fumerist in that her comedy deals both with feminist politics (on a macro- and micro-scale) and also clearly displays her anger at the injustices and inequalities experienced by women. As Cynthia Willett, Julie Willett and Yael Sherman observe, 'Just as ridicule and humor provide an arsenal of tools that can reinforce these norms and practices, so too this arsenal can tear those conventions down' (2012: 230). Christie's comic arsenal is extensive and, as such, she is well placed to undertake the rhetorical demolition of the patriarchy, upon which her material rests.

The clearest example of how Christie's approach to deconstructing gendered norms has evolved across her career is to be found in the comparison of her 2010 show *A.Ant* and her current style as evident in *A Bic for Her* (2013), *An Ungrateful Woman* (2014) *A Book for Her* (2015), *Because You Demanded It* (2016), *What Now?* (2018) and, most recently, *Who Am I?* (2021). Although there is a consistency in the inclusion of material that skewers gender stereotypes, her performance style has changed significantly from an initial focus on character comedy prior to 2013. Christie explains her decision to engage with gender politics in her routines in the following way:

> I read some reviews of female comedians and noticed they were full of irrelevant information about their looks and clothes, cooking skills, how well they could throw a ball, their fertility capabilities, how many previous boyfriends they'd had [. . .] There wasn't too much about their actual material. It really annoyed me, so I started talking about it on stage. (Christie 2015: 54)

Christie's show *A.Ant* dealt with the complexities of being a woman on the live comedy circuit. However, rather than tackle this issue head-on, Christie concocted the premise of being an ant, dressing in a home-made costume and angrily demanding equality for ant comics working on the circuit. A.Ant (the character) was livid at the compère for introducing them to the stage as an 'ant' comedian, complaining that this, as well as playing music by Adam Ant as they took to the stage, simply gave the audience a chance to recall and process all their preconceptions about ants not being funny. The humour of this routine was reliant upon both familiarity with the key stereotypes about women and comedy, in the spirit of the infamous Christopher Hitchens' article of 2007, but also in the incongruity of these arguments being applied in the context of an insect comedian.

The content of the *A.Ant* performances played directly with the stereotype that women comics produce material that is only ever about 'being a woman' and therefore will only be accessible to other women. As Christie comments in her published work *A Book for Her* (2015):

> I'd read out lots of ant jokes from a small red notebook, which were rubbish and just a play on the word 'ant'. This bit often went down much better than the actual routine, especially with audiences who hadn't quite understood the metaphor, which is perfectly understandable. (2015: 72)

This section of the routine (the reading of ant jokes from a book) again highlighted the way a cisgender male universality is applied in the comic arena. Comedy produced by those identifying as male is often seen and discussed as accessible to all, whereas those positioned as 'other' (along gendered, or in terms of this routine, species lines) are expected to only ever perform jokes about their identity, thus rendering their comedy less universally understandable. By removing the human gender stereotypes and replacing them with insects, she enabled the prejudice described to be laid bare and ridiculed by all present, irrespective of the audiences' own gender identity. Thus, humour provided a way to challenge the gender stereotypes at play in relation to performed comedy. There is also an argument to be made here that by removing the gendered aspect of the critique within the performance, or at least masking it, literally and metaphorically, behind the face of an ant, Christie was less likely to come up against overt resistance from those who disagreed with her identification of sexism on the circuit. This could apply to both resistance from male audience members and those booking Christie to play at their clubs or events.

In the case of the character of A.Ant, however, the more surreal nature of the delivery potentially obscured the message and prevented it from being accessible to wider audiences. Christie was also aware that the context of these performances impacted on the way audiences understood and connected with her act. She comments:

> My ant act went well if I did it in a proper venue with a decent sized audience, in front of a comedy-savvy crowd, for example at the Soho Theatre for one of Alexei Sayle's curated gigs, or as part of a really good bill, but it always bombed at new-material and open mic nights. (2015: 72)

I first saw Christie perform as A.Ant as part of Robin Ince's *School for Gifted Children* at Bloomsbury Theatre, London on 29 March 2010, and was so willing to accept the premise of the performance, the concept of an ant comedian, that I almost completely missed the underlying critique of gender stereotypes. I would argue that this demonstrates the complexity of the approach Christie was taking during this period of her work. She had to navigate a path between contexts where the suspension of disbelief may not be sufficient to enable access to the humour, in more mainstream comic environments, and also where, if anything, an audience would be too willing to accept the premise unquestioningly in traditionally theatrical spaces, again resulting in the humour (and indeed the feminist message) being missed. This is a challenging line to walk when your name as a comic is less familiar to an audience, as Christie's certainly was at this point in her career. Audience members may enter the performance space without any awareness of the style or approach to comedy that they are about to witness.

Christie's move away from more surreal strategies coincided with her increased presence on BBC Radio 4 comedy shows, culminating in her own radio series *Bridget Christie Minds the Gap*, first broadcast in April 2013. Arguably the constraints of radio prompted the opportunity to explore some less visual ways of conveying comic meaning to an audience and provided a space to develop a persona that was a 'heightened version' of herself. The topic of her radio show, which was re-commissioned for a second series then broadcast in 2015, was gender equality, and this formed the foundation of her subsequent live work. With her post-2013 approach much more aligned with traditional stand-up form, there is far less opportunity for audiences to miss the political messages of her work.

Although the content of the shows she has produced subsequent to *A Bic for Her* is openly feminist, tackling complex and emotive subjects such as rape and domestic violence, Christie has mastered the ability to make these unlikely topics humorous. She routinely comments that she would rather be talking about something else, but she has been provoked into focusing on these issues by society. A quotation from *A Book for Her* highlights this point: '[T]he problem is that misogyny, like those girl's shiny leggings, has made an unexpected comeback' (Christie 2015: 90). It is through adopting this tone of self-aware 'comic reluctance' that she manages to ensure the show does not feel like a lecture whilst, at the same time, does not belittle or lessen the severity of the subjects being discussed.

We can make use of Joanne Gilbert's (2004) identified comic postures as a way to frame Christie's performances, although we have to accept that there are always limitations to any approach that suggests a finite number of available options. In her live comic performances, we can see Christie operate across what Gilbert describes as the 'reporter', 'kid' and 'bitch' postures.

Christie's performance is founded above all else on the relatively androgynous posture of the 'reporter': 'The reporter persona is clearly opinionated, but because she offers socio-cultural – and occasionally political – critique through an observational lens, she does not appear threatening' (Gilbert 2004: 124). In my own experience of Christie's performance, I would be inclined to agree with Gilbert's argument here.

However, just because I do not find the content of her performances threatening, as I believe I hold many similar values to those advocated in Christie's performances, this does not mean it would be unthreatening to everyone. Christie is clearly angry about the injustices she is exploring in her work and thus her comedy could be perceived as challenging to those who are less aligned to left-wing or feminist ideologies.

It is key to note that Christie's notoriety subsequent to the success of *A Bic for Her* will have changed the make-up of her audience. As Christie herself observes, 'they've come to hear what the "feminist" comedian has to say for herself, on behalf of all the women in the world' (Christie 2015: 248). Her increased public profile, despite an unwillingness to engage with social media, means that potentially audiences already know a bit more about the content of her shows than they once did, and this could mean that her performances attract audiences who already hold similar values to those espoused in her comedy.

Gilbert comments in relation to the reporter posture, 'This persona also muses, often telling humorous anecdotes as a way to voice mild irritation, frustration, or incredulity' (2004: 124). This posture is demonstrated when Christie describes taking her young children to the supermarket and her horror that 'lads' mags' (magazines aimed at young men which contain significant amounts of imagery sexually objectifying women) have been put alongside the children's comics. In this, and many other such anecdotes, she utilizes a personal story in order to make a bigger political point, in line with Gilbert's observations.

As well as her use of the reporter posture, we can also consider Christie's current performance style in terms of the 'kid': 'The kid posture is based on ingratiation. Kids want to be liked and the playfulness they exhibit endears them to others' (Gilbert 2004: 128). Christie exudes a kind of playfulness even when dealing with quite challenging topics. Her casual and relatively androgynous costume choices, and her integration of, slightly manic, physical comedy (as showcased extensively in her earlier work), can be seen as aspects of the kid posture. For a significant part of her current routines, she operates from a de-sexualized position.

In addition to these two principal postures, due to the way Christie's performances can also be seen as more argumentative than that of the 'reporter', we can see aspects of the 'bitch' persona evidenced, as 'the bitch is the angriest female comic persona' (Gilbert 2004: 108). Although Christie does not make use of the 'put-down humor' central to the 'bitch' posture, which was epitomized by the late Joan Rivers, who was the most notable comic who made use of this approach (in terms of both the public awareness of her work and academic consideration), Christie is certainly angrier than other 'reporter' comics. I would argue that, for myself as an audience member, her anger actually makes her more, rather than less, likeable, complementing the kid-like ingratiation her physical comedy provokes. As an audience member, I am angry at the same things as Christie and so can identify with the material.

What elevates Christie's performance style above the somewhat formulaic comedy that simply combining these comic postures might create is that she is dealing explicitly with political and feminist material. Aspects of Gilbert's critique seem an uneasy fit for analysing Christie and this is possibly because Christie is a product of a time and cultural context different from early 2000s America, which was Gilbert's focus in her writing. Christie has adapted aspects of the bitch persona for the modern context, creating a posture that does not hide her anger whilst, at the same time, shuns any reliance on either putting down or critiquing other women, or indeed using herself, as the butt of her jokes.

Gilbert comments:

> Certainly both the kid and the reporter comics seem to deny or at least ignore any gender boundaries in the world of comedy. By downplaying their gender, these comics simply follow the rules and present non-controversial material and personas. (2004: 131)

But this is simply not true in relation to Christie. Although she is operating in a way that is likeable and non-threatening, this does not make the content of her material any less controversial (e.g. very few comedians would attempt to deal with such a complex or serious matter as female genital mutilation), and nor does she, at any point, attempt to deny or obscure her gender identity. Although she does not present herself as overtly sexual or feminine, she is not negating or downplaying her gender as her routine is explicitly about being a woman. The fact that she presents as an average woman is seemingly what makes her more likeable and relatable to her audiences and thus gives her room to explore these more challenging topics. De-sexualized is not the same as de-gendered. To visually downplay gender to avoid sexual objectification does not have to result in a complete disavowal of the performer's identity as a woman, as Christie's material amply demonstrates.

At a time when increasing numbers of women comics are entering the industry, and in the context of multiple and sometimes contradictory notions of feminism, the question that cannot be avoided is: What makes Christie's comedy feminist rather than postfeminist in tone and content? This is pertinent in spite of the whiteness of her material and to some extent the whiteness of the feminism that underpins it.

Her choice of subjects is a good place to start. Christie covers a huge amount of ground in her more recent shows, focusing on female genital mutilation (FGM), the No More Page 3 campaign and stationery-based pervasive sexism in *A Bic for Her*. As part of a critique of vaginaplasty, Christie implored her audience, during her tour of *An Ungrateful Woman*, to never consider altering the natural state of their vaginas through surgery as each one is unique. Christie rendered this idea comic by creating the delightfully constructed metaphor, 'they are like snowflakes made of gammon'. Subsequent to this observation, she moved on to criticizing the tampon tax and sexist advertising in *A Book for Her* and *Because You Demanded It*.

Even when Christie makes use of personal anecdotes as a way of initiating the topic (her story about encountering a flatulent bookstore employee seamlessly enabling her to bring up the importance of early feminists such as Simone de Beauvoir and Virginia Woolf), these narratives always have an underlying political message. The topics do not only relate to Christie as an individual. She makes the connections between her own embodied experiences and the wider context for women. She discusses the need for a collective reaction to the policing of women's bodies. Christie is not an FGM survivor, and the practice overwhelmingly impacts women of colour, but that does not mean that she cannot understand, and encourage others to understand, how much of a violation these procedures must be. Her approach across all her shows subsequent to 2013 has been predicated on the necessary unification of women against societal controls, rather than against each other in a competitive way. Her message is that we must collectively protest the sexist tampon tax and we must collectively hide or destroy copies of *The Sun* to prevent sexist imagery continually pervading our culture, describing how our small acts of rebellion as individuals can contribute to wider campaigns for change in our society.

Christie is addressing people of all genders in her work and calling for collective action to relieve everyone of the burden of stereotypical notions of difference. Christie then does not deal with the personal 'self-improvement' or empowerment narratives, which are a focus of modern postfeminist media and performance.

Postfeminist comedy: Luisa Omielan

As Limor Shifman and Daphna Lemish argue in their analysis of internet humour, it is important to distinguish not only between sexist and feminist humour but also between feminist and postfeminist humour, as this is another aspect of the ways in which comedy, in the post-2013 context, engages with the notions of gender difference. This is especially relevant to the current UK circuit where the number of women in the industry has significantly increased over the last ten years, and there exist multiple and contradictory understandings of feminism. They comment:

> The analysis of humour on gender, along the axis running from conservative/sexist to subversive/feminist is important and fundamental. However, we believe that in order to properly assess

contemporary humour, a third construct – postfeminist humour – must be conceptualized and assessed. (Shifman and Lemish 2010: 872)

The attributes of postfeminist humour outlined by Shifman and Lemish (2010: 875), which are in line with the analysis of postfeminist media cultures, can be summarized as follows:

- A renewed focus on gender differences.
- The targeting of both men and women rather than just one gender.
- The de-politicization of feminist concepts – the 'context of postfeminist humour is the world of leisure and consumption rather than politics or work' (875).
- Focus on the individual, the female body and 'sexuality as a means of empowerment and goal achievement' (875).

Although it is possible for comedians of any gender identity to be sexist in their material, it is my contention that the comedy on the current circuit, performed by women, operates predominantly at the postfeminist end of this proposed axis. Alongside the overtly feminist and political humour evidenced by Christie, we also have a large number of women comedians dealing in what can be termed postfeminist humour, in line with the aforementioned definition.

As cultural theorist Angela McRobbie noted in 2009, 'in popular culture there is a process which says feminism is no longer needed, it is now common sense, and as such it is something young women can do without' (McRobbie 2009: 8). Since McRobbie's initial writing on postfeminism, we can see a more multifaceted engagement with 'feminism' occurring; this is evident in not only a dismissal of its continued necessity but also multiple reclamations of the word and versions of feminisms, including celebrity feminisms. There is certainly more direct acknowledgement of feminism(s) in mainstream and commercial comic performances by women than there was before Christie's win of 2013. Arguably women comedians working on the circuit operate, in the majority, from a postfeminist standpoint where gender equality is seen, as McRobbie articulates, as common sense.

The live work of many successful comics working in the UK, including Katherine Ryan and Sara Pascoe, often provides evidence of this 'common sense' or de-politicized stance, where collective political action is, by implication, positioned as unnecessary in favour of an individual neoliberal self-actualization. It is Luisa Omielan's work, however, that will provide the focus for considering postfeminist comedy on the current circuit.

Omielan outlines in her autobiography (Omielan 2016) how, after several years of gigging on the UK live circuit and performing her critically and commercially successful solo show *What Would Beyoncé Do?!* (first performed in 2013 and so contemporary to Christie's *A Bic for Her* of the same year), she found it difficult to make the jump to televised forms. Inspired by her hero, the pop icon Beyoncé, Omielan decided to do things her own way rather than compromise her style, or wait for the interest of a broadcaster. She managed to crowdfund the money to enable her to record her second solo show, *Am I Right Ladies?!*, which she filmed in front of a live audience at the Bloomsbury Theatre in London in 2015.

Later, in 2017, Omielan started to reach a wider audience via broadcast television. She was invited to record *What Would Beyoncé Do?!* for BBC3, having successfully toured the show nationally, and internationally, for four years. The recording of the show was released online on St Valentine's Day and subsequently repeated on BBC One later that year. A significant part of the publicity for the show's release, as well as the decision to release it on the most 'commercially' romantic day of the year, was linked to the notion of Luisa being the 'voice' of single, millennial women. Shane Allen, BBC comedy commissioner, commented, 'Luisa spins a time of personal rejection into a riotous, uplifting comedy banshee cry. It's for anyone who has ever had their heart broken.'[4] Setting aside the clearly gendered language at play in this quotation (the term 'banshee' referring to a shrieking Irish mythological spirit and often used pejoratively to refer to women 'making a scene'), we can see that foregrounding the romantic comedy themes of Omielan's show formed a central part of the marketing strategy.

This again demonstrates a postfeminist approach to the marketing of Omielan and a reassertion that plays into existing stereotypes about comedy performed by women – that her comedy is *for* women.

This assumption is further evidenced in the way a series of clips were used as part of BBC3's social media campaign around the release of the show. These comprised short sections of Omielan's performance, each around one minute in length, which were titled with feminized names such as 'Bootylicious' and 'Independent woman' in line with the songs of Beyoncé. These clips were used as trailers on Twitter to encourage viewers to stream the show from iPlayer and later on to watch the repeat on BBC One. The exposure she achieved via her BBC3 special enabled her to reach a wider audience than previously with her live work and brought her to the attention of other comedians, including Dawn French, who enthusiastically championed Omielan's work over social media.

Omielan is highly aware of the way in which her comedy could easily be pigeonholed for being commercial and speaking to a specific, female, demographic. *What Would Beyoncé Do?!* and *Am I Right Ladies?* created a hen-party-like atmosphere with loud pop music, dancing, glitter and extensive interaction between performer and audience. The hyper-feminized space created by Omielan for these performances is easy to dismiss as frivolous. Omielan, however, has challenged those people criticizing the commercial nature of her shows, by pointing out that men aren't criticized for wanting to be successful, but that often the desire to succeed is used against powerful women to keep them in a place of submission (Omielan 2015).

The opening section of *Am I Right Ladies?* provides an example of how Omielan uses the language of pop culture and women's magazine-style empowerment to set up jokes that cut through this language with blunt sexually explicit punch lines which assert a heterosexual norm.

> It seems to me right, no matter how well things are going, or however long it takes you to achieve something, once you finally get to a place where things are going all right there is always something to get in

the way – isn't there? There's always some reason to feel not quite completely good enough. And it's weird because in my life I've learnt my happiness is so important. I realise what's important to me and what I need in my life for fulfilment and, actually, it's so simple, it's so obvious, all I need to be happy, all I really want in life to be happy [shout] is I just want a penis. Right? I just want a penis, I have got lots of willies but they are in the drawer I want a penis with a man on the end. That's what I want, bitches (*Am I Right Ladies?* 2015)

This is indicative of the tone of Omielan's comedy. This section of her show evidences the way her work both advocates for sexual experience and desire without shame (is body- and sex-positive), whilst simultaneously situating heteronormative sexual and emotional relationships as a central part of her ambitions – focused on individual goal achievement in line with the neoliberal contexts of postfeminism.

Her obvious appeal to younger demographics, due to her extensive social media presence and the proliferation of pop-culture references in her work, has not gone unnoticed. In 2018 Omielan started to develop material for her BBC3 commission *Politics for Bitches,* and she performed several live shows to develop the idea before performing an Edinburgh Fringe Festival run in 2018. Mirroring a Beyoncé-like trajectory, this show was much more political in focus than her previous work. *Politics for Bitches* responded to the traumatic death of Omielan's mother the previous year, and the systemic failures of the NHS, due to underfunding by the Conservative government.

Apart from her undeniable, self-driven success, Omielan is a stand-up comic whose work provides an example of a comedian using her body to reclaim the reading of her physical presence in the room in a positive way, rejecting self-deprecatory address. Her solo shows to date, and her numerous comedy club sets, provide effective examples of someone refusing existing readings of their body. As with Christie, her performance can also be read through the lens of Gilbert's comic postures. We can see Omielan perform in both bawd and bitch postures due to the way in which she is aware of, and manipulates, her sexuality.

Her command of the performance space can be read in terms of Gilbert's description:

> Clearly aggressive, often angry, the bitch comic critiques male sexual technique and apparatus as well as male inadequacies in intimacy and communication. Whereas the bawd may seduce and titillate male audience members, the bitch seems unconcerned about being liked by them. (Gilbert 2004:129)

Omielan makes use of these postures throughout her routines. Because she discusses the intimate details of her sexual experiences and the trouble she has attracting partners, her material is often explicit and scatological. Whilst this is not really a case of her trying to titillate the audience as such, although she does go amongst the crowd and grind on the laps of audience members, she demonstrates her techniques for attracting potential partners and therefore draws attention to herself as an emancipated sexual being. There is also undoubtedly an air of intimidation at play here:

> A comic who is obviously in control of her sexuality may appear to be in control, period. Because the bawd is often conflated with the bitch posture, it is not surprising that the bitch is based on intimidation. (Gilbert 2004: 129)

This posture links back to the hen-party feel of the spaces she creates for her performances and the way in which she creates a group identity by repeatedly referring to all audience members as her 'bitches'. The way Omielan moves amongst the crowd, invading their personal space and being overtly sexual towards them, means that whilst she comes across as extremely personable, audience members may also get the sense that she is aggressively forcing herself into people's space to make a point. She is empowered, and should you be the person selected for interaction, you will experience this by being overpowered by the way she interacts with you. Often her expression of sexual power towards male audience members would make the recipients of the interaction appear uncomfortable (as was the case when I first saw her live, when the person attending with me was treated to a kind of lap dance and laughed uncomfortably throughout, avoiding eye contact). Her material makes it very clear that she is more than a sexual object and so performing these physical gestures to/with the audience often highlights how repressed or disempowered they are sexually, as they are clearly much less confident expressing their (hetero)sexuality when confronted, so starkly, with hers. This disparity is rendered comic through the excess with which she expresses her sexual power in the performance space and amongst the audience.

Omielan's overall approach can be considered postfeminist in tone and content, in relation to Shifman and Lemish's definitions noted earlier. The way in which her material heavily references celebrity feminisms and often reinforces a binary gender division is a key aspect of this: 'Whereas in sexist humour the hierarchy between the feminine and masculine features is clear, postfeminist humour will tend to obliterate the hierarchical component and focus only on differences' (Shifman and Lemish 2010: 875).

The intermingling of feminist positions, evidenced in Omielan's empowered 'girl power' stance, with non-feminist or postfeminist positions, as her comic material is often maintaining a gender binary and a heteronormative goal of 'finding a man', is part of the complexity of the current postfeminist comedy context. Her use of 'Mars and Venus humour' (Shifman and Lemish 2011) is evident throughout her material. As a specific example of this, she often laments the way men have low personal hygiene standards, especially in relation to their genital areas, which can make certain sex acts less than enjoyable for women. Unlike the work of Christie, which unifies the audience in a political way against an ideology, Omielan's work focuses on unifying men and women as separate groups with the notion that, whilst equal, we are unavoidably different from each other.

The problematic aspects of her postfeminist approach aside, we can see certain sections of her work as undeniably empowering for audiences. Omielan directly rejects the negative meanings imposed on her body by others and is able to assert a more positive meaning, reclaiming her body shape and size through comedy. Throughout her routines, both in comedy club sets and her solo shows, she repeatedly challenges the control of women's sexuality (and media representations of this) as well as the pressures body image and being a 'single woman' can exert on women's mental health. She also directly within her routines considers the problems with self-deprecation, highlighting how, when complimented in social settings, women have a tendency to immediately self-deprecate. Omielan advises that we do the opposite – telling everyone to 'upgrade yourselves, bitches', in line with the current confidence culture discussed by Orgad and Gill (2022).

The unavoidable nature of the body for stand-up comedy means that material that addresses its presence within performance will continue to be written and performed. Self-objectification in comedy by women has, in previous eras, tended to be self-deprecatory. However, Omielan can be seen as someone self-objectifying in a way that moves beyond self-deprecation.

I feel it is necessary to note here that I am not in any way opposed to postfeminist styles of comedy, but the focus is very often on the personal rather than political. This is one of the defining characteristics of postfeminist sensibilities, as Rosalind Gill notes:

> One of the most striking aspects of postfeminist media culture is its obsessive preoccupation with the body. In a shift from earlier representational practices, it appears that femininity is defined as a bodily property rather than a social, structural or psychological one. (2007: 149)

Although the body as a site of protest has long been a feminist concern, it is the de-politicization of the body as a tool of collective resistance to gender norms that is evident in these shows. Omielan regularly eludes to a 'natural' difference between men and women, often with reference to behaviour in relationships. Arguably the context that current women comedians are operating within leads to this complicated relationship with feminism, as comedy both references and reflects the cultural attitudes of the time. Irrespective of whether the show is explicitly politically engaged with feminism, as evidenced by the work of Christie, or simply reflecting a postfeminist normalizing of a perceived (if not genuine) gender equality and empowerment narratives, as is the case with Omielan's earlier shows, we can see that women performing in the current context have moved towards a less self-deprecatory tone.

It is clear that the situation is more nuanced than a simple 'more women in comedy equals more feminist comedy' argument. The women currently on the circuit have been raised within a patriarchal society and so it is hardly surprising (even when we consider age differences) that some comedy by women simply reinforces cultural norms. Self-deprecation or self-objectification in the hands of one comic can produce a completely different effect to another's use of similar techniques due to the myriad other factors that can come into play when creating comedy.

This chapter is not about women competing against one another either: in the current cultural context, feminism is often used as a tool with which to berate others. There is often an unhelpful approach to contemporary feminism that attempts to pit different factions against each other rather than to push for collective action. Whilst of course being mindful to not get stuck with white feminism's reductive narrative or shutting myself off from learning from the experience of others, I acknowledge that many women, comics included, are simply doing their best from their own position. Therefore, I am not attempting to place a value judgement on the work of any woman comic who chooses not to deal explicitly with gendered issues in their routine. The comedy industry has space for the multiplicity of perspectives articulated by male comics and the same range of voices should be heard from women too. However, in terms of progressing an inclusive feminist agenda through comedy, simply being a comic and identifying as a woman is not enough.

The focus of those seeking to create a more diverse and inclusive comedy industry in the UK should be squarely on the backlash against women and feminist comics entering the industry, rather than attempting to create a sense of competition between them. It is this backlash that the following chapter will consider.

6

An (un)equal and opposite reaction
The backlash and barriers facing feminist comedy

Just as quickly as fumerists such as Bridget Christie, and to a certain extent her postfeminist contemporaries such as Luisa Omielan, are challenging and confronting gender stereotypes, other comedians, overwhelmingly white cisgender men, are busy rebuilding and reinforcing them, often with the support of large media organizations. This chapter will explore how certain kinds of feminist comedy have struggled to find a space within more mainstream outlets for comedy in Britain, focusing specifically on UK television. To illustrate the difficulties of inclusion (without structural change), I will return to Christie and Omielan. Both comedians, despite their critical and commercial success in the live arena, have faced challenges when trying to get their voices heard more widely through mass media forms.

The increased profile of feminist public rhetoric and feminist comedy has, as with every step forward for women into male-dominated areas, engendered a backlash. The existing progress that women in Western society have achieved with regard to gender equality remains under constant threat. We only need to look at what is occurring in the United States in relation to abortion access and attempts to overturn *Roe v. Wade* (Bland 2022), as well as the continued erosion of LGBTQ+ rights in the UK (Brooks 2022), to see how fragile some of the wins for equality are. In relation to how this is reflected on the UK comedy circuit, arguably these threats to equality form part of a much wider cultural nostalgia for traditional and uncomplicated Britishness. This has been evidenced by the political and media discourses around events such as the UK's departure from the European Union (EU) (aka Brexit) and moral panics related to 'free speech' and 'anti-wokeness'. As Anita Superson and Anne E. Cudd explain when considering the various negative reactions to feminist thought within academia, 'In its normative use, "backlash" connotes something to be avoided, something that is excessive in its zeal and reactionary in aim' (Superson and Cudd 2002: 5). It is this definition of backlash that will underpin the analysis contained within this chapter.

Emboldened public displays of retro-sexism, racism, homophobia and transphobia in the wake of the election of Donald Trump, in 2017, to the American presidency, the outcome of the UK's referendum on membership of the EU, in 2016, Boris Johnson's ascendance to the office of UK prime minister, in 2019, as well as the continued rise of the Alt-right, Incel and TERF cultures (Nagel 2017, Phipps 2020), have enabled gendered inequalities to continue. Additionally, in the UK, the impact of extensive and continued government austerity measures (in place since 2010), and more recently the impact of Covid-19, has had an extremely detrimental effect on services and support for women. In the last few years, after the Brexit referendum in the UK, there has also been a (perceived) culture war playing out on the media. This can be summarized broadly as a clash of ideology between those with progressive attitudes towards equality and inclusion and those who are destabilized by their attitudes no longer being socially acceptable. Much of the media discussion of these ideological differences is very reminiscent of the 1990s/2000s 'political correctness gone mad' discourse. The press over the last five years have repeatedly proclaimed that people (with often racist, homophobic or transphobic views) are being 'cancelled' (Ng 2020 2022) by being denied a platform for their views. It is often the case, however, that we hear even more from the 'cancelled' *after* their moment of fame, as they bellow, 'I am being silenced' from a myriad of new welcoming platforms.

Humour in this political context continues to be a place where racism, sexism, homophobia and transphobia find a home. Outside of performed comedy, the cultural association between men and humour, or 'banter', continues to hold strong, and the caveats of 'just joking' or 'a bit of fun' are still regularly deployed as a defence for problematic sexist comments in a range of social and political situations. Rosalind Gill comments:

> Most significantly [...] in postfeminist media culture irony has become a way of 'having it both ways', of expressing sexist, homophobic or otherwise unpalatable sentiments in an ironized form, whilst claiming this was not actually 'meant'. (Gill 2007: 159)

This use of irony is a key feature of the context within which the women comics discussed in this book work. This is especially true in relation to recent controversies around freedom of speech as noted earlier – which often the UK press conflates with freedom from the consequences of speech.

We can consider this resistance to gender equality and restatement of traditional masculinities through irony from an industrial perspective. Lindsey German, in *Material Girls: Women, Men and Work* (2007), analysed women's struggle for inclusion within the paid labour sector and work outside the home. German describes how the increased participation of women in the workplace, across all industries, has historically provoked men to reassess their identities and the concept of masculinity.

> So we see the reassertion of traditional male values, at least amongst a layer of men: lap dancing clubs, lad magazines, an insidious campaign against the notion of 'date rape', a resurgence of sexist language, and continuing high levels of violence against individual women. (2007: 115)

This position is true for the British comedy industry which has historically been a male industry operating within a male space (most public spaces being male-dominated but specifically working men's clubs and more recently macho mainstream comedy clubs), making it doubly difficult for women to infiltrate. This situation bears many similarities to academia, which evidences some of the same contextual traits and rhetorical resistances to feminism. Superson and Cudd, in their consideration of academia, comment:

> Physical violence is the most obvious but not the only sort of reaction to progress. In the academy, where physical violence is rare (but not unheard of), backlash usually comes in the form of institutionally sanctioned, or at least unprevented, abuses of power. (Superson and Cudd 2002: 4)

Even in professions that appear on the surface enlightened by the inclusion of women, where women are more visually present than ever before, and where there have not been significant changes to the kind of labour being performed, as is the case with say, manufacturing industries, we still see resistance and backlash play out. We can take the comparison between stand-up comedy and academia further by considering how both professions have evolved from male-only spaces and continue to be male dominated, especially at the top of the hierarchies. Women (comics and academics) work alone within physical spaces where once they were excluded precisely because of their gender (within older institutions); they stand up in front of crowds publicly voicing their own observations and are often hired on the basis of people's awareness of their work as an individual. It is also noteworthy that we are now seeing the uncovering of more physical ways of controlling women within these industries, which will be discussed in the next chapter.[1]

The inclusion of women into the competitive and predominantly male comedy industry has resulted in a crisis of cisgender male identity and an insistence on traditional masculinity, which has played out through reactionary humour over the last ten years. To elucidate upon this point I will now consider several examples of this backlash to the increasing diversity of the UK comedy circuit in action.

Andrew Lawrence

In contrast to Christie's work, which through comedy vocalizes the problems faced by women and attempts to engage all genders as equals, several comedians have taken an approach that re-establishes a binary gender divide and attempts to reassert a hierarchy of active men and passive women. A cisgender male comic who demonstrates this backlash is comedian Andrew Lawrence, whose work evidences a right-wing sensibility. Alongside working on the mainstream club circuit since the early 2000s, Lawrence has been regularly broadcast on BBC Radio 4, where he has written and performed several comedy shows. Within his work, as well as via his online presence, we can see a direct retaliation against what he terms 'political correctness' or 'wokeness'.

Lawrence publicly shared posts via Facebook in October 2014 that specifically highlighted his attitude towards the diversification of the comedy circuit. Comedy website Chortle reported:

> Lawrence – who makes much of his bitter disillusionment with the comedy industry in his act – also berated 'moronic, liberal back-slapping on panel shows like *Mock The Week* where aging, balding, fat men, ethnic comedians and women-posing-as-comedians, sit congratulating themselves on how enlightened they are about the fact that UKIP are ridiculous and pathetic'. (Chortle, 2014)

Lawrence was widely condemned by other comedians for his comments, especially in relation to the way he othered both 'ethnic' comics and women – who in the initial post are cast as not really comedians at all – simply pretenders to the throne. However, his public comments are certainly indicative of some of the attitudes explored in the interviewing process of this research, both in terms of hostile audience responses to material from comics identifying as women and feminists and in the way these views reassert the stereotype that women are simply not funny.

He aligns himself within these comments with the discursive position of the UK Independence Party (UKIP), a minority political party which campaigned to leave the EU. UKIP were criticized around the time Lawrence made these comments for making use of far-right rhetoric and racist scaremongering within their publicity, for example, the populist trope of Britain being invaded by foreign 'others' (Gander and Wright 2014). Lawrence's comedy seeks to normalize attitudes that see white men (especially those who would fall into the politically contentious white working-class demographic) as somehow 'under threat', and as a universal norm against which everyone else should be measured. The intensely problematic aspects of the 'white working-class' debate are unpicked at length in the work of Reni Eddo-Lodge, who highlights the way in which this kind of rhetoric both feeds into far-right ideology and implies that for this demographic, class and race are two 'separate disadvantages' (Eddo-Lodge 2017: 202).

In a post-EU-referendum UK, we can see the xenophobic aspects of Lawrence's work as indicative of the isolationism and backward-looking nationalism capitalized upon by the referendum campaigns (Tomsett and Weidhase 2020). It is not possible to establish whether the attitudes he displays on stage are those he personally holds or whether (similar to populist politics) he is perhaps simply capitalizing on these views in order to further his career. To provide a more recent example of Lawrence's humour, the following quotation provides an update to his material in the light of high-profile sexual assault scandals and acts of terrorism in the UK. In a public Facebook post from 1 November 2017 he muses, '[I] need some press coverage to promote the tour, just got to decide whether to sexually harass a bunch of people or drive a truck into them.'[2] This again evidences a humour that is based on shock factor and controversy. This is nothing new. The humour of the working men's clubs traded in this provocation technique extensively (Gray 1994, Tomsett and White 2024) and much of his work can be read in relation to superiority perspectives. However, it is clear how Lawrence's humour is actively attempting to re-establish a white male norm in response to the current political climate, especially as fears of terrorism were played upon by the Vote Leave campaign, as part of the 'taking back control' narrative of the UK's EU membership referendum and subsequent parliamentary elections.

Lawrence (either personally or through his comic persona) is seemingly reacting to a threat to his own survival as a comic within an increasingly diverse comedy industry. Alongside this defensiveness, we can also see the continued trivialization of violence against women in the comedy content of Lawrence and several others operating in the current context. He is clearly aware of the impact his controversial views have in terms of attracting and audience. In 2018 Lawrence performed his hour-long Edinburgh show *Clean* and addressed some of the controversies he had been involved in. He delivered this show without profanity, as if to make the point that he is capable of being family-friendly. Towards the end of the show, which I experienced live for research purposes, Lawrence extemporized about how a comment on social media could quickly become taken out of context and interpreted as hate speech. To my mind, his decision to perform a clean set was an odd one, as it appeared to imply that people had previously objected to his use of profanity or vulgarity, both of which are commonplace within live comedy contexts, rather than the actual content of his comments about women and minority groups (which I'd argue does not have an ambiguous relationship to hate speech). His framing of his social media activity within this performance placed himself squarely as the victim of 'woke' cancel culture, being punished for exercising his right to free speech. To those in the audience without an awareness of the content of his actual comments, this part of his routine would have seemed like quite a reasonable take on the situation, his ability to claim innocence was bolstered by his presentation as a 'clean' comic for this show.

Dapper Laughs

In the UK context, the 2014 controversies surrounding comedian Dapper Laughs (real name Daniel O'Reilly) afford us the ultimate example of a reactionary humour that objectifies women and trivializes violence against them. Dapper's work provides an almost polar opposite to the work of his contemporary Bridget Christie – so much so that he could arguably be referred to as the Anti-Christie. Having attracted thousands of followers by vlogging online before transferring to what would be a brief period on ITV2 (September to November 2014), Dapper's work was allegedly presented as a satirical take on modern 'lad culture' with the aforementioned 'just joking' and 'banter' caveats. Yet, much of his work was indistinguishable from straightforward sexism. *Dapper Laughs: On the Pull* (2014) involved Dapper giving members of the public dating advice and demonstrating behaviours, often in line with outdated gendered stereotypes, that they could adopt to attract partners. Telling comparisons were made to real-life pick-up artists being covered in the media of the time, such as the much-discussed Julien Blanc (Li 2014), who make a living by instructing men how to attract women – often by advocating sexually aggressive behaviours. These comparisons only served to highlight that the distance between the real behaviour and the 'satirical, exaggerated behaviour' displayed by Dapper was simply too close to call or indeed non-existent.

Whilst receiving heavy criticism, and in reaction to an online petition from other comics and members of the public for ITV2 to remove him from broadcast, statements were often released by the broadcaster and Dapper himself, in line with the 'not actually meant' argument Gill articulates in her analysis of postfeminist media culture. Although character-based satire is a very successful and familiar tradition within the British stand-up scene, one can only assume that there was insufficient consideration by the broadcaster as to whether the irony (if they believed it to be irony) would be clear to the television audience, or whether the humour would be received or understood on a less sophisticated level. This case certainly demonstrates a willingness of broadcasters to find space for more regressive and reactionary forms of humour from the most dominant voices, at a time when the live circuit included more women and people of colour than ever before.

Due to a public outcry regarding a video clip of Dapper Laughs addressing the media criticism of his TV work in one of his live shows, and his comment to a woman in the audience that she was 'gagging for a rape', ITV finally bowed to pressure from complainants and dropped the ITV2 show. Whilst his comments in his live shows were considered by ITV as part of the decision to drop the show, they still maintained that the content of *Dapper Laughs: On the Pull*, his television show, was 'carefully considered and compiled' (Burrell 2014).

If we reflect, however, on the statement made by ITV (and the production companies Hungry Bear Media and Big Minded) initially announcing the commissioning of this series, it is clear they were well aware of the problematic aspects of his act at the outset. In the statement, Kate Maddigan (the commissioning editor from ITV) commented, 'I'm excited to bring him and his risqué brand of humour to ITV2'.[3] Additionally, both producers from Hungry Bear and Big Minded articulate their excitement in the statement at having been given the opportunity to share Dapper's work with a wider audience. The press release signs off with the following statement: 'Dapper Laughs said, "I can't wait to bring my brand of comedy to the ITV2 viewers, [sic] who says you can't sleep your way to the top"'.

In the aftermath of this scandal, Daniel O'Reilly repeatedly said he would put the character to bed – if audiences could still believe there was a character at all.[4] This most memorably occurred when he appeared without characterization (or, arguably, performing a different characterization) on the BBC's *Newsnight* on 11 November 2014, and clearly stated, 'Dapper Laughs is gone'. Throughout this interview, O'Reilly repeatedly reiterated the difference between himself as a 'real person' and Dapper. This was visually indicated to viewers through his decision to dress in a sombre black polo neck jumper, as if attending the character's funeral. At one point he asked interviewer Emily Maitlis, in an incredulous tone, if she really thought him capable of the actions depicted in the online videos of Dapper, specifically in relation to a clip shown at the start of the show where he demonstrates how to remove a woman's bra quickly, by holding up a knife and saying 'take your fucking top off'. When arguing that in many ways this character had ruined his life, O'Reilly artfully avoided labelling himself a victim by replying to Maitlis' question, 'so you feel like a bit of a victim now?' with 'a victim of my own mistakes maybe'.

Despite this clear mea culpa, by early 2015 Dapper had headed out on a live tour again, recording his *Res-erection* show and releasing it as a DVD. Disconcertingly, considering his clear assertion that Dapper Laughs was a character and that critics should credit the audience with a bit more intelligence than assuming they would take the act at face value, here again, within this performance, we see O'Reilly blurring these boundaries, and being deliberately provocative and offensive. This is especially evident in the section where he recalls being interviewed on *Newsnight* (doubly confusing when, seemingly, it was O'Reilly rather than Dapper who was interviewed) commenting that the whole time he was looking at Maitlis thinking, 'You fucking want it, don't ya?' (Logan 2015). This directly contradicts the idea that the character and the person are different entities.

Al Murray's well-known Pub Landlord character provides a useful counterpoint to Dapper Laughs. Murray has faced similar criticism in the past in relation to the ways his performances as the Pub Landlord can be read on multiple levels (see Double 2014: 124–6). Both performers are playing with stereotypes, but whereas Dapper's work seemed to advocate that others act in a similar way to his character, The Pub Landlord, famed for his problematic patriotism and white working-class traditional values, does not seem to be advocating specific behaviour to his audience (beyond, maybe, just enforcing the consumption of wine and beer along gendered lines). Murray is clearly provoking his audience to ridicule the Pub Landlord's outdated views, and there is sufficient distance between Al Murray the comic, and the performed character of the Pub Landlord, for him to achieve this, and so no caveat is therefore necessary. For Dapper's comedy, the women targeted by his pick-up lines or 'antics' were the butt of the jokes, rather than Dapper himself. Further complexity arose as the audience were unaware of any discrepancy between the comic, Daniel O'Reilly, and the character of Dapper Laughs. The distance between performer and character and the way in which Murray's act does not incite others to behave in a similar way are crucial factors in understanding Murray's work. Murray's comedy as the Pub Landlord has been regularly televised and is more clearly read by an audience as satire because this double meaning is detectable and as such can be understood as part of the challenge to patriarchal norms, achieved through ridicule, present in much post-alternative movement humour. In contrast, Dapper's work, arriving in the cultural context of 2014, highlights a more aggressive insistence of old-school macho humour and a reaction against political correctness. The double meaning necessary for an audience to read a performance as irony was very difficult to observe – so difficult that one wonders if it is irony at all. This amply demonstrates German's (2007) point that traditional masculinity seeks to reassert itself in the wake of increased gender diversity in workforces. In this instance, specifically, this is through humour and in reaction to the increasing inclusivity of the British comedy circuit, since male comics such as Lawrence and O'Reilly saw an opportunity to push back against progressive thought within their work so as to reassert a dominant male position.

At the start of 2018 O'Reilly (although again constantly interchangeably referred to as Dapper Laughs in the press) was invited to enter the *Celebrity Big Brother* (2001–18) house. This particular series of the popular reality TV show had been initially advertised as completely women-focused, in celebration of the 100-year anniversary since the voting franchise was extended to some women in the UK. This is an obvious example of the commodification of feminism by Channel 5, who sought to exploit the centring of women for entertainment. O'Reilly's inclusion within a show designed to (somehow) honour women's suffrage is intentionally provocative and offensive given his clear disregard for women's rights. His participation in such a high-profile show forces us to consider exactly what this comic would have to say before he was denied any further platform. It seems that formats and channels in the UK are quick to find a way to accommodate this kind of sexist humour in a way simply not afforded to feminist comedy, which one can only surmise is still disappointingly considered a 'minority perspective'.

Women comedians accessing wider platforms

Despite coming to wider attention at the same time as Dapper Laughs, the inclusion of Bridget Christie's humour in mainstream formats has been much trickier to achieve than that of her male equivalents. This is epitomized by the example of her problematic inclusion into some panel shows. On 2 May 2014, Christie was a panellist on the long-running BBC satirical panel show, *Have I Got News for You?* (1990 to present). This was her first appearance on the show. In a poignant echo of the complaints made by the character A.Ant about poor introductions affecting audiences' preconceptions, Christie's position was undermined before she had even said a word. Christie's introduction, welcoming her onto the show, was delivered by the guest host, comedian Jack Dee:

> On Ian's team tonight is a comedian who collected the Foster's Comedy Award wearing a T-Shirt saying No More Page 3, and she got an extra round of applause when she took it off. Please welcome Bridget Christie.

The No More Page 3 campaign challenges the use of sexualized images of topless women on page three of the national newspaper *The Sun*. Christie protested this introduction at the time and has been quoted in an interview with *The Guardian* as saying she will never return to the show, asking, 'Have they ever introduced a male comedian with a joke about his cock?' (Lawson 2014). This comment, at the start of the show, immediately cast Christie as an outsider and focused on her difference, her gender and her feminism, rather than her status as a comedian. The joke not only undermined Christie as an individual but also made light of a campaign with serious objectives.

The rest of this episode effectively illustrated how Christie's feminist position has the potential to make it difficult for her to contribute to shows dealing with politics and the media. This is not a fault of Christie's, but because so much of this broadcast culture is still, we can reasonably conclude, from an 'old school' patriarchal perspective. For example, at the time of the recording and broadcast of the particular episode of *Have I Got News for You?* under discussion, the trial of PR guru Max Clifford (for sexual assault) and Operation Yewtree (concerning historical paedophile networks within the entertainment industries) were in the news and, therefore, were covered as part of the show.[5] Christie's live comedy is diametrically opposed to humour that makes light of the impact of sexual harassment or assault and therefore it would understandably have been difficult to participate in this kind of humour without compromising her views or comic persona.

Despite the uncomfortable nature of Christie's inclusion on this show being made public, she was nominated for the British Comedy Awards Best Female TV Comic for this one appearance on television. This nomination could be read in relation to the way in which the wider industry wishes to be understood as inclusive whilst actively reinforcing a gender divide. The industry achieves this by othering women when they do appear on TV panel shows, in terms of the introductions they receive, which mark them out as different from the established male panellists. Also, by maintaining their gender-specific categorization for the Comedy Awards the celebration plays into the long-established 'funny for a woman' discourse.

To evidence that Christie's experience of patriarchal humour in this environment is not an isolated incident, it is important that we consider the show as a whole, rather than this one episode. Several pertinent examples present now themselves. In 2017, *Have I Got News for You?* found itself at the centre of debate about the reporting of revelations of sexual assault being made on both sides of the Atlantic. In an episode broadcast on BBC1 on 3 November 2017, the guest host, comedian Jo Brand, corrected long-term team captain Ian Hislop (editor of UK satirical magazine *Private Eye*) when he dismissed aspects of harassment as trivial (Agerholm 2017). When discussing the media reports of a serving member of parliament taking his personal trainer to the cinema, and how this contributed to a culture of harassment, he quipped, 'Some of this is not high-level crime, is it, compared to Putin or Trump?'. Brand, with an air of reluctant fatigue (having no doubt, like many women, had to explain the impact of harassment to those who choose to live in ignorance), responded:

> If I can just say – as the only representative of the female gender here today – I know it's not high-level, but it doesn't have to be high-level for women to feel under siege in somewhere like the House of Commons.

This was met by facial expressions of shock from the male panellists, possibly at being publicly corrected rather than the content of Brand's polite and concise rebuttal, and loud cheers from the audience for the recording. Whilst, of course, the programme has been edited together, and we switch between shots of Brand, Hislop and the other team captain Paul Merton in quick succession, it seems clear this is not a scripted or 'approved' joke and that Brand is reacting in the moment with little regard to the embarrassment of the team captains or to making her point humorous. It is notable that this moment made it into the edit of the show at all.

Whilst the content of Brand's response is of course praiseworthy, the real importance of this moment for me was that it revealed the unquestioned patriarchal humour that often passes without comment and goes unnoticed by the audience. Comments and actions that belittle or 'other' women are rife on this show, which has run in a prime-time slot for over thirty years (with many other panel shows equally problematic in this regard). Within the same episode guest panellist Quentin Letts described right-wing commentator Julia Hartley-Brewer as a 'girl'; the expression was also picked up, and corrected to 'woman', by Brand.

A further example of this pattern of 'othering' of women in action can be found in the decision by *Have I Got News for You?* producers on 16 December 2016 to replace Conservative MP Nicky Morgan with a designer handbag when she cancelled close to the day of recording. The handbag was not a randomly chosen object. It directly related to the argument between Morgan and the then prime minister Theresa May over the message high-cost fashion sends out to struggling, austerity-burdened constituents. This choice, however, resulted in no women being included in that episode of the show (Bulman 2016). The decision taken to field a handbag rather than one of the numerous capable women comedians who would have loved a shot at that programme is one of the most telling signs that these shows have failed to change in line with the live circuit.

In April 2018, as part of promoting the new series of *Have I Got News for You?*, hosts Ian Hislop and Paul Merton provoked the ire of many by suggesting that women MPs and comedians were regularly asked to appear but simply chose not to. Hislop, revealing some of his deeper held and possibly unconscious biases, concluded that this was because men are simply more willing to 'have a go' at something, whereas women are more naturally modest. Merton compounded this by stating that, in his opinion, the show had actually had a lot of women as hosts, demonstrating a questionable grasp of basic maths (Davies 2018). I can appreciate that the replacement of Morgan with a handbag was supposed to be read as a joke and was a callback to the episode of 4 June 1993, when MP Roy Hattersley (who had repeatedly cancelled his appearance) was replaced by a tub of lard. However, this, in a 2016 context, was a very literal objectification of women – the handbag could be the object of humour just as well as a woman panellist.

The 'Jo Brand incident' on *Have I Got News for You?* in 2017 highlighted how little awareness those who hold powerful positions within the comedy industry really think about or understand gender inequality. Just as Brand's comment highlighted the way small instances of harassment and sexism build up, so too do the small throwaway comments and jokes in televised comedy (Ruddick 2017). These also build up to create an environment hostile to any humour that seeks to challenge the patriarchal norms that much mainstream televised humour perpetuates.

In a response to the complaints received about the Brand and Hislop harassment exchange on the show, the BBC commented that the show 'doesn't deliberately set out to offend viewers' and that they 'accept that tastes vary enormously'. This, to my mind, demonstrates how the BBC has yet again failed to fully understand the reaction to this incident. The response to this small part of the show was not about taste or the assumption that Hislop was attempting to be intentionally offensive, but the way the show is still overwhelmingly articulated from a white cisgender male perspective, and Brand's inclusion highlighted why further consideration of representation on this show is so important.

Another key point in relation to Brand's work here is the way her long-standing career *enables* her to be in a position to challenge these views. It is hardly surprising that many of the instances of the belittlement of women or the downplaying of harassment that occurs on panel shows goes unchallenged by the very few women panellists who are present. In 2016, data scientist Stuart Lowe of the Open Data Institute conducted and then published a rigorous analysis of the gender split across TV and radio panel shows, in terms of both regular and guest appearances. The data, which clearly breaks down the gap between men and women participants, made for depressing, if not surprising, reading and confirmed a significant gender gap in bookings.[6]

Panel shows are very hard to get on to in the first place, and so anyone wanting to subvert or challenge the existing humour being perpetuated would already need to be at a certain stage in their career to be confident doing so without jeopardizing future employment. It is in moments such as her appearance on *Have I Got News for You?* that we can truly see the significance of Jo Brand as a comedian in the current UK comedy context. She has survived a changing industry and built a career that enables her to be as vocal and challenging to the patriarchy as she first was when performing live as part of the alternative comedy scene (Figure 5).

Figure 5 Image of Jo Brand in conversation with Dr Kate Fox at Manchester Literature Festival 2018. Photograph by the author.

Whilst Brand has certainly undergone a process of change in the style of her comedy in order to be accommodated by television formats, she uses her position within the industry to challenge and provoke change with awareness that she has attained power and has the chance to use it to benefit others, as evidenced in this example. In the UK, we still do not have Black women or women of colour at a point in their comedy careers to be able to successfully challenge things in the same way – especially as so many feel compelled to move to the United States to access wider opportunities. This means that many of the debates about diversity in TV comedy continue to rest on the white men versus white women dynamic alone, without any significant attention to intersectionality.

It is not only panel shows that pose problems for the inclusion of those with a more feminist or postfeminist comic approach. We can also see how Omielan's increase in profile provides a pertinent example of the difficulties of transitioning from live comedy to TV, and why women still need to reject meanings imposed by others on their bodies in these televised spaces.

Omielan was approached to be one of the many presenters for the 2017 *Comic Relief* (1986 to present) broadcast. She co-presented various links throughout the night, with the programme culminating in presenter Graham Norton interviewing a huge number of guests on an extra-long sofa as part of a world record attempt. Omielan was the last guest to take up a place on this sofa, and, due to time constraints, each guest had only around a minute to talk with the host. With Omielan, Norton only talked about what she was wearing (she had changed outfit from earlier in the night) and spent the entire short duration telling her to cover herself up. This exchange was subsequently reported in the reviews of the show in a similar 'cover yourself up love' tone, with Ally Ross writing the following day for *The Sun*:

> It came to an ugly head during the *Graham Norton Chat Show*/celebrity circle jerk thing, which featured 33 famous people and someone called Luisa Omielan who felt the lash of the host's tongue for dressing like an Albanian stripper. (Ross 2017)

Norton did not use that particular wording to describe Omielan's dress, although he had focused solely on her appearance. This incident provides a further example of how even when a comedian takes ownership of their sexuality and body, and even when they are in fact *renowned* for it within their live work, others are quick to control and denigrate them when in new mediated spaces.

It is important to challenge the default position of male-dominant televised comedy programming because the representations of women in this environment both compound gender stereotypes and help normalize patriarchal attitudes towards women. Although both my examples here have been white women, it is clear that women of colour and those with disabilities are also underrepresented in the television comedy arena and face discrimination across multiple indices of difference from the white cisgender male norm. It is these norms which are in need of disruption in order for political feminisms to have a wider voice within comedy programming. It is not just a matter of formats, although we can see through the foregoing examples how these often place restrictions on who can be included. It is, crucially, the predominantly white male sense of humour these shows perpetuate.

When Black women are included in newly developed formats often the reaction to their inclusion is disproportionately negative and they experience 'misogynoir', defined as anti-Black racist misogyny (Bailey and Trudy 2018). Sophie Duker's 2020 experience as a guest on *Frankie Boyle's New World Order* (2017 to present), a comedic debate format, provides an example. Duker, as part of a section discussing the concept of Black Power, used the phrase 'kill whitey' as part of a joking routine. This resulted in over 1,000 complaints to the BBC (which the BBC dismissed), and a significant amount of online abuse directed at Duker (Dosani, 2020). The reaction seemed to stem from the audiences' shock of having a Black woman express a political opinion, still a relative rarity in UK politics and media programming. This example evidences that the dominant social group (white cisgender men) are very quick to make use of and legitimize the 'just joking' defence when it serves their own purposes but very quick to dismiss the humorous intent of a professional comedian, making a joke on a comedy television show if they are Black and a woman.

Shows that normalize public space (televised space) as male and white must be challenged to be more inclusive and reflective of wider society. In an interview with Channel 4 news presenter Krishnan Guru-Murthy for the *Ways to Change the World* podcast series, Reni Eddo-Lodge comments:

> I don't believe that middle-aged white men are the most talented in society. But if I looked around at people who are in positions of power that would be the conclusion that I would draw. But I don't believe it.
> (*Ways to Change the World* 2018)

Whilst Eddo-Lodge is talking more broadly about politics and cultural institutions, we can certainly apply this critique to television comedy. The current representation of women, working-class people and people of colour on UK comedy programming falls woefully short of reflecting the wealth of comedy talent available on the live circuit. It is this very lack of diversity that effectively maintains hegemonic notions about the comic capabilities of anyone who does not fit a very specific mould and so prevents feminist comedy from reaching a comparable audience to that of the humour of retro-sexist lad culture.

To briefly consider a counterargument, it could be said that the form of comedy evidenced by Dapper Laughs or even Andrew Lawrence is simply articulating a differing, and perhaps more distinctly 'young white cisgender male' viewpoint of the world. However, this position runs into problems when we consider the vehicles afforded Christie and Dapper's humour and the inequality between them. It is not just the case that a male comic was afforded a wider opportunity than a female contemporary – although this is, of course, worthy of note. The backlash, which goes beyond simple inequality, originates *within the content* of the comedy afforded this wider platform. Christie is an award-winning comic with years of experience, yet her non-live work has so far been confined to those areas sometimes referred to as 'niche feminism' – the pages of *The Guardian* (for which she has previously written several columns), and BBC Radio 4, for example. These niches for feminism almost always are focused on white middle-class cisgender women's experiences too. The televising of Dapper's work, however briefly, created the impression of mainstream endorsement and enabled a comic renowned for sexism and promoting sexually aggressive behaviours access to a much wider audience. Although, at the time of writing, Bridget Christie is a participant in series thirteen of comedy entertainment show *Taskmaster* (2015 to present) and has a television show in development, it is clear that across the last ten years the same level of opportunity provided to those male comics with 'controversial' takes on gender equality has not been afforded to feminist humour despite an upswing in popularity and commercial success within the live circuit.

It is clear then that current televised output in the UK, which remains the dominant route to accessing a wider audience in the live circuit, remains resistant to the inclusion of feminist humour. The pace of change within narrative forms such as sitcom has outstripped comedy entertainment shows where stand-up comics are mostly found. New technologies such as streaming services and social media platforms provide innovative routes for women entering the industry, but these are often challenging spaces to infiltrate too. Even when women comedians are successful both commercially and critically in a live environment, it does not guarantee them an automatic, or indeed comparable, transition to a wider audience, especially when trying to integrate into existing or long-running shows. That both Christie and Omielan who are only now, ten years after their initial significant successes in the live arena, starting to find ways of accessing televised audiences evidences this.

7

Comedy too

Taken in isolation a comedian being brought on to the stage as 'the lovely . . .', or being booked as the only woman on a line-up, may feel surmountable – particularly to those external to the industry who hold an outsider perspective. However, these barriers specific to stand-up comedy, identified and examined throughout this book, intersect with a wider Cultural and Creative Industry (CCI) context, where gendered power hierarchies can easily be exploited. This exploitation of women working in entertainment industries can result in sexual misconduct, sexual abuse and rape. This chapter will consider the ways that historic and contemporary abuses of power, and violations of women comics, have been facilitated, reported, discussed and responded to by the industry. The chapter will draw on both the findings of netnographic work undertaken as part of this research and observations made as a participant-observer within women-only comedy spaces.

UK Cultural and Creative Industries context

The UK government's Department for Digital, Culture, Media and Sport (DDCMS) defines the Creative Industries as 'those industries which have their origin in individual creativity, skill and talent and which have a potential for wealth and job creation through the generation and exploitation of intellectual property' (DDCMS 2001: n.p). This is a wide definition which includes a variety of professions, that collectively, according to recent government data, 'contributes almost £13 million to the UK economy every hour' (DDCMS 2020:

n.p). Live comedy, in respect of this definition, is clearly a part of the wider CCI sector, although data about the live comedy industry is rarely captured in isolation and thus sits (obscured) within data about music, performance and live arts. Working as a comedian is absolutely aligned with individual creativity, talent and the exploitation of intellectual property in the form of comic material. Comedy as a profession, however, occupies a liminal position. It is often positioned as an illegitimate art form or one requiring less skill than say musical or acting talent. When included within the broad conception of 'the arts', comedy is routinely conflated with other kinds of performance cultures in terms of data, and this conflation hides the specificities of comedy as a professional space.

The freelance and informal nature of creative work often results in disparate un-unionized workforces and workforces that are homogenous in their class, gendered and racial make-up. Orian Brook, David O'Brien and Mark Taylor (2020) note, in their analysis of the Office for National Statistics' Labour Force Survey of 2019, that in regard to social class breakdown 'in every creative occupation we see those from managerial and professional origins dominate the occupations, as compared with those from working-class origins' (2020: 63). In total, 85 per cent of those working in music, performance and visual arts (the category which includes live comedy) are white, and the gender breakdown for the same category shows that 54 per cent in this field are women (2020: 60–1). What this survey data of course does not tell us is the way the class, gender or racial breakdown operates at different stages of the hierarchies within each profession encompassed by this category. The authors note that 'while occupations as a whole might present a particular pattern, specific roles, such as very senior leadership in prestigious institutions, or who wins music awards, might still be skewed away from the general pattern' (2020: 61). Crucially, the data does not allow for the differentiation between different industries that fall within this category. It leaves us asking questions such as: are all the men or people of colour included in this statistic in the music industry? Or fine artists? Is comedy as an industry better or worse than the statistical picture formed through uniting data from music, performance and visual arts? The picture remains incomplete in terms of the currently available data. Anecdotally, however, and as the previous chapters have explored in detail, the dominance of men and people racialized as white in UK comedy is well known. Also clearly apparent are the economic barriers to working-class people who do not have the financial resources to build up stage time by undertaking free or low-paid labour. These inequalities will only be compounded by the UK's 2022 cost-of-living crisis where energy bills have skyrocketed, resulting in people having to make increasingly difficult decisions about their financial resources without sufficient state support.

In relation to the working practices of the CCIs, the informality of the sector is often framed as a 'good thing', enabling individual creative workers some autonomy. The connotation of the word 'informal' is much more inviting than the just as relevant word 'precarious'. As Rosalind Gill notes, the informal practices of the CCIs 'also significantly contributes [sic] to their inequality, becoming a space in which subtle forms of sexism can flourish, outside any requirements for accountability' (2014: 519). This was certainly true of my own experience working in a UK CCI organization prior to academia and also speaks to some of the examples provided by my interviewees. Gill is discussing 'subtle sexism' as a symptom of the informal and flexible structures of work found within the creative industries. This is in contrast, she argues, to the very stark overt sexism that characterized the increased inclusion of women into paid labour outside the home in the 1970s.

Sexism alone does not automatically result in violence and abuse of women. It does, however, play a part in perpetuating and normalizing rape myths – for example that women are asking for it, the problem is their behaviour rather than men's behaviour and so on. An informal environment where sexism, of any kind, is normalized or downplayed can contribute to the normalizing of sexual aggression and a blurring of boundaries (Koepke et al, 2014, Rollero and Tartaglia 2019). Overt and more subtle forms of sexism have been a mainstay of live comedy since the inception of the form, and whilst (as the introduction of this book explored) it is now less acceptable to articulate sexist remarks overtly, it is far from an extinct ideology. As Gill comments, 'sexism itself, [. . .] is increasingly dynamic, mobile, and agile, requiring more nuanced vocabularies of critique' (Gill 2014: 511). Sexism is a key part of the context of sexual abuse and assault, in that behaviours that dismiss women's agency by ignoring the need for consent feed off of the wider disenfranchisement and low status of women, by making their voices easier to ignore. Being exposed to and, more importantly, being pressured to contribute to talk that normalizes sexism, in the case of comedy in the form of onstage and green-room banter, can have an impact on how men understand masculinity and their belief in rape myths (Cole et al. 2020).

Significantly, studies of inequalities in the CCIs conducted in the UK have rarely focused on live comedy. For example, the excellent work of David Hesmondhalgh and Sarah Baker (2015) on gender segregation and sexism in CCIs considered television, magazine journalism and music. Rosalind Gill's (2014) work was similar in emphasis, also using Skillset data, but not considering performance. Lenny Henry and Marcus Rider's (2021a) work focused on inequalities in the film and television industries. The lack of specific consideration of the live comedy industry, at grassroots level, is perhaps because of its fragile ecology.

In addition to the issues present across the CCIs in the UK, comedy has further complexities in terms of being *seen and valued* as a credible industry. There is a huge discrepancy between highly commercial successful arena tours at the top and low or no-pay labour undertaken by those entering on the local live scene. At the male-dominated top of the industry, it is difficult for comedy to be seen *as anything but* a commercial enterprise, with huge financial gains attached. In this high-earning end of the industry, individual comics have representation in the form of agents or publicists, and thus have a protection afforded to them not experienced prior to reaching this level of success. Conversely, at the grassroots level, where more women and minority comedians operate, it can be hard for jobbing un-represented comics to be taken seriously as cultural workers, rather than hobbyists or dabblers who, as freelancers, often have their labour exploited in exchange for 'exposure' or the (non-binding) promise of future work. This framing is aided by the fact that many comics starting out have multiple jobs to support their creative pursuits. Where people source their main income from is often perceived as their 'main job', rather than as simply the facilitator of their creative ambitions. The downplaying of comedy as a viable job (and creative arts professions more broadly) is problematic and is connected to wider ideas of what constitutes work under capitalism. As Horgan notes that 'because of the background unfreedom – the fact that we are compelled to work – challenging bad workplace practices, such as not having proper safety equipment, routine unpaid overtime, even harassment and discrimination all become harder' (Horgan 2021: 71). Since being able to work as a comedian, or artist, actor or other creative vocation, is socially positioned as a privilege, any action that might risk that position, for example by challenging questionable industry practice, is more difficult to achieve.

I would argue that the fight to have the creative and artistic aspects of comedy respected, in line with other dramatic or musical arts, has resulted in an over-compensation which obscures or downplays the idea of comedy as a workplace and industry. When work as a comedian is dismissed intentionally or unintentionally as *not art*, individual comics combat this by foregrounding the creative aspects of the work, rather than the more complex or mundane aspects of creative labour. This evidences what Gill describes (when considering CCIs, more broadly) as a 'favouring an entrepreneurial individualistic mode that disavows structural power relations' (Gill 2014: 509). If the public focus is always on the individual, who is scrutinizing the system that enables that individual to succeed or fail? Trying to get the creative merit of comedy recognized (especially by the UK's Arts Council) has inadvertently obscured some of the workplace practices the industry includes. The difference, in terms of professional practices at the contrasting ends of the comedy industry spectrum, is significant and relevant, when we consider how sexual assault or harassment is enabled. And this industrial background is important when we consider the reports of abuse and misconduct made by women in comedy; it is within this complicated industrial context that the impact of #MeToo has been felt within the UK comedy circuit. Unfortunately, a key feature of the live comedy industry has been the creation and sustaining of contexts which facilitate the potential for abuse. Many aspects of the comedy industry overlap with critiques of wider CCIs, although there are distinctions which set comedy apart. This chapter will focus on the way the live comedy industry has been a place of gendered abuses of power and the reasons why this industry diverges in some ways from other, more formally recognized, entertainment industries.

#MeToo and comedy

I commenced my research into the UK comedy industry before the 2017 #MeToo revelations which drew into sharp focus the experiences of women in the entertainment industries and beyond. Although 2017 can be seen as a particularly notable moment in disclosures of sexual violence and harassment, Karen Boyle (2019) highlights that we can differentiate this *moment* from a longer feminist activist *movement* against rape culture. Boyle rightly considers Tarana Burke's MeToo activism, which pre-dates the hashtag and is centred on and led by Black and marginalized women, as an example of *ongoing labour* to address rape culture and violence against women. This kind of activism is labour-intensive, emotionally draining and time-consuming. Boyle distinguishes Burke's work from the more visible public disclosures of abuse spurred on by the #MeToo moment of 2017, which has been criticized as being white-centric. The #MeToo discourses more broadly have also frequently focused on privileged white women (as considered by Angela Onwuachi-Willig 2018, Karen Boyle 2019 and Alison Phipps 2020), and these white-centric testimonies can actually be used to obscure the kinds of exploitation and abuse faced by marginalized women of colour, who often do not have the option to be heard, or feel they will be believed. This is not to say that #MeToo has not made a significant impact; and, as I will argue in this chapter, for the comedy industry #MeToo has provided a template for how to make public the ongoing problems of sexual harassment. However, disclosure via social media is not an end point; rather, it is the first step to addressing these issues, through tangible work to build a better society or industry.

It is only subsequent to the #MeToo moment of the late 2010s, specifically following the public outing of Harvey Weinstein in October 2017, four years into the period of my research, that women have felt more emboldened to share their stories from the UK comedy circuit. This shift in the culture of disclosure does not mean that the abusive behaviour being highlighted is a new thing or that women did not try and speak out prior to this, but that a significant increase in awareness and action occurred following this period. None of the interviewees I spoke to in the mid-2010s (pre #MeToo) mentioned explicit examples of sexual abuse. Again, this does not mean that it was not a factor in the industry at the time of the interviews. My interviewees knew they were not being anonymized and my line of questioning may well have prevented or precluded this kind of conversation. As part of these conversations, I did hear things that shocked me and made me think that this kind of working environment was exactly the kind of space where abuses of power could become commonplace – as some of the testimonies in previous chapters make clear.

The public outing of those who had committed sexual violence and harassment against women (overwhelmingly cisgender men), both before and during the #MeToo moment, included high-profile figures in the US comedy scene. Bill Cosby, who started out in live comedy in the 1960s before becoming an internationally recognized comic actor in *The Bill Cosby Show* (1969–71) and *The Cosby Show* (1984–92), had been the focus of allegations long before #MeToo. What is particularly interesting here is the way attention to Cosby's behaviour was highlighted *within* stand-up comedy in the mid-2010s (a space much less regulated than mediated comic spaces), but allegations were not formalized until 2018. Comedian Hannibal Buress explicitly drew attention to the historic pattern of rape accusations against Cosby in his 2014 live set, which was subsequently recorded and circulated on social media (Graves 2018). Adrienne Truscott, in her show *Asking for It*, specifically addressed the accusations made about Cosby noting that his 'family man' persona was exactly why he was able to get away with his behaviour for so long. Comedy's role in society as outside the normal social contract, and its ability to break taboos, means that often the 'outing' of problematic behaviour can be incorporated into comic routines. Whether disclosures that occur within these liminal spaces of comic performance, and that can, as a result, be dismissed easily as humour, are taken seriously or acted upon is, of course, another matter.

American comic Louis C.K. (real name Louis Székely), who publicly acknowledged the sexual harassment allegations against him were true (C.K. 2017), remains probably the most high-profile example of a comic caught up in the #MeToo moment of 2017. C.K. was accused by multiple women of masturbating in front of them without their permission, in a demonstration of behaviour that both projected his power within the industry (who would believe the women; they had much more to lose than him career-wise? and so on) and a total disregard for consent. I will return to both C.K. and Cosby later in this chapter in relation to the lack of consequences for this kind of behaviour.

In 2020 there was a more public reckoning with the issues of sexual harassment in live comedy in the UK and Ireland specifically. As many of the revelations related to the UK circuit were made public during the Covid-19 pandemic lockdown period, when comedy venues were closed by the government as part of measures to control the spread of the virus, it could be argued that this period of enforced rest from the live circuit provided an opportunity for comedians to reflect upon their industrial practices (Tomsett et al. 2021). The live circuit was paused in-person and shifted online, and so people (both comedians and the public) were able to think about what a better, more inclusive circuit could look like when in-person live gigs returned. This thinking was particularly apparent in relation to disabled access which has long been an issue for live comedy. As, with the introduction of online gigs, there were more opportunities for neurodiverse people, and those with physical disabilities, to access live comedy experiences from home. Many comedians then had the chance to consider the unwanted and exclusionary behaviour they encountered, and how these had been normalized within existing workplaces.

A significant amount of the online disclosures regarding the UK circuit were provoked by a clip resurfacing online from a 2011 episode of the American podcast *The Joe Rogan Experience* (2009 to present) where guest, US comedian Joey Diaz, is discussing the sexual exploitation of young women comics entering the American live circuit. The specific behaviour being described is the forcing of new women comics to give sexual favours (in this discussion, oral sex) to Diaz in exchange for his help to furthering their careers. In the clip, this behaviour, casually discussed, was laughed off by Rogan and so completely normalized. The abuse of power inherent in what was being discussed was not considered at all by those involved in the podcast recording as exploitation or abuse. In addition, at the same time as this clip being re-circulated in 2020, there was widespread reporting of accusations levelled at another US comedian, Chris D'Elia, in relation to problematic behaviour with under-aged fans (Michallon 2020). The fact that both examples came from the US circuit (which has close ties to the UK circuit, with many comedians moving between them) meant that women online, especially on the Twitter platform, were keen to highlight that this kind of exploitation was not confined to an American context, and therefore dismissible as something unique to the US industry. There were many comments online from women comics regarding several examples of just this kind of abuse occurring within the UK and that, at some future point, these issues will come to light with respect to some of Britain's well-known comedy stars (Healy 2020). As Karen Boyle observes, 'Men are made newly vulnerable when behaviour which has historically been rewarded or joked about is denaturalized and problematized by refocusing the narrative on how these behaviours were/are experienced by women' (Boyle 2019: 70).

Online, women were starting to wrestle the narrative away from the men who dismissed this behaviour as a normal part of the industry.

It is worth noting here the difficulties of the 'this is widely known' narrative of sexual exploitation and abuse. Boyle (2019) comments that by framing the reports of sexual violence and harassment as something 'everyone knew', as was typically the case during this outpouring of online disclosures related to the UK circuit, such a framing can unhelpfully be conflated with a 'well if they knew, why did they not do something?' approach. Such a response to disclosure shifts the focus of these instances to the behaviour of women (what they did or did not do at the time), rather than identifying the men abusing their power.

Comedy as a workplace susceptible to gendered abuse

A key question we might ask is: Why is live comedy a special case? Why might the live comedy industry be *more susceptible* to these kinds of sexual harassment and abusive behaviours than other performance or other CCIs?

First, as succinctly observed by Kiri Pritchard-McLean in the title of her article for iNews, 'There's no HR department in comedy' (Pritchard-McLean 2020). This is, of course, also the case for other creative careers where the dominant mode of employment is freelance and insecure. However, specific *comic framing* of the social/professional interactions we find in the live comedy environment contributes in unique ways that exacerbate the opportunity for sexual harassment. If we make use of Pritchard-McLean's concept further and think about the role of a Human Resources (HR) department in more traditional workplace structures, we can see that HR functions as a way of maintaining norms of appropriate behaviour and professionalism in a workplace. The problem is that, for comedians, part of their professionalism is their ability to make jokes, engage with taboos and test boundaries, and this *serves to mask* inappropriate behaviour and blur the line as to what is allowable. In my own workplace (within a UK university), it would not be acceptable to use the kinds of language, sexual objectification or sexism that is still very much alive and well in the comic material of many stand-ups working on the live circuit. This kind of behaviour is very clearly beyond the scope of that which is considered appropriate in an educational setting. The issue for live comedy is that harassment, objectification and even unwanted physical attention or assault can be easily integrated into normalized workplace behaviours. Hidden within green-room 'banter', or off-stage playfulness, can lurk more violent or violating behaviours that cannot be clearly seen, and therefore remain unchallenged. For live comedy, the informality of CCIs more broadly interrelates with the comic framing of interactions between comedians, which then makes comedy venues additionally challenging places to navigate safely as a woman.

There are two well-used rhetorical defences to those calling out sexual harassment and sexism within the comedy industry, drawn from a wider postfeminist cultural setting. First, the person performing the offensive or abusive behaviour can claim they were 'just joking'. This, crucially, does not deny that the offending behaviour did not occur, or that it was a mistake as such, but that the *intent* was humour. This defence is more likely to be accepted as an 'excuse' when working in a space where joking around is the expected, and in many ways the default, way of interacting. It also potentially serves to implicate others too, in that 'everyone jokes around' and this therefore has the potential to make other (mostly male) comics feel that they too could have their own intentions easily misinterpreted in the current climate, provoking defensiveness. In contrast to other professions, where explicit language or informal physicality are abnormal and discouraged, warning signs can be easily missed in comic environments as the boundaries are so mutable. This easily exploitable situation may of course be additionally complex when we consider how certain comics are known for their near-the-knuckle or controversial sexist humour, and the performance of this material makes money for the club/promoter as well as the individual comic. In certain instances, there will be an economic incentive to tolerate behaviour or make minimal fuss about any complaints received, if the comic is profitable for the venue/promoter.

Second, the problematic or abusive person can simply claim that the target of this abuse 'can't take a joke', drawing on and reinforcing the stereotypes that women, and more specifically feminists, are killjoys. This kind of rhetorical defence has consequences for women comics in a way that it does not in other non-comic industries. Again, to use a comparison, if I, in my workplace, call out sexism and am told I cannot take a joke, it does not undermine my ability to do my job. My work is not contingent on my sense of humour, and the criticism therefore speaks to me as a person rather than my abilities or professionalism related to my career. For women comics, who already have overcome a huge number of barriers to work within the industry, being undermined in this way is *an attack not only on them personally but also on their professional abilities*. A good sense of humour is framed as a part of comic professionalism and so an accusation of not being able to take a joke, or being humourless, has a very different meaning and set of implications for future employment in a comedy industry context. We can therefore see why women may well laugh along in instances where they feel uncomfortable to avoid conflict which, in this instance, would be both interpersonal *and* professional.

When allegations of sexual misconduct do come to light, we can see that this notion of comedy industry professionalism becomes relevant for both accused and accuser as 'the discursive context in which their behaviour is situated: is it criminal, immoral, unprofessional and/or old-fashioned?' (Boyle 2019: 71) is enacted. Instinctively, people try to fit reported behaviour into these frameworks and attach differing levels of 'seriousness' to an allegation as a result. The difficulty here is that 'unprofessional behaviour' means something different in comedy. The form of comedy is somewhat resistant to this 'professionalism narrative' in favour of a focus on vocational talent. Boyle describes how 'There is a conflation of consequences in much of this commentary where reputational damage (however temporary) is itself described in a language of violation so that men-behaving-badly are recast as victims of indiscriminate moral righteousness' (Boyle 2019: 60). This is perhaps of particular relevance for professions that are framed as vocational and talent based, where the individual person(ality) is a key part of their employment, rather than the function they provide within a team, where they are seen as more easily replaceable.

This again relates to the structure of the UK comedy industry and the significant differences between the white male-dominated top of the industry and the grassroots of the industry, where women and minority comedians are often held for longer before being able to progress, if allowed to progress at all. The America open mic circuit, explored by Stephanie Brown (2020), with a focus on Chicago, also perpetuates issues that prevent women and people of colour from progressing into the industry from this initial space. As comedians work as individual freelancers and do not have formal 'colleagues' as such, there is often no one in a position to push back on abusive behaviour, so this can continue unchecked. As women often work in isolation amongst men, and these men may well not encounter the same women in a professional context ever again, the opportunity to take advantage of these unique dynamics is clear.

The freelance nature of the work of live comedy, as explored by Nick Butler and Dimirinka Stoyanova Russell (2018), means that a huge amount of emotional labour is required to navigate the precarity of this professional environment. Being seen to be available and willing to undertake poorly remunerated or even unpaid gigs in order to progress is completely normalized at the entry end of the circuit. Women working in this context know that the consequences of speaking out against a more powerful male comic will potentially be significant for their careers. The impact of speaking out is also very difficult to definitively prove in this context too. What I mean by this is that it is almost impossible for a freelancer to know whether they are not being booked again because of the accusation they levelled at another comic (e.g. retaliation, denial and dismissal of their disclosure) or for some other unspecified and intangible reason that may also result in their not being booked again, such as the personal taste of the promoter, or the perceived fit with the audience – which is part of the existing inbuilt precarity of the circuit.

Campaigns and initiatives

The international #MeToo campaign and its various iterations across multiple sectors have brought sexual harassment in entertainment and creative workplaces to mainstream attention. The death of Australian comedian Euridice Dixon, killed on her way home from work after performing in Melbourne, was widely reported internationally and served as a reminder of the vulnerability of women in performing industries (Alcorn 2018). This incident directly inspired UK comedians Angela Barnes, Sameena Zehra and Pauline Eyre to establish the Home Safe Collective, an initiative to help get women and non-binary comedy performers home safely after late-night gigs. This initiative, which was piloted at the 2018 Edinburgh Festival, won the Fringe Panel Prize that year and was widely praised as a way of making working women comedians safer by removing ambiguity related to returning home or to their accommodation after a gig (Masso 2018).

After the revelations of 2020, further work has been undertaken to make positive changes to the industry. The Live Comedy Association, established in 2021 and co-founded by Brid Kirby and Owen Donovan, is a networking and lobbying group dedicated to the UK live comedy circuit.[1] As part of its work to date (which due to the pandemic context has focused overwhelmingly on the needs of the circuit during and after the Covid-19 response), the group has also attempted to address some of the safety and harassment concerns of the UK circuit. The association's board, which changes fairly regularly, has several positions dedicated to inclusion and representation, and their Code of Conduct explicitly references their dedication to equality and diversity across the sector. Since their establishment they have successfully run the #SaveLiveComedy campaign in order to lobby Arts Council England to include comedy in the Culture Recovery Funding for arts venues and organizations – something ACE has refused to do multiple times in the past. Their website has a resources page dedicated to signposting victims of sexual assault and harassment to relevant support as well as suggesting training for promoters who wish to better understand how to prevent this behaviour. In terms of making a change in the industry, this organization is significant in that it provides a collective voice for comedians and promoters – something that so far has been sorely missing. The importance of collective action cannot be understated when discussing cultural changes to workplace discrimination as it relieves the burden on individual women (or in relation to racism, people of colour) from jeopardizing their own careers as individuals.

Also in 2021, comedians Kiri Pritchard-McLean and Nina Gilligan established Get Off Live Comedy which positions itself as an HR service for the live comedy industry.[2] The crux of the group's work is to get comedy promoters and venues to join as members, to undergo training in creating safe comedy workplaces, to publish (and crucially adhere to) sexual harassment policies, and then to access the HR services the organization provides when necessary, when preventing sexual harassment or indeed dealing with disclosures or complaints. This initiative, in its infancy, has attracted significant press, bringing it to wider attention (Healy 2021). In Ireland, the Comedy Safety Standards (CSS) group, established in 2020, has also emerged, led by comic performers who volunteer their time.[3] This group has partnered with the Dublin Rape Crisis Centre to provide resources, advice and training to educate comedy professionals on rape myths, relevant laws in relation to harassment and assault and, crucially, bystander intervention. The focus on practical training to prevent harassment is a key aspect of their work and again makes the issue one that the industry, as a whole, are responsible for fixing, not the individual survivors of abuse.

Alongside the productive approaches to addressing sexual harassment and abuse on the comedy circuit, there is also evidence that there are some well-meaning, yet fundamentally flawed, approaches to allyship occurring through encouraging disclosure. Tweets were put out by various organizations (an example here would be the Comedy 50: 50 campaign) stating that anyone who had suffered abuse within the comedy industry could get in touch with them to disclose and report this behaviour, as they wanted to know. What was unclear was exactly what would be done with this information: Was the idea that those organizations or individuals inviting disclosure would no longer work with anyone accused of this behaviour? Would they put people disclosing in touch with the relevant support? What were the legal ramifications of this for both those disclosing and those accused informally in this way (e.g. vulnerability in the form of freedom of information requests)? The actual reasons why disclosure in this way would be necessary, and what outcomes could be expected, were very unclear. I appreciate that Twitter is not great for nuance, but these key questions struck me upon reading tweets encouraging disclosure as important to ask *before* welcoming an outpouring of information that could potentially retraumatize people or have tangible impacts on their careers. The UK Comedy industry is a small world, so these are not unreasonable things to consider, and these invitations to share information speaks to concerns that Boyle describes as disclosure 'becoming culturally mandated' (Boyle 2019: 55). Requests, however well-meaning, for people to come forward and disclose (in this case to untrained comedy industry professionals, with personal or professional links that are not made clear), play into the mindset that if you do not speak up or disclose, to anyone who provides that option, at a later point you'll be told, 'well, you did not speak up'. This kind of offer, to hear a disclosure, without tangible outcomes for those reporting and relevant support, is simply performative allyship and has the potential to cause a lot more harm than good.

Conclusion

Comedy as a workplace is markedly different from other CCIs when it comes to creating an environment where abuse and harassment can flourish. The humour frameworks within which comedians operate both on and off-stage obscure and can in certain instances enable abusive behaviour that then goes unnoticed or is downplayed. Boyle comments that 'violence against women is entirely compatible with how masculinity, and heterosexual masculinity specifically, is personally, politically, culturally and socially enacted' (Boyle 2019: 51). This compatibility is also (as explored in the previous chapter) very much in line with how masculinity has been performed by stand-up comics over the last ten years as part of both a backlash against contemporary feminisms (including fourth-wave initiatives such as #MeToo) and the continuation of the male dominance of the form. White cisgender male supremacy has been built into the UK comedy industries' evolution due to spatial injustices in the live and recorded forms and the constant reinforcing of binary gender stereotypes, and this creates an environment where the voices of women and minority groups are easy to dismiss.

We have seen in the UK how sexist humour is regularly excused and reintegrated back into the comedy circuit after a nominal time period has elapsed (as discussed in the previous chapter in relation to Dapper Laughs). Worryingly, we can also see this reintegration play out with comedians who have enacted abuse and harassment. Despite the huge amount of column inches dedicated to the concept of 'being cancelled', we can see that, certainly for the high-profile American examples explored previously in this chapter, there is a lack of significant consequences. Notably, in 2022, Louis C.K., who had publicly admitted his wrongdoing, won a Grammy Award for Best Comedy Special. The show awarded this accolade, the self-released *Sincerely* (2020), featured the comedian downplaying and making humour out of his sexual misconduct (Wagmeister 2022). So, far from being 'cancelled', C.K. has gone on to integrate back into both live spaces of comedy, despite much condemnation from women working in these spaces, and the critically successful upper echelons of US comedy. It only took five years for this trajectory to be complete. Bill Cosby's 2018 conviction for sexual assault was overturned in mid-2021 due to a Pennsylvania court deciding that he could not be tried due to a technicality: a deal having been made with a previous prosecutor for the same crime (Betancourt 2021). Cosby was not exonerated by the judge in this case, but the fact that he is no longer in prison, despite the original length of his sentence, sends a very clear message about the provisional nature of consequences for those with sufficient resources to hire legal teams. Cosby has recently publicly stated his intention to return to touring his comedy as early as 2023, despite ongoing legal issues (Parkel 2022). Neither of these approaches – a carceral one in the case of Cosby, and a full public admission and censure in the case of C.K. – can be seen as providing justice to the women abused or have addressed the consequences that the behaviour of these powerful men had on the victims personally, or professionally.

Comedy as an industry seems to be particularly quick to try and rehabilitate people, in terms of both their problematic material and abusive behaviours, and achieves this in many instances through its steadfast adherence to the rhetorical defence of 'just joking'. The landscape of the current UK circuit is challenging for women and minority groups in that many of the industry practices that facilitate and harbour abusers are still to be addressed – or are arguably inbuilt, into the precarity of employment in live comedy.

8

Conclusion

Reflections on UK comedy's glass ceiling

This book has explored the context of women's stand-up comic performance over the last ten years, as well as the content of feminist and postfeminist stand-up comedy. In outlining the development of the UK comedy industry since the working men's club era, I have sought to situate new knowledge, developed through primary research, within a wider comedy history. Through discussions with those working within the industry, this research has shed light on the continued challenges women face when performing in spaces, contexts and formats designed and dominated by men. As comedian Daphna Baram noted when interviewed for this project, the 'glass ceiling', created by structural barriers to women's inclusion within comedy, is well known and widely discussed.

> There is not even an argument about the glass ceiling of women in comedy, it's not really made of glass everybody can see it. It's basically the glass of the television screen.

The increased awareness of structural barriers preventing inclusion in comedy does not mean that the common gendered issues are being dealt with effectively. This disparity, between *awareness* of barriers and *action* leading to resolution of the inequality experienced by women, was evident and evidenced in interviews with performers and audiences and through analysis of selected case studies.

The societal pressures placed on women comedians on stage, and the more specific issues that feminist performers encounter, demonstrate the complex and continually evolving state of the comedy industry. Whilst some of the identified issues relating to inclusion in comedy are wider than gender identity and relate to marginalized groups such as Black and minority ethnic performers, women do meet specific gendered barriers. This is because gender stereotypes are deeply entrenched within the language of comedy. By this I mean, first, in the literal language, in this case English, with gendered words such as 'feisty' and 'comedienne' highlighting gender difference and being regularly deployed in criticism and introductions by compères. But, second, gender is highly pertinent to the formal language structures of comedy itself, such as joke structures which require incongruous and shocking punchlines or self-deprecatory jokes which are used to address power imbalances in performance situations. In many instances, men have invented these languages of comedy and have dominated and restricted their uses both socially (re. social humour) and as part of performance.

Changes to the comedy industry and feminisms during the research period

This research has been conducted at a time of significant change for women's rights. The rise of fourth-wave and celebrity feminisms has provoked a reclamation of a word to which few have laid claim to in the previous decade. This upswing in a public rhetoric of feminism is coupled with a surge in right-wing politics in the United States, the United Kingdom and across Europe that harks back to a mythical 'golden era' of uncomplicated patriotism and old-fashioned binary gender politics – as can be seen within examples of exclusionary feminism in the UK too.

In 2013, when initiating my research, feminist comedy was at its peak in terms of acclaim on the live circuit. Now, at the time of writing, the idea of women comedians identifying as feminist or talking about women's rights on stage (in the live comedy environment) has become almost clichéd. What would have been strikingly bold in 2013 has now become normalized as part of the comedy scene. This was particularly apparent to me as I watched performances by women comics at the 2018 Edinburgh Festival (pre-pandemic) where, almost uniformly, gender was addressed in some way by those I watched perform.

Despite wide-ranging journalistic considerations of gender across performance industries, it is clearly very difficult for individual women to speak out against sexist and gendered practices in the comedy industry. This difficulty is due to the way that work on the circuit is always precarious and, in many instances, managed in an informal manner. In 2017, at Mixed Bill's Women and Comedy symposium at the University of Salford, Sameena Zehra made the point that it is not enough for women to boycott sexist promoters or shows. This boycotting results in women shouldering the economic and emotional burden of changing the industry, when a more inclusive industry is better for everyone, irrespective of their gender identity. Zehra called on cisgender male comics to show solidarity with their women and non-binary contemporaries, to act collectively to take a stand and make a change. Just as Zehra advocates for collective action, it is my hope that this research can be used to demonstrate that gendered challenges and experiences are not as individual as we are led to believe. Experiences of sexism are still common and by collecting the thoughts and testimonies of multiple performers I hope this point is amplified. Experiences of sexism in the UK comedy industry, whilst slowly becoming less frequent, are not in any sense exceptional.

Women comics, live comedy spaces and barriers to inclusion

In the contemporary context, the spatial injustice apparent during stand-up comedy's development has yet to be fully addressed, and the effects of the gendered evolution of the form are still evident. This claim was substantiated repeatedly in the interviews I undertook with performers and promoters, who highlighted that women often still perform alone amongst men on the mainstream circuit – as white cisgender men continue to dominate the spaces of comic performance. Although the alternative comedy movement of the 1980s made progress towards changing the content of stand-up comedy away from explicitly racist and sexist comedy, it arguably did little to address the spatial injustices felt by women in the comedy industry outside London, or indeed mainstream/commercial performance spaces. It was the way that the post-alternative comedy circuit left unchallenged this existing male dominance that resulted in women taking things into their own hands in the late 1990s and early 2000s. This has been followed, more recently, by minority groups establishing their own spaces to address intersectional aspects of their exclusion from the circuit (Black, minority ethnic, LGBTQ+, Disabled and working-class comedians).

This research highlights that the development of women-only spaces for comedy was a direct reaction to male dominance and industry sexism on the UK circuit. The action taken by the people and organizations consulted as part of this research (Lynne Parker of Funny Women and Hazel O'Keefe of Laughing Cows Comedy and the Women in Comedy Festival) to develop women-only nights and events has, in this book, been documented thoroughly for the first time. The contributions of these pioneering women have been contextualized as part of the diversification of the form of stand-up comedy and the spatial and industrial changes within British comedy.

The industrial structure of the current live comedy industry continues to include gendered spaces at the grassroots level, as the gendered issues these nights were established in the late 1990s to address continue to be a problem for those trying to enter the industry. Post-2013 the comedy industry in the UK has taken some steps towards the inclusion of women and minority voices. However, even subsequent to key periods of progress such as the alternative movement of the 1980s and the establishment of women-focused comedy organizations in the 1990s/2000s, as well as the critical success of feminist comedy in 2013, the specific challenges remain and function as barriers to the inclusion of women. These barriers can be summarized in the following way: individuals being understood (or perceived to be understood) by the public to represent all women, sexist audience reactions, poor introductions, sexism from industry professionals, badly advertised women-only nights, economic disparities and aesthetic pressures. These seven issues relate to the observed behaviours of industry professionals, comedy critics and journalists as well as the public and perpetuate past injustices by upholding a (white) male norm from which women are cast as deviating. This does not mean that the current industry has not started to consider the issue of inclusion, but that there is still some significant way to go to make the industry fully accessible to all who wish to participate.

In addition to the themes identified earlier, a general hostility towards women-only comedy nights was discussed during interviews with performers. I also experienced and observed first-hand this general hostility, both online and in-person. I believe this hostility stems from a wider societal resistance to quotas and affirmative action. When commencing this research, I had suspected that women-only nights would meet with general dismissal (or disrespect) in line with most labour performed by women more generally and attitudes towards sectors that employ mostly women. However, several performers highlighted how women-only nights were seen as less of a challenge for performers by the wider industry, and also as something distinct from, and of less value than, mainstream spaces in terms of experience and audience. This attitude from the wider industry (perceived by those working professionally in the context under discussion) is reflective of the wider social context and is an experience unique to women and minority performers who may develop their own spaces to combat their exclusion from existing comedy nights/venues/festivals.

This experience is combined with the way that often comedy performed by women is referred to explicitly or by implication as 'women's comedy', where gender automatically becomes a genre. This is frustrating for women performers and unique to them, as they are working in an industry, and a wider social context, that still holds the assumption that comedy by women is in some way *for* women. This continual foregrounding of gender was apparent many times when conducting my digital ethnographic work, as women comics regularly reported being told by, sometimes well-meaning, audiences that they were 'funny, for a woman'.

My research evidences that sexist attitudes from comedy audiences are not a thing of the past – even when these audiences are attending women-only comedy events specifically. Popular feminisms have resulted in a rise in popular misogyny, as explored extensively by Sarah Banet-Weiser (2018). Therefore, women working in this current industrial context still labour under the shadow of the entrenched stereotypes around gender and humour, even if these attitudes are not as explicitly articulated as they once were. Whilst most performers were aware that these attitudes about women-only nights exist, they maintained a belief in the necessary function of women-only nights and this was foregrounded many times within interviews.

The current circuit operates in a way that both horizontally and vertically segregates women. This is achieved by forcing women into a position where, in order to build up sufficient stage time, they first have to work in women-only spaces (which continue to be less respected than mainstream spaces). This occurs simultaneously with the industry's reproduction of barriers to women's inclusion at the top end of the mixed-gendered live comedy circuit and television industry. This horizontal and vertical segregation plays out concurrently with the industry's attempt, as a whole, but also as individual organizations and broadcasters, to present itself as more inclusive. When the data used to make these claims is interrogated, as in *The State of Play Report* (Mermiri et al. 2014), the picture is different to that which the commercially focused industry presents.

In the current industrial context, organizations on the surface may appear changed by their diversity initiatives. This appearance is often achieved, however, without any structural change. It is relatively easy for a comedy club to host a women-only comedy night (either regularly or as a one-off), but it is harder to ensure inclusion is considered and achieved across the whole of a venue's programme. Television comedy can be considered through a similar lens. Comedy produced by women is often lauded as part of publicizing increased diversity on screen, only to then be axed or fail to be recommissioned after the kudos of including women has been accrued for the broadcaster. Unsurprisingly, broadcasters and platforms are less keen to shout about the comedy shows produced by women that they are axing, often after significant critical success – Channel 4's *Raised by Wolves* (2013–16) provides an example here as the show was both commercially popular and critically successful, winning the Rose D'Or for Best Sitcom in 2016 but was still not recommissioned.

It should be noted that not all comics wish to participate in the television comedy industry or see it as a destination (or progression) of their live careers. However, in terms of increasing audiences for live shows, participation in television comedy continues to be important for careers, as evidenced in my audience study. Of my 336 surveyed participants, 88 per cent also watched television comedy (double the 44 per cent figure for radio comedy). This relates to Kuiper's understanding that 'knowledge always precedes appreciation: you have to be aware of something in order to like, hate or be indifferent to it' (Kuipers, 2006: 360). Television comedy plays an important role in relation to awareness of specific women comedians and also can assist in dismissing the idea of 'women's comedy' as a genre, as with more exposure to a range of women performers this would very quickly be disproved.

A crucial role that women-focused organizations such as Funny Women and the Women in Comedy Festival play is that of advocacy for inclusion. This was of particular importance for the UK circuit in a time before more industry-wide collectives, such as the Live Comedy Association, were in place. Organizations have a unique opportunity to challenge unethical, discriminatory or abusive processes and practices, which individuals may not be in a position to undertake and to collaborate with the wider industry to showcase women performers. For example, Funny Women continue to work with high-profile organizations (such as Women in Film and TV and ITV) to create and promote initiatives to address under-representation across all areas of comedy. The link between the Women in Comedy Festival and the Manchester venue, The Frog and Bucket, has certainly impacted on further integration of women across all events at the venue. Jessica Toomey, who manages The Frog and Bucket, and more recently took up directorship of the festival itself, has made significant progress in including women across all mixed-bill nights at the venue over the last ten years. Women-only comedy nights and events provide space for women to develop the stage time required to progress in their careers – stage time they are not able to accrue as easily on the mainstream circuit due to a continued reluctance by promoters to book multiple women on the same bill.

A further contribution that these spaces make to the current industry is through the ways in which they provide an opportunity for women comedians to work with each other and share experiences. Not only is working with other women significant in terms of being able to see and be inspired by the work of others (along 'see it to be it' lines) but this arrangement has implications for the industrial conditions that women face. By providing a space for women to work together and share experiences, the opportunities for collective action or challenges to existing conditions increase. When women, in any industry, work in isolation they are more vulnerable to exploitation and it is easier for employers to dismiss instances of sexism or discrimination as a 'one-off' if the complaint is raised by one person. An obvious example here, and something that came out unexpectedly within the interview data, would be the silence that exists around women's pay (both in a wider sense and also, in relation to this study, within the live comedy industry). The way women rarely work together in the mainstream comedy industry means that there is little awareness of the rates people get for their work – or whether they are being paid at all, when offered spots so they can 'gain experience'. This can mean that it is hard to know when people are being under-remunerated for their labour. By creating spaces where women can come together, an opportunity to discover these issues exists, and this is the first step towards addressing the issues.

Whilst there are clear positives for women working together, there was still a concern that some audiences or industry professionals see these nights as ghettoizing women and, by implication, suggesting that 'women's comedy' is a genre in and of itself. This is not helped, and sometimes actively perpetuated, when certain women-only nights cash in on a reductive binary to create 'ladies nights'. These kinds of nights were uniformly dismissed within the interviews with performers as unhelpful to inclusion due to their retro-sexist tone and approach. For many, these badly thought-through nights simply reinforced the perception that women's comedy is a genre. It would be wrong to fully dismiss commercial gain as a motivation for the founding of women-only comedy organizations or nights; the chance to build a market, or capitalize on an under-served market is, of course, relevant. However, if the motivation for commercial gain is coupled with a general lack of awareness about gender stereotypes or a lack of care when assembling the event, as with poorly executed journalism about women comics, 'ladies nights' clearly have the potential to do significant damage in terms of the perception of comedy performed by women.

In the past five years, there has been a significant rise in the number of women and non-binary performers organizing their own mixed-gendered comedy nights. Many of these new live comedy nights and initiatives, such as Kiri Pritchard-McLean's *Suspiciously Cheap Comedy*, nights ran by *The LOL Word*, a queer comedy collective ran by Jodie Mitchell, Chloe Petts, Chloe Green and Shelf,

Sian Davies' *Best in Class* and Sophie Duker's *Wacky Racists*, have an overt inclusion agenda and provide a space for a diverse range of acts from across the gender spectrum. Thus, whilst women-only comedy spaces provide a useful and formative space for women to develop careers, they are now not the only spaces to be prioritizing gender diversity in performers and comic material. The nights and events found at the grassroots end of the industry evidence a much more thoughtful and nuanced commitment to diversity than many of the much bigger (and commercially or publicly funded) organizations can.

Women comics and mediated spaces

The continued adoption of social media over the last ten years has had a huge impact on the UK comedy industry. Many of these changes have been positive in relation to the evolution of who takes on gatekeeping functions for the wider industry. Information about new comedians has never been more accessible and platforms such as Twitter provide an unprecedented opportunity for self-presentation as well as interaction with audiences outside of the space of performance. This has a direct impact on the live comedy industry. This research contributes to the existing literature in the field by developing arguments made by Sam Friedman (2014) about the role of gatekeepers, considering how this may be altered by the online environment and what this means for women.

Whilst the online environment, specifically the Twitter platform, undoubtedly has benefits for women comics seeking to enter the industry (such as building a following, testing material and gaining confidence), the digital environment in many ways replicates the gendered policing of space and public speech found in existing physical spaces. The barriers women face to speaking up, having an opinion or engaging in public discourse, are replicated online through aggressive behaviours such as trolling. The resistance and aggression that women (especially Black women, women of colour and trans women) face online should not be overlooked in future discussion of online comedy.

Despite a rise, over the period of this research, in the number of women featured in television comedy, it remains a male-dominated space and one that is not accessed as easily by female comics with the same degree of experience as their male contemporaries. Women are therefore often developing their own paths to enter the industry, and many of these paths are directly facilitated by new technology. There are three indicative examples of this. First, there has been a rise in the crowdfunding of projects using online donation sites such as Kickstarter or Go Fund Me – promoting the initiative through Facebook, Instagram and Twitter. Luisa Omielan undertook this process, to record and release a DVD of *Am I Right Ladies?*. Second, there has been increased engagement by women comedians with the new opportunities presented by streaming services such as Netflix or Amazon, who record live shows as 'specials' to be featured on their sites. And, last, there has been an increase in women comics developing self-produced work that embraces the possibilities and freedoms of audio production. This is achieved through podcasting and developing an audience for future live and broadcast work. Both the work of Sofie Hagen and that of Kiri Pritchard-McLean exemplify this practice.

When women do make it into the long-running spaces of broadcast comedy, such as high-profile panel shows, *it is possible* for hegemonic norms around gender roles to be challenged. However, as resistance or refusal to engage with the patriarchal nature of these spaces, as discussed in relation to Bridget Christie, can prevent further employment in these arenas, very few women are currently in a position in their careers to provoke this change.

When considering the success of women comedians within the current comedy industry, it is clear, through extensive observation of live, online and television comedy, that some women are breaking through to play a more active role at the top of the industry.

However, it is also clear that the majority of these women are white, cisgendered, able-bodied and middle-class, thus replicating for producers the 'T-Shirt comic' ingredients that, as Friedman (2014) identifies, have been so successful for their male contemporaries. In addition to the kinds of women who manage to make this final leap into inclusion on TV (so accessing a wider audience), the dominant material found within these televised spaces tends to be aligned with postfeminist comedy (as discussed in Chapters 5 and 6). In the current context, we therefore see frequent appearances from specific women (e.g. Sara Pascoe, Katherine Ryan, Holly Walsh, Kerry Godliman and Cariad Lloyd), and more needs to be done to ensure the field is widened to be more inclusive in general, but also specifically for women of colour and women with disabilities. Steps are being made towards this inclusion, and we can point to the recent rise of Rosie Jones, Sophie Duker, Kemah Bob and Desiree Burch as examples – but the fact we can point to only a handful of women evidences that there is still a significant way to go to achieve parity. It would not be possible, or perhaps take much longer, to name all the cisgender white male comedians booked for television appearances. Postfeminist comedy is easier to include within existing mediated formats, as it does not challenge the patriarchal assumptions that underpin much of the comedy already found in these spaces.

Comedy content

This research concludes that self-deprecatory comedy has changed over the last decade due to the dominance of 'empowerment' narratives to which Western societies now overwhelmingly subscribe, as evidenced through celebrity feminisms. Even when some women performers (specifically those who self-identify as feminist in their work) do not want to make self-deprecatory jokes, they still seem to do so.

This is because of the placatory function self-deprecation can serve in addressing gendered power imbalances in performance situations (as I have argued previously, Tomsett 2018).

Contemporaneous to the use of self-deprecation and in line with current feminisms, several comics, including those explicitly discussed in this book, adopt an approach that focuses on body positivity, rejecting humour that makes their bodies, and by extension the similar bodies of those in the audience, the butt of the jokes. Comedy that takes a more body-positive approach has the potential to be feminist or postfeminist in line with the definitions provided by Shifman and Lemish (2010) and my research evidences that both kinds of comedy are evident on the current UK circuit. The hallmarks of feminism or postfeminism can be apparent in many ways within performances by women comics, such as the use of imagery to promote solo shows, the choice of costume, use of the performers body and the content of the jokes contained within the acts.

There is a huge range of comedy approaches and styles performed by women evident on the current UK live comedy circuit. This conclusion was arrived at as a result of extensive observation of women comics over the period of this research, observations which emphatically evidenced a diversity of talent. However, the diversity of this talent, in terms of both the diversity of the performers themselves and the content of the material, is not currently reflected within broadcast comedy, especially on television. Postfeminist comedy that continues to uphold a binary between men and women, where the focus is on non-political topics and themes, is much easier to incorporate into existing comedy formats. This kind of comedy is reflective of a process which Angela McRobbie (2009) refers to as double entanglement and includes humour which invokes a kind of feminist collective action (an updated 'Girl Power'), whilst simultaneously implying an irrelevance of (or a lack of need for) the action, as an approximation of equality has now been reached. As a result, often when women are included in the spaces of broadcast comedy, they perform material that does not challenge gender norms or make gender political points to ensure a seamless fit with the material provided by the cisgender men who occupy these spaces regularly (e.g. hosts and team captains).

In addition to the presence of feminist and postfeminist comedy on the UK circuit performed by women comedians, there is also evidence of direct resistance to increased inclusion of women and minority groups in the comedy industry found *within* the content of comedy by male performers (as discussed in Chapter 6). This can be seen as evidence of what Angela McRobbie (2009) refers to as the complexification of a backlash to feminism. Comedy as a form is very open to content that takes an ironic, or 'political-correctness-gone-mad', approach to gender inclusion and some comedians are utilizing the freedom of comic licence to reassert a male dominance through gender stereotypes. It is well documented that all industries that include labour performed outside the home, especially labour that does not conform or connect to traditional feminized gender roles (such as caring, cleaning and teaching), have been initially resistant to including women. It is therefore worth restating, irrespective of the creativity of the artform, that comedy is an industry. Thus it is not surprising that a rise in the number of women attempting to 'infiltrate' the industry has met with resistance.

Attempts to diversify

Whilst I conducted this research, the comedy industry slowly started to talk openly about diversity across all aspects of identity. However, much of this diversity work continues to be tokenistic or (even worse) reliant upon stereotypes. To provide a tangible example, I will briefly outline a representative instance of the BBC's attitude towards diversity by relating an exchange I personally had with the corporation's representatives in 2017.

The launch of the Caroline Aherne Bursary for Funny Northern Women took place at MediaCity, Salford, in July 2017. I attended, with a colleague, in the hope that this was the first step in the BBC's acknowledgement that their gender representation in comic output is insufficient. The following recollection may seem judgemental in tone. This is a risk I am willing to take, however, as I am in a unique position to provide a critique of this event, as one of only a handful of people present not looking to apply for the scheme, seeking employment with the BBC, or indeed working for the corporation already.

This event took place a full three years after the 'no all-male' panel show announcement by Danny Cohen and the bursary was for one lucky woman to receive a radio commission with the BBC. What struck me immediately was the lack of diversity on the panel. The panel was made up of five cisgender white women: director of BBC Children's and BBC North Alice Webb (who performed the role of host), BBC Comedy commissioning editor Alex Moody, comedy producer Rebecca Papworth and comedy writer-performers Gemma Arrowsmith and Frog Stone. Of the two performers on this panel, one had attended drama school (despite being from a working-class background) and the other had been a member of the Cambridge Footlights. Although there is nothing inherently 'wrong' about these routes into the industry, it is far from the majority experience of comedians on the current circuit. During the launch, video clips of the panel's comedy heroes were played and these, again, were entirely white women.

The event started with Webb welcoming the audience, commenting, 'It's nice to see a few brave men in the audience'. This comment could be dismissed as minor. However, as this book has evidenced, there is a continued positioning of comedy by women as *for* women, and comments like this play into the assumption that men should take no interest in diversifying the industry. This was compounded by one of the panelists repeatedly using the term 'comedienne' throughout the event, differentiating women comics from their male contemporaries.

The event launching the bursary was conducted without any seeming awareness of *why* it might be necessary to diversify comic output or include more women in comedy, specifically northern women at that. As such the bursary was very much positioned like a 'one in one out' scenario – in that UK comedy has sadly lost Aherne, and she must be replaced. This event took place just two weeks after the high-profile discussions of the BBC's racial and gender pay gap, with various BBC presenters banding together to protest against this inequality (McIntyre et al. 2017). To not acknowledge or even mention this political context may be understandable – from observing the number of staff passes on those in attendance, many of those few 'brave men' in the audience undoubtedly worked at the BBC. To field an all-white panel, however, was shocking and indicative of complacency.

Therefore, having sat through the launch politely, hoping that someone might bring up the obvious lack of consideration for people of colour and incredibly retro-sexist binary discussion, in the spirit of constructive criticism I wrote to the BBC's diversity department after the event. In the email I outlined both my thoughts on the make-up of the panel and extremely reductive content of the discussion. Whereas my email was acknowledged after three weeks, it took the organization, which is publicly funded and has a *diversity department*, a full eleven weeks to respond fully.[1]

The response, when it did arrive, chose not to tackle my comments on the content of the panel but simply corrected my reading of the panel as all-white and privileged. The response contained the line that whilst 'ostensibly the panel may have appeared quite uniform it did include women from different backgrounds, (two women from the North) and a panel member who is a lesbian'.[2] It concluded that although diversity was a priority for the BBC when assembling the panel, the final line-up was down to a need to have a variety of expertise and their availability on the date.

As Sara Ahmed writes in *Living a Feminist Life* (2017) in relation to academic institutions, often: 'Diversity becomes about changing perceptions of whiteness rather than changing the whiteness of organizations' (2017: 105). This panel was about changing perceptions of maleness in comedy, without recourse to other aspects of intersectional identity. Here we can see that *the perception* of the BBC being more diverse in their decision-making is clearly more important than making structural or significant change. The BBC decided to launch a bursary to add more women into a system that has proven to be discriminatory against them based on gender and race. Ahmed continues:

> [W]e can see a key difficulty here: even if diversity is an attempt to transform the institution, it too can become a technique for keeping things in place. The very appearance of a transformation (a new more colourful face for the organisation) is what stops something from happening. (2017:105)

If we were to consider the inclusion of Bridget Christie and Luisa Omielan in television comedy output, we can see that, in terms of ticking a box on a spreadsheet, their inclusion on TV shows will (on paper) make these shows more diverse, as will the inclusion of a select few women comedians on panel shows. However, it is the way these women comedians are treated by those who already occupy this space, and the structures at play within them, that often reassert notions of difference. This maintains the norm of women as 'other'. These industry decisions, in terms of both launching a bursary and including specific women on panel shows, undermine the BBC's commitment to diversifying voices. We have to ask ourselves; if the BBC cares so much about diversifying voices, why do we keep hearing so much from the same people? This failure is relevant because the BBC remains the biggest commissioner of comedy content across television, online and radio, in the UK.

In addition to large media corporations considering diversity in a structural and significant way, a key conclusion of my work is that Arts Council England (ACE) has to readjust its attitude to comedy in order to ensure diversity is possible in comedy. There is a direct link between the live comedy sector and mediated forms, and yet (at the time of writing) no funding goes into the live sector for individual comics. Some positive steps towards this have commenced in relation to the Culture Recovery Fund, which, for the first time, enabled comedy festivals and venues to apply for funding. But this recent change of position does not go far enough or indeed undo the longer-term harm ACE has enacted by ignoring comedy in the past. Prior to the pandemic, ACE had recently placed diversity at the heart of its objectives, by reiterating its commitment to what it terms the 'Creative Case for Diversity'.[3] The Creative Case sets out an argument for arts organizations to embrace diversity to benefit their creative work. The crux of this argument is that without embracing diversity, society is missing out on the creative voices of many with something to say, or a talent to share. However, at the time ACE released this document, there was still a narrow, biased and discriminatory approach that prevented them from considering comedy as an art form. In order to diversify comedy, investment into organizations and events that seek to challenge the white male norms of the form is crucial, as is the funding of individuals to a comparable level to other live performance forms.

Diversity across the arts cannot merely be about broadening participation in existing, high-culture forms such as dance and opera. It is necessary for ACE to consider *how* the conclusion that comedy is a self-funding industry has been reached, as this has repeatedly been their justification for not funding comedy prior to the decimation of the cultural sector during the pandemic, rather than any wording that would make the organization seem biased against such a 'low' cultural form. As it stands, the argument that comedy can self-sustain (or could, pre-Covid) is only applicable to a narrow strata of comedy (the top level of mainstream comedy – that exists above the glass ceiling). Numerous gendered barriers exist below this preventing women from participating at this top level of the mainstream industry.

If ACE are serious about inclusion and access to the arts for all, as both audiences and artists, this has to include funding comedy going forward. And this funding should not just include the festivals and organizations ACE engaged with as part of the Culture Recovery Fund, since this excludes a huge number of freelancers working, or trying to work, in the sector. If ACE do not fully reconsider their attitude to comedy at all levels they remain effectively complicit in the silencing of women (as well as working-class people and people of colour) in this art form, and this entirely undermines their hubristic claims related to diversity in the arts.

It is complicated

This book does not provide a universal statement about the status of 'women in comedy' at this current time, as a key finding of my research is that it is not possible to do so (for the comedy industry or indeed any industry). To make such wide-ranging statements would also go against the fundamental intersectional methodological underpinning of this research, which sought to highlight the pitfalls of simply unifying individuals based on gender alone. The research has revealed that there are many differing and conflicting aspects of the industry, and every woman's experience of this industry is different based on a variety of factors (such as age, ethnicity, sexuality, ability, genre of comedy performance, geography and so on). Whilst themes were identified from my research which impact on all women, these have varying positive and negative outcomes for individuals. Therefore, any singular statement that fails to acknowledge the extreme complexity of the UK comedy industry, its many levels, the impact of technology and the differences between performance contexts will do the women I have engaged with as part of this research a disservice. A key finding of the research is that to present women's experiences of the industry as uncomplicated and unified in the current context is actively unhelpful, distorts understanding of the way the industry operates and helps perpetuate gendered barriers.

What can be said in order to conclude, however, is that my work is a step in moving beyond sweeping uncomplicated statements (originating from the industry) about women in contemporary UK comedy that are reductive and problematic. Listening further to those who work within the comedy industry is central in order to unite theoretical writing on comedy and practice, as well as to hopefully make tangible changes to the industry for minority groups.

Notes

Introduction

1 More information on these projects can be found using the following links. See http://everydaysexism.com, http://nomorepage3.org and http://vagendamagazine.com (accessed 15 May 2022).
2 The research of Baron-Cohen, who is the cousin of comedian Sacha Baron-Cohen, is mainly in relation to autism and whether testosterone in-utero impacts on this.
3 It is important to note that Hitchens never moved his position in the light of the responses of others, including the work of Alessandra Stanley. He wrote a follow-up article the snappily entitled (in both senses of the word 'entitled'), 'Why women still don't get it' (Hitchens, 2008).
4 I am grateful to all who participated in contributing to this project and hope that the forthcoming analysis reflects a more comprehensive and nuanced analysis of their experiences than can be found in the superficial journalism on the topic.
5 Many of these meetings took place in the back room of The King's Arms in Salford and Gulliver's Bar in Manchester's Northern Quarter.

Chapter 1

1 It is worth noting that in recent years there has been an unearthing of historical records, highlighting the role of women in theatrical performance much earlier than the general public have been led to believe. Pamela Allen-Brown and Peter Parolin's edited collection, *Women Players in England 1500–1660: Beyond the All-Male Stage* (2005), is an example of a text engaging with the overlooked contribution of women to theatrical performance more broadly during this period.
2 Double (2017) has also found use of the term 'stand up' (without hyphenation) in a 1911 edition of *The Stage*. However, in this instance, it was unclear whether the term was used to denote the literal 'standing up'

of a performer singing comic songs. Either way it certainly indicates an earlier usage of the term than originally believed.

3   In the 1960s Britain still only had three television channels. ITV only started broadcasting in 1955 and BBC2 was launched in 1964, which meant that viewing figures were significantly higher for these programmes than comparable shows in today's context.

4   During much of the 1960s, homosexuality was still illegal in the UK, so the inclusion of openly LGBT+ performers at this time would have been totally impossible. The Sexual Offenses Act came into force in England and Wales in 1967 partially decriminalizing homosexual activity, specifically, activity between men over the age of twenty-one in private settings. The LGBT+ community still faced overwhelming vilification and prejudice during this era and thus sexuality would not have been openly discussed in public, let alone on stage in front of a working men's club crowd. Public expression of sexuality during this time was often obscured behind coded language such as Polari as explored by Baker (2002).

5   See http://funnywomen.com and http://www.dulcetsounds.co.uk/live/laughingcowscomedy (both accessed 15 May 2022).

Chapter 2

1   See https://www.comedy.co.uk and http://www.chortle.co.uk (accessed 15 May 2022).

2   Whilst I know the name of the male comedian Willan is referring to (as I was at the event in question), it was her decision during the interview not to name him directly. I will therefore respect her wishes and remain consistent with her use of the term 'male comedian'.

Chapter 3

1   A previous analysis of some aspects of this audience data, and what this might mean for the concept of gendered comedy 'safe spaces' is included my book chapter '"Less dick jokes": Women-only comedy line-ups, audience expectations and negotiating stereotypes' in Double and Lockyer (2022) *Alternative Comedy Now and Then: Critical Perspectives*.

2. The comedians named in the report are Michael McIntyre, Peter Kay, Lee Evans, Miranda Hart, Sarah Millican, John Bishop, Jimmy Carr, Billy Connolly, Russell Howard, Kevin Bridges, Jack Dee, Frankie Boyle, Ken Dodd, Alan Carr and Harry Hill.

Chapter 4

1. All quotations from David Schneider originate from Tomsett, E. (2019) *Reflections on UK Comedy's Glass Ceiling: Stand-Up Comedy and Contemporary Feminisms*. Available online. http://shura.shu.ac.uk/26442/ (accessed 20 September 2022).
2. To view Jenny Bede's YouTube videos, see https://www.youtube.com/user/bedey100/videos.

Chapter 5

1. This chapter includes some aspects of material published in my 2017 and 2018 articles for *Comedy Studies*.
2. http://www.adriennetruscott.com/asking-for-it/ (accessed 15 May 2022).
3. A previous version of this analysis of Christie is the focus of my published article. See Tomsett, 2017.
4. See http://www.bbc.co.uk/mediacentre/latestnews/2017/what-would-beyonce-do (accessed 15 May 2022).

Chapter 6

1. At the time of writing there is also widespread campaigning to highlight the issues of sexual harassment within UK academia (see #TimesUpAcademia). So, whilst Superson and Cudd, writing in 2002, comment that violence is 'not unheard of' within academia, the physical policing of women within this male-dominated space is becoming increasingly visible. Sara Ahmed who publicly quit her institution in May

2016 due to its poor handling of sexual harassment continues to raise awareness of this issue (Ahmed 2016).
2. Lawrence's full post and the responses to it can be found on his public Facebook page. Posted 1 November 2017. See https://www.facebook.com/andrewlawrencecomedy (accessed 6 January 2018).
3. See http://www.itv.com/presscentre/press-releases/dapper-laughs-pull (accessed 2 January 2018).
4. In November 2014, O'Reilly appeared on BBC *Newsnight* to address the controversy of his ITV2 show cancellation. A contrite O'Reilly can be seen in action attempting to defend his work in the following clip from the BBC *Newsnight* YouTube channel. https://www.youtube.com/watch?v=lBt3fr5viAE (accessed 6 January 2018).
5. For more information on how the British entertainment industry has historically failed to protect the vulnerable or take allegations of sexual harassment and abuses of power seriously, the BBC's internal investigation, overseen by Dame Janet Smith, into the Jimmy Savile and Stewart Hall years, thoroughly examines the failings of the institution to keep people safe (BBC Trust 2016). See: https://www.bbc.co.uk/bbctrust/dame_janet_smith.html (accessed 1 September 2022).
6. To access Lowe's panel show data, which was last updated December 2017, see http://strudel.org.uk/panelshows/index.html (accessed 13 April 2018).

Chapter 7

1. https://livecomedyassociation.co.uk (accessed 10 May 2022).
2. https://getofflivecomedy.co.uk (accessed 10 May 2022).
3. https://comedysafetystandards.com (accessed 10 May 2022).

Chapter 8

1. Positioning is, of course, an issue here. Many of those asked to speak about the topic of women and comedy publicly have done very well out of the existing system, or rely upon it for their livelihood. I'm not a performer

and I don't rely on many of the institutions I am critiquing within this book for work. Therefore, I am relatively free to be critical and that is a position of privilege. However, the current situation, evidenced by this panel, results in those who have been successful, within a highly faulty system, not being able to articulate criticisms about that faulty system in order to improve it.
2 Nicola Crowther, 2017, 'BBC Writersroom Women in Comedy Panel – Feedback' (private email correspondence), 11 October.
3 See https://www.artscouncil.org.uk/diversity/creative-case-diversity (accessed 25 May 2022).

References

Abramson, Kate. (2014), 'Turning Up the Lights on Gaslighting', *Philosophical Perspectives*, 28 (1): 1–30.

Ackerly, Brooke and Jacqui True. (2010), *Doing Feminist Research in Political and Social Science*, Basingstoke: Palgrave Macmillan.

Agerholm, Harriet. (2017), 'Jo Brand Silences All-Male Panel on Have I Got News For You with Perfect Explanation of Why Sexual Harassment Isn't Funny', *The Independent*, 4 November. Available online: https://www.independent.co.uk/arts-entertainment/tv/news/jo-brand-have-i-got-news-for-you-hignify-video-sexual-harassment-ian-hislop-quentin-letts-a8037276.html (accessed 9 May 2022).

Ahmed, Sara. (2010), *The Promise of Happiness*, London: Duke University Press.

Ahmed, Sara. (2012), *On Being Included: Racism and Diversity in Institutional Life*, London: Duke University Press.

Ahmed, Sara. (2013), 'Making Feminist Points', *Feminist Killjoys*, 11 September. Available online: https://feministkilljoys.com/2013/09/11/making-feminist-points/ (accessed 9 May 2022).

Ahmed, Sara. (2016), 'Resignation', *Feminist Killjoys*, 30 May. Available online: https://feministkilljoys.com/2016/05/30/resignation/ (accessed 9 May 2022).

Ahmed, Sara. (2017), *Living A Feminist Life*, London: Duke University Press.

Ahmed, Wasim, Peter Bath, and Gianluca Demartin. (2017), 'Using Twitter as a Data Source: An Overview of Ethical, Legal, and Methodological Challenges', in Kandy Woodfield (ed), *The Ethics of Online Research. Advances in Research Ethics and Integrity*, 79–107, Bingley: Emerald.

Alcorn, Gay. (2018), 'Eurydice Dixon: How One Woman's Death Put Focus on 'Male Rage' in Australia', *The Guardian*, 19 June. Available online: https://www.theguardian.com/australia-news/2018/jun/19/eurydice-dixon-death-male-rage-australia-women-men-attitudes (accessed 9 May 2022).

Allen-Brown, Pamela and Peter Parolin, eds (2005), *Women Players in England 1500–1660: Beyond An All-Male Stage*, Aldershot: Ashgate.

Am I Right Ladies? (2015) [video] Luisa Omielan.

Aston, Elaine and Geraldine Harris. (2015), *A Good Night Out for the Girls: Popular Feminisms in Contemporary Theatre and Performance*, London: Palgrave Macmillan.

Bailey, Moya and Trudy. (2018), 'On Misogynoir: Citation, Erasure and PLAGIARISM', *Feminist Media Studies*, 18 (4): 762–8.

Baker, Paul. (2002), *Polari: The Lost Language of Gay Men*, London: Routledge.
Bakhtin, Mikhail. (1984), *Rabelais and His World*, Bloomington: Indiana University Press.
Banet-Weiser, Sarah. (2018), *Empowered: Popular Feminism and Popular Misogyny*, London: Duke University Press.
Baron-Cohen, Simon. (2003), *The Essential Difference: Men, Women and the Extreme Male Brain*, London: Allen Lane.
Barreca, Regina. (2013), *The Used To Call Me Snow White . . . but I Drifted: Women's Strategic Use of Humor*, 2nd edn, Lebanon New Hampshire: University Press of New England.
Barry, Andrea. (2021), 'We Cannot Allow the Pandemic to Set Gender Parity Back Decades.' Joseph Rowntree Foundation. Available online: https://www.jrf.org.uk/blog/we-cannot-allow-pandemic-set-gender-parity-back-decades (accessed 31 March 2021).
BBC Trust. (2016), 'The Dame Janet Smith Review – Investigation Report'. 25 February. Available online: https://www.bbc.co.uk/bbctrust/dame_janet_smith.html (accessed 9 May 2022).
Beale, Sam. (2020), *The Comedy and Legacy of Music Hall Women 1880–1920*, Cham: Palgrave Macmillan.
Beard, Mary. (2017), *Women and Power: A Manifesto*, London: Profile Books.
Belanger, Jillian, M. (2015), 'Comedy Meets Media: How Three New Media Features Have Influenced Changes in the Production of Stand-up Comedy', *Comedy Studies*, 6 (2): 141–7.
Bennett, Steve. (2013), 'Canadians of Comedy: A Review', *Chortle*, 2 August. Available online: https://www.chortle.co.uk/review/2013/08/02/29247/canadians_of_comedy (accessed 9 May).
Betancourt, Sarah. (2021), 'Bill Cosby's Sexual Assault Conviction Overturned by Pennsylvania Court', *The Guardian*, 30 June. Available online: https://www.theguardian.com/world/2021/jun/30/bill-cosby-sexual-assault-conviction-overturned-by-pennsylvania-court (accessed 11 May 2022).
Bing, Janet. (2007), 'Liberated Jokes: Sexual Humor in All-Female Groups', *Humor – International Journal of Humor Research*, 20 (4) 337–66.
Blackwell, Lindsay, Nicole Ellison, Natasha Elliott-Deflo and Raz Schwartz (2019), 'Harassment in Social Virtual Reality: Challenges for Platform Governance', *Proceedings of the ACM on Human-Computer Interaction*, 3:CSCW: 1–25.
Bland, Archie. (2022), 'Supreme Court Abortion Law Leak: What Happened and Why Does It Matter?', *The Guardian*, 3 May. Available online: https://

www.theguardian.com/world/2022/may/03/supreme-court-abortion-law-leak-roe-v-wade (accessed 24 May 2022).

Bourdieu, Pierre. (1993), *The Field of Cultural Production: Essays on Art and Literature*, New York: Columbia University Press.

Boyle, Karen. (2019), *#MeToo, Weinstein and Feminism*, Cham, Switzerland: Palgrave Macmillan.

Brinkmann, Svend, and Kvale, Steinar. (2015), *Interviews: Learning the Craft of Qualitative Research Interviewing*, 3rd edn, Los Angeles: Sage.

Brizendine, Louann. (2007), *The Female Brain*, London: Bantham Press.

Brizendine, Louann. (2010), *The Male Brain*, London: Bantham Press.

Brook, Orian, David O'Brien and Mark Taylor. (2018), 'Panic! Social Class, Taste and Inequalities in the Creative Industries'. *AHRC*. Available online: https://createlondon.org/wp-content/uploads/2018/04/Panic-Social-Class-Taste-and-Inequalities-in-the-Creative-Industries1.pdf (accessed 9 May 2022).

Brook, Orian, David O'Brien and Mark Taylor. (2020), *Culture Is Bad for You: Inequality in the Cultural and Creative Industries*, Manchester: Manchester University Press.

Brooks, Libby. (2022), 'UK Falls Down Europe's LGBTQ+ Rights Ranking for Third Year Running', *The Guardian*, 12 May. Available online: https://www.theguardian.com/world/2022/may/12/uk-falls-down-europes-lgbtq-rights-ranking-for-third-year-running (accessed 24 May 2022).

Brown, Stephanie. (2020), 'Open Mic? The Gendered Gatekeeping of Authenticity in Spaces of Live Stand-Up Comedy', *Feminist Media Histories*, 6 (4): 42–67.

Bulman, May. (2016), 'Nicky Morgan Replaced by Handbag on Have I Got News for You After Late Cancellation', *The Independent*, 17 December. Available online: https://www.independent.co.uk/news/uk/politics/nicky-morgan-have-i-got-news-for-you-handbag-cancellation-education-theresa-may-a7481601.html (accessed 9 May 2022).

Burrell, Ian. (2014), 'Dapper Laughs ITV Show Cancelled Over Vlogger's "Rape Comedy Routine"'. *The Independent*, 10 November. Available online: https://www.independent.co.uk/arts-entertainment/tv/news/dapper-laughs-itv-under-fire-over-dating-show-vlogger-s-rape-comedy-routine-9852224.html (accessed 9 May 2022).

Butler, Nick and Dimirinka Stoyanova Russell. (2018), 'No Business: Precarious Work and Emotional Labour in Stand-up Comedy', *Human Relations*, 71 (12): 1666–86.

Chatman, Dayna. (2015), 'Pregnancy, Then It's 'Back to Business'': Beyoncé, Black Femininity, and the Politics of a Post-feminist Gender Regime', *Feminist Media Studies*, 15 (6): 926–41.

Chitnis, Ketan S., Avinash Thombre, Everett M. Rogers, Arvind Singhal, and Ami Sengupta. (2006), '(Dis)similar Readings: Indian and American Audiences' Interpretation of *Friends*', *The International Communication Gazette*, 68 (2): 131–45.

Chortle (2014), 'What a Rant!', 26 October. Available online: http://www.chortle.co.uk/news/2014/10/26/21186/what_a_rant (accessed 9 May 2022).

Christie, Bridget. (2013), 'The "Are Women Funny?" Debate Is as Dead as Christopher Hitchens'. *The Guardian*, 1 October. Available online: https://www.theguardian.com/commentisfree/2013/oct/01/are-women-funny-lee-mack (accessed 9 May 2022).

Christie, Bridget. (2015), *A Book For Her*, London: Century.

C.K., Louis. (2017), 'These Stories Are True', *New York Times*, 10 November. Available online: https://www.nytimes.com/2017/11/10/arts/television/louis-ck-statement.html (accessed 9 May 2022).

Cohen, Dave. (2013), *How to be Averagely Successful at Comedy*, London: Acorn Independent Press.

Cole, Brian P., Margaret Brennan, Emily Tyler and Ryan Willard (2020), 'Predicting Men's Acceptance of Sexual Violence Myths Through Conformity to Masculine Norms, Sexism, and "Locker Room Talk"', *Psychology of Men and Masculinities*, 21 (4): 508–17.

Condron, Stephanie. (2007), 'Women Win Equality at Working Men's Clubs', *The Telegraph*, 2 April. Available online: https://www.telegraph.co.uk/news/uknews/1547345/Women-win-equality-at-working-mens-clubs.html (accessed 9 May 2022).

Cooke, Rachel. (2014a), Danny Cohen: 'TV Panel Shows Without Women Are Unacceptable'. *The Observer*, 8 February. Available online: https://www.theguardian.com/media/2014/feb/08/danny-cohen-bbc-director-television-tv-panel-shows (accessed 9 May 2022).

Cooke, Rachel. (2014b), 'Where Is Britain's Lena Dunham? Who Cares? We should Celebrate British TV Talent', *The Guardian*, 30 May. Available online: https://www.theguardian.com/tv-and-radio/2014/may/30/where-is-britains-lena-dunham (accessed 9 May 2022).

Cox, David. (2016), '#OscarsSoWhite: Who Is Really to Blame for the Oscars' Lack of Diversity?'. *The Guardian*, 26 February. Available online: https://

www.theguardian.com/film/2016/feb/25/oscarssowhite-right-and-wrong-academy-awards-audience (accessed 9 May 2022).

Crenshaw, Kimberlé (1991), 'Mapping the Margins: Intersectionality, Identity Politics, and Violence against Women of Color', *Stanford Law Review*, 43 (6): 1241–99.

Croziet, Jean-Claude and Theresa Claire. (1998), 'Extending the Concept of Stereotype Threat to Social Class: The Intellectual Underperformance of Students from low Socioeconomic Backgrounds', *Personality and Social Psychology*, 24 (6): 588–94.

Cuboniks, Laboria. (2018), *The Xenofeminist Manifesto: A Politics for Alienation*, London: Verso.

Daly, Emma. (2014), 'Sarah Millican Tops List of Best-Selling Female Stand-up Comedians as Ticket Sales Boom', *Radio Times*, 1 October. Available online: https://www.radiotimes.com/tv/comedy/sarah-millican-tops-list-of-best-selling-female-stand-up-comedians-as-ticket-sales-boom/ (accessed 9 May 2022).

Davies, Helen and Sarah Ilott, eds. (2018), *Comedy and the Politics of Representation: Mocking the Weak*, Cham: Palgrave Macmillan.

Davies, Caroline. (2018), 'Women Too Modest to Host Have I Got News for You, Hislop Claims', *The Guardian*, 3 April. Available Online: https://www.theguardian.com/tv-and-radio/2018/apr/03/host-have-i-got-news-for-you-hislop-merton-women-presenters (accessed 9 May 2022).

Department for Digital, Culture, Media and Sport. (2001), *Creative Industries Mapping Documents*, 9 May. Available online: https://www.gov.uk/government/publications/creative-industries-mapping-documents-2001 (accessed 9 May 2022).

Department for Digital, Culture, Media and Sport. (2020), 'UK's Creative Industries Contributes Almost £13 Million to the UK Economy Every Hour', 6 February. Available online: https://www.gov.uk/government/news/uks-creative-industries-contributes-almost-13-million-to-the-uk-economy-every-hour (accessed 9 May 2022).

Doan, Petra L. (2010), 'The Tyranny of Gendered Spaces – Reflections from Beyond the Gender Dichotomy', *Gender, Place and Culture*, 17 (5): 635–54.

Dosani, Rishma. (2020), 'Comedian Sophie Duker Sparks Ofcom Complaints with "Kill Whitey" Joke on Frankie Boyle's New World Order', *Metro*, 17 September. Available online: https://metro.co.uk/2020/09/17/comedian-sophie-duker-sparks-ofcom-complaints-with-kill-whitey-joke-on-frankie-boyles-new-world-order-13288089/ (accessed 17 May 2022).

Double, Oliver. (2014), *Getting the Joke: The Inner Workings of Stand-up Comedy*, 2nd edn, London: Bloomsbury.

Double, Oliver. (2017), 'The Origin of the Term "Stand-up Comedy"', *Comedy Studies*, 8 (1): 106–9.

Double, Oliver and Sharon Lockyer, eds (2022) *Alternative Comedy Now and Then: Critical Perspectives*, Cham: Palgrave Macmillan.

Dowell, Ben. (2013), 'Mary Beard Suffers "Truly Vile" Online Abuse After Question Time', *The Guardian*, 21 January. Available online: https://www.theguardian.com/media/2013/jan/21/mary-beard-suffers-twitter-abuse (accessed 9 May 2022).

Eddo-Lodge, Reni. (2017), *Why I'm No Longer Talking to White People About Race*, London: Bloomsbury Circus.

Ellison, Nicole, Rebecca Heino and Jennifer Gibbs. (2006), 'Managing Impressions Online: Self-Presentation Processes in the Online Dating Environment', *Journal of Computer Mediated Communication*, 11 (2): 415–41.

Evans, Dayna. (2015), 'Kristen Wiig Is Tired of the "Women in Comedy" Question', *The Cut*, 26 October. Available online: https://www.thecut.com/2015/10/kristen-wiig-no-more-women-in-comedy-questions.html (accessed 9 May 2022).

Fine, Cordelia. (2010), *Delusions of Gender: The Real Science Between Sex Differences*, London: Icon Books.

Fox, Kate. (2017), 'Humitas: A New Word for when Humour and Seriousness Combine'. *The Conversation*, 24 August. Available online: https://theconversation.com/humitas-a-new-word-for-when-humour-and-seriousness-combine-82556 (accessed 9 May 2022).

Franzini, L. R. (1996), 'Feminism and Women's Sense of Humour', *Sex Roles*, 35: 811–19.

French, Dawn. (2008), *Dear Fatty*, London: Century.

Freud, Sigmund. ([1905] 1976), *Jokes and Their Relation to the Unconscious*, London: Penguin.

Friedman, Sam. (2014), *Comedy and Distinction: The Cultural Currency of a 'Good' Sense of Humour*, London: Routledge.

Gander, Kashmira and Oliver Wright. (2014), 'UKIP Election Posters: Nigel Farage Defends "Racist" Campaign Anti-immigration Campaign Ahead of Europe Elections', *The Independent*, 22 April. Available online: https://www.independent.co.uk/news/uk/home-news/ukip-accused-of-scaremongering-in-antiimmigration-poster-campaign-ahead-of-european-elections-9273100.html (accessed 1 October 2022).

German, Lindsey. (2007), *Material Girls: Women, Men and Work*, London: Bookmarks.

Gilbert, Joanne R. (2004), *Performing Marginality: Humor, Gender and Cultural Critique*, Detroit: Wayne State University Press.

Gilbert, Joanne. (2017), 'Laughing at Others: The Rhetoric of Marginalized Comic Identity', in Matthew Meier and Casey Schmitt, eds, *Standing Up, Speaking Out: Stand-up Comedy and the Rhetoric of Social Change*, 57–69, New York: Routledge.

Gill, Rosalind. (2007a), 'The Difficulties and Dilemmas of Agency and "Choice" for Feminism: A Reply to Duits and van Zoonen', *European Journal of Women's Studies*, 14: 69–79.

Gill, Rosalind. (2007b), *Gender and the Media*, Cambridge: Polity Press.

Gill, Rosalind. (2014), 'Unspeakable Inequalities: Post Feminism, Entrepreneurial Subjectivity, and the Repudiation of Sexism amongst Cultural Workers', *Social Politics*. 21 (4): 509–28.

Gold, Tanya. (2012), 'Have You Heard the One About Rape? It's Funny Now', *The Guardian*, 17 August. Available online: https://www.theguardian.com/commentisfree/2012/aug/17/heard-one-about-rape-funny-now (accessed 9 May 2022).

Graves, Lucia. (2018), 'Hannibal Buress: How a Comedian Reignited the Bill Cosby Allegations'. *The Guardian*, 26 April. Available online: https://www.theguardian.com/world/2018/apr/26/hannibal-buress-how-a-comedian-reignited-the-bill-cosby-allegations (accessed 9 May 2022).

Gray, Frances. (1994), *Women and Laughter*, Charlottesville: University of Virginia Press.

Gunaratnam, Yasmin, and Hamilton, Carrie. (2017), 'The Wherewithal of Feminist Methods', *Feminist Review*, 115: 1–12.

Harding, Sandra, ed. (1987), *Feminism and Methodology: Social Science Issues*, Milton Keynes: Open University Press.

Harman, Harriet. (2017), 'Labour's 1997 Victory was a Watershed for Women – But Our Gains Are at Risk', *The Guardian*, 10 April. Available online: https://www.theguardian.com/commentisfree/2017/apr/10/labour-1997-victory-women-101-female-mps (accessed 9 May 2022).

Healy, Rachael. (2020), "I've had Men Rub Their Genitals Against Me': Female Comedians on Extreme Sexism in Stand-up', *The Guardian*, 5 August. Available online: https://www.theguardian.com/stage/2020/aug/05/creepy-uncomfortable-sexism-harassment-assault-faced-by-female-standups (accessed 9 May 2022).

Healy, Rachael. (2021), 'New Organisation Launched to Tackle Sexual Harassment in Live Comedy', *The Guardian*, 19 November. Available online: https://www.theguardian.com/stage/2021/nov/19/new-organisation-launched-to-tackle-sexual-harassment-in-live-comedy-get-off (accessed 11 May 2022).

Henry, Lenny and Marcus Ryder. (2021a), *Access All Areas: The Diversity Manifesto for TV and Beyond*, London: Faber.

Henry, Lenny and Marcus Ryder. (2021b), *Black British Lives Matter: A Clarion Call for Equality*, London: Faber and Faber.

Hesmondhalgh, David and Sarah Baker. (2015), 'Sex, Gender and Work Segregation in the Cultural Industries', *The Sociological Review*, 63 (1): 23–36.

Hitchens, Christopher. (2007), 'Why Women Aren't Funny', *Vanity Fair*, 1 January. Available online: https://www.vanityfair.com/culture/2007/01/hitchens200701 (accessed 9 May 2022).

Hitchens, Christopher. (2008), 'Why Women Still Don't Get It', *Vanity Fair*, 3 March. Available online: https://www.vanityfair.com/culture/2008/04/hitchens200804 (accessed 9 May 2022).

Hole, Anne. (2003), 'Performing Identity: Dawn French and the Funny Fat Female Body', *Feminist Media Studies*, 3 (3): 315–28.

Holpuch, Amanda. (2012), 'Daniel Tosh Apologises for Rape Joke as Fellow Comedians Defend Topic', *The Guardian*, 11 July. Available online: https://www.theguardian.com/culture/us-news-blog/2012/jul/11/daniel-tosh-apologises-rape-joke (accessed 9 May 2022).

Horgan, Amelia. (2021), *Lost in Work: Escaping Capitalism*, London: Pluto Press.

Hughes, Christina. (2002), *Key Concepts in Feminist Theory and Research*, London: Sage.

Huxley, David. (1998), 'Viz: Gender, Class and Taboo', in Stephen Wagg, ed, *Because I Tell A Joke or Two: Comedy, Politics and Social Difference*, 273–90, London: Routledge.

Huxley, David and David James. (2012), 'No Other Excuse: Race, Class and Gender in British Music-Hall Comedic Performance 1914–1949', *Comedy Studies*, 3 (1): 17–28.

Izade, Elahe. (2016), 'Tina Fey, Kristen Wiig and Mindy Kaling Answer the Dumbest Questions About Female Comedians', *The Independent*, 9 February. Available online: https://www.independent.co.uk/news/people/tina-fey-kristen-wiig-and-mindy-kaling-answer-the-dumbest-questions-about-female-comedians-a6862481.html (accessed 9 May 2022).

Jones, Alice. (2019), 'London Hughes: 'If I Was a White Dude Would I Be at the Edinburgh Fringe or Would I Be Selling Out Arenas?", *inews*, 21 September. Available online: https://inews.co.uk/culture/london-hughes-edinburgh-2019-interview-podcast-328683 (accessed 9 May 2022).

Kalviknes-Bore, Inger-Lise. (2017), *Screen Comedy and Online Audiences*, New York: Routledge.

Kanter, Jake and Kasia Delgado. (2013), 'BBC: Comedy Panel Shows Should Include Women', *Broadcast Now*, 13 December. Available online: https://www.broadcastnow.co.uk/bbc-comedy-panel-shows-should-include-women/5064733.article (accessed 9 May 2022).

Khamis, Susie, Lawrence Ang and Raymond Welling (2017), 'Self-branding, "Micro Celebrity: and the Rise of Social Media Influencers', *Celebrity Studies*, 8 (2): 191–208.

Khan, Omar and Faiza Shaheen (2017), 'Minority Report: Race and Class in Post-Brexit Britain', *Runnymede Trust*. Available online: https://www.runnymedetrust.org/publications/minority-report-race-and-class-in-post-brexit-britain (accessed 9 May 2022).

Koepke, Sabrina, Friederike Eyssel and Gerd Bohner (2014), '"She Deserved It": Effects of Sexism Norms, Type of Violence, and Victim's Pre-Assault Behavior on Blame Attributions Toward Female Victims and Approval of the Aggressor's Behavior', *Violence Against Women*, 20 (4): 446–64.

Kotthoff, Helga. (2006), 'Gender and Humor: The State of the Art', *Journal of Pragmatics*, 38: 4–25.

Kozinets, Robert, V. (2015), *Netnography: Redefined*, 2nd edn, London: Sage.

Krefting, Rebecca. (2014), *All Joking Aside: American Humor and Its Discontents*, Baltimore: Johns Hopkins University Press.

Krefting, Rebecca and Rebecca Baruc (2015), 'A New Economy of Jokes?: #Socialmedia #Comedy', *Comedy Studies*, 6 (2): 129–40.

Kuipers, Giselinde. (2006), 'Television and Taste Hierarchy: The Case of Dutch Television Comedy', *Media, Culture and Society*, 28 (3): 359–78.

Kuipers, Giselinde (2012), 'The Cosmopolitan Tribe of Television Buyers: Professional Ethos, Personal Taste and Cosmopolitan Capital in Transnational Cultural Mediation', *European Journal of Cultural Studies*, 15: 581–603.

Lawson, Mark. (2014), 'Bridget Christie: "It's Trickery, Hiding Serious Bits within a Comic Framework"', *The Guardian*, 29 August. Available online: https://www.theguardian.com/culture/2014/aug/29/bridget-christie-trickery-hiding-serious-bits-comic-framework (accessed 9 May 2022).

Lee, Stewart. (2010), *How I Escaped My Certain Fate: The Life and Deaths of a Stand-up Comedian*, London: Faber and Faber.

Letherby, Gail. (2003), *Feminist Research in Theory and Practice*, Buckingham: Open University Press.

Li, Jenn. (2014), 'Julien Blanc Is a Racist Sexual Predator Teaching Men to Prey on Women Like Me – and He Must Be Stopped', *The Independent*, 6 November. Available online: https://www.independent.co.uk/voices/comment/julien-blanc-is-a-racist-sexual-predator-teaching-men-to-prey-on-women-like-me-he-must-be-stopped-9843939.html (accessed 9 May 2022).

Lockyer, Sharon. (2015), 'From Comedy Targets to Comedy Makers: Disability and Comedy in Live Performance', *Disability and Society*, 30 (9): 1397–1412.

Lockyer, Sharon and Lynn Myers (2011), 'It's About Expecting The Unexpected: Live Stand-Up Comedy from the Audiences' Perspective', *Participations: Journal of Audience and Reception Studies*, 8 (2): 165–88.

Logan, Brian. (2015), 'Should Dapper Laughs Be forgiven?', *The Guardian*, 23 November. Available online: https://www.theguardian.com/stage/2015/nov/23/dapper-laughs-daniel-o-reilly-lads-comic-dvd (accessed 9 May 2022).

Lumsden, Karen and Heather Morgan (2017), 'Media Framing of Trolling and Online Abuse: Silencing Strategies, Symbolic Violence, and Victim Blaming', *Feminist Media Studies*, 17 (6): 926–40.

Maguire, Gráinne. (2015), 'Why I'm Tweeting the Taoiseach My Periods', *The Guardian*, 8 November. Available online: https://www.theguardian.com/commentisfree/2015/nov/08/tweet-taoiseach-periods-enda-kenny-abortion-law (accessed 9 May 2022).

Maguire, Gráinne. (2016), 'Great People Making Great Choices Extract'. Available online: https://www.youtube.com/watch?v=DF6v6ED7SSU (accessed 23 May 2022)

Mahdawi, Arwa. (2017), 'The Daily Show's Gina Yashere: "In England, I'd still be the Token Black Face on Mock the Week"', *The Guardian*, 11 June. Available online: https://www.theguardian.com/stage/2017/jun/11/the-daily-show-gina-yashere-in-england-id-still-be-the-token-black-face-on-mock-the-week (accessed 10 May 2022).

Masso, Giverny. (2018), 'Free Taxi Scheme for Vulnerable Workers at Edinburgh Fringe Wins at Edinburgh Comedy Awards', *The Stage*, 28 August. Available online: https://www.thestage.co.uk/news/free-taxi

-scheme-for-vulnerable-workers-at-edinburgh-fringe-wins-at-edinburgh-comedy-awards (accessed 10 May 2022).

McIntyre, Niamh, Chico Mares and Harry Robertson (2017), 'BBC Salary Data Shows Huge Pay Gap Between White and BME Stars', *The Guardian*, 19 July. Available online: https://www.theguardian.com/media/2017/jul/19/bbc-salary-data-shows-huge-pay-gap-between-white-and-bme-stars (accessed 10 May 2022).

McKeague, Matthew. (2018), 'Is Vlogging the New Stand-up? A Compare/Contrast of Traditional and Online Models of Comedic Content Distribution', *Comedy Studies*, 9 (1): 84–93.

McRobbie, Angela. (2004), 'Post-feminism and Popular Culture', *Feminist Media Studies*, 4 (3): 255–64.

McRobbie, Angela. (2009), *The Aftermath of Feminism: Gender, Culture and Social Change*, London: Sage.

McRobbie, Angela. (2020), *Feminism and the Politics of Resilience: Essays of Gender, Media and the End of Welfare*, Cambridge: Polity.

Mermiri, Tina, Sophia Rawcliffe, and Thomas Rea (2014), *State of Play: Comedy UK*. Live Analytics, Ticketmaster International.

Merrill, Lisa. (1988), 'Feminist Humor: Rebellious and Self-affirming', *Women's Studies: An Interdisciplinary Journal*, 15 (1): 271–80.

Michallon, Clemence. (2020), 'Chris D'Elia: YOU Star and Comedian Responds to Underage Sexual Misconduct and Grooming Allegations', *The Independent*, 17 June. Available online: https://www.independent.co.uk/arts-entertainment/tv/news/chris-delia-allegations-you-comedian-underage-sexual-misconduct-grooming-response-a9571986.html (accessed 10 May 2022).

Mills, Brett. (2009), *The Sitcom*, Edinburgh: Edinburgh University Press.

Mintz, L.E. (1985), 'Standup Comedy as Social and Cultural Mediation', *American Quarterly*, 37 (1): 71–80.

Mizejewski, Linda. (2014), *Pretty/Funny: Women Comedians and Body Politics*, Austin: University of Texas Press.

Morrish, Ed. (2014), 'It's Great to Have One Woman on a TV Panel Show, but You Need More than That', *The New Statesman*, 10 February. Available online: https://www.newstatesman.com/culture/2014/02/its-great-have-one-woman-tv-panel-show-you-need-more (accessed 10 May 2022).

Mort, Frank. (2007), 'Striptease: The Erotic Female Body and Live Sexual Entertainment in Mid-Twentieth-Century London', *Social History*, 32 (1): 27–53.

Nagel, Angela. (2017), *Kill All Normies: Online Culture Wars from 4chan to Tumblr to Trump and the Alt-Right*, London: Zero Books.

Nally, Claire and Angela Smith, eds (2013), *Naked Exhibitionism: Gendered Performance and Public Exposure*, London: I.B. Tauris.

Negus, Keith. (1999), *Music Genres and Corporate Cultures*, London: Routlegde.

Neuman, William Lawrence. (2014), *Social Research Methods: Qualitative and Quantitative Approaches*, Harlow: Pearson.

Ng, Eve. (2020), 'No Grand Pronouncements Here . . .: Reflections on Cancel Culture and Digital Media Participation', *Television and New Media*, 21 (6): 621–7.

Ng, Eve. (2022), *Cancel Culture: A Critical Analysis*, Cham: Palgrave Macmillan.

Olbrys Gencarella, Stephen. (2017), 'Returning the Favor: Ludic Space, Comedians, and the Rhetorical Constitution of Society', in Matthew Meier and Casey Schmitt, eds (2017), *Standing Up, Speaking Out: Stand-up Comedy and the Rhetoric of Social Change*, 237–49, New York: Routledge.

Omielan, Luisa. (2015), 'Why I Strip Off for My Stand-up Show', *The Guardian*, 12 February. Available online: https://www.theguardian.com/stage/2015/feb/12/luisa-omielan-strip-off-standup-comedy-show-am-i-right-ladies (accessed 10 May 2022).

Omielan, Luisa. (2016), *What Would Beyoncé Do?!*, London: Century.

Onwuachi-Willig, Angela. (2018), 'What about# UsToo?: The Invisibility of Race in the #MeToo Movement', *Yale Law Journal Forum*, 128: 105–20.

Oppenheim, Maya. (2022), 'Women "Brutally Exposed" to Cost-of-Living Crisis after Bearing Brunt of Soaring Poverty', *The Independent*, 28 April 2022. Available online: https://www.independent.co.uk/news/uk/home-news/women-poverty-cost-of-living-crisis-b2067579.html (accessed 10 September 2022).

Orgad, Shani and Rosalind Gill (2022), *Confidence Culture*, Durham: Duke University Press.

Power, Kate. (2020), 'The COVID-19 Pandemic has Increased the Care Burden of Women and Families', *Sustainability: Science, Practice and Policy*, 16 (1): 67–73.

Parkel, Inga. (2022), 'Bill Cosby Reveals Plans of 2023 Tour Amid Sexual Abuse and Battery Lawsuit', *The Independent*, 29 December. Available online : https://www.independent.co.uk/arts-entertainment/tv/news/bill-cosby-2023-tour-lawsuit-b2252795.html (accessed 29 December 2022).

Penny, Laurie. (2011), 'A Woman's Opinion Is the Mini-Skirt of the Internet', *The Independent*, 4 November. Available online: https://www.independent.co.uk/voices/commentators/laurie-penny-a-woman-s-opinion-is-the-miniskirt-of-the-internet-6256946.html (accessed 10 May 2022).

Phipps, Alison (2020), *#MeToo Not You: The Trouble with Mainstream Feminism*, Manchester: Manchester University Press.

Plunkett, John. (2015), 'BBC Should Not Have Announced Ban on All-Male Panels, Says Jason Manford', *The Guardian*, 10 March. Available online: https://www.theguardian.com/media/2015/mar/10/bbc-should-not-have-announced-ban-on-all-male-panels-says-jason-manford (accessed 10 May 2022).

Porter, Laraine. (1998), 'Women and Representation in British Comedy', in Stephen Wagg, ed, *Because I Tell a Joke or Two: Comedy, Politics and Social Difference*, 65–93, London: Routledge.

Pritchard McLean, Kiri (2020), 'There's no HR Department in Comedy and Sexual Predators Thrive', *iNews*, 26 June. Available online: https://inews.co.uk/opinion/sexual-harassment-exploitation-comedy-456463 (accessed 10 May 2022).

Quirk, Sophie. (2018), *The Politics of British Stand-up Comedy. The New Alternative*, Cham, Switzerland: Palgrave Macmillan.

Ramaswarmy Chitra. (2018), How the Fallout from Mary Beard's Oxfam Tweet Shines a Light on Genteel Racism, *The Guardian*, 19 February. Available online: https://www.theguardian.com/lifeandstyle/2018/feb/19/mary-beard-oxfam-tweet-genteel-racism (accessed 10 May 2022).

Raskin, Victor. (1985), *Semantic Mechanisms of Humor*, Dordrecht: D. Reidel Publishing.

Roberts, Helen, ed. (1981), *Doing Feminist Research*, London: Routledge.

Robins, Mel. (2017), 'Hilary Clinton Lost Because of Sexism'. *CNN*. 3 May. Available online: https://edition.cnn.com/2017/05/03/opinions/hillary-clinton-interview-sexism-robbins/index.html (accessed 10 May 2022).

Rollero, Chiara and Stefano Tartaglia (2019), 'The Effect of Sexism and Rape Myths on Victim Blame', *Sexuality and Culture*, 23: 209–19.

Ross, Ally. (2017), 'Red Nose Day? This Shambles Was Red Face Day as It Fails to Deliver "Funny for Money" Promise for Comic Relief', *The Sun*, 28 March. Available online: https://www.thesun.co.uk/news/3192390/ally-ross-red-nose-day-fails-to-deliver-for-comic-relief/ (accessed 10 May 2022).

Rowe Karlyn, Kathleen. (2011), *The Unruly Woman: Gender and the Genres of Laughter*, Austin: University of Texas Press.

Ruddick, Graham. (2017), 'Have I Got News for You Where Jo Brand Rebuked All-Male Panel Tops Complaints', *The Guardian*, 16 November. Available online: https://www.theguardian.com/media/2017/nov/16/have-i-got-news-for-you-where-jo-brand-rebuked-all-male-panel-tops-complaints (accessed 10 May 2022).

Russell. Danielle. (2002), 'Self-deprecatory Humour and the Female Comic: Self-destruction or Comedic Construction?', *Thirdspace: A Journal of Feminist Theory & Culture*, 2 (1). Available online: http://journals.sfu.ca/thirdspace/index.php/journal/article/viewArticle/d_russell (accessed 10 May 2022).

Rutter, Jason. (2000), 'The Stand-up Introduction Sequence: Comparing Comedy Compères', *Journal of Pragmatics*, 32: 463–83.

Saha, Anamik. (2018), *Race and the Cultural Industries*, Cambridge: Polity Press.

Saïd, Edward. (1993), *Culture and Imperialism*, London: Vintage.

Salter, Anastasia and Bridget Blodgett (2017), *Toxic Geek Masculinity in Media: Sexism, Trolling, and Identity Policing*, London: Palgrave Macmillan.

Saunders, Jennifer. (2013), *Bonkers: My Life in Laughs*, London: Viking.

Schmader, Toni. (2001), 'Gender Identification Moderates Stereotype Threat Effects on Women's Math Performance', *Journal of Experimental Social Psychology*, 38: 194–201.

Schmader, Toni, Michael Johns and Chad Forbes (2008), 'An Integrated Process Model of Stereotype Threat Effects on Performance', *Psychological Review*, 115 (2): 336–56.

Shapiro, Michael. (1996), *Gender in Play on the Shakespearean Stage: Boy Heroines and Female Pages*, Ann Arbor: University of Michigan Press.

Sherwin, Adam. (2014), 'Miranda Hart and Sarah Millican Named Highest-Selling Female Comedians', *The Independent*, 1 October. Available online: https://www.independent.co.uk/arts-entertainment/comedy/news/miranda-hart-and-sarah-millican-lead-female-comedy-breakthrough-9765423.html (accessed 10 May 2022).

Shifman, Limor and Daphna Lemish (2010), 'Between Feminism and Fun(ny)mism', *Information, Communication & Society*, 13 (6): 870–91

Shifman, Limor and Daphna Lemish (2011), '"Mars and Venus" in Virtual Space: Post-feminist Humor and the Internet', *Critical Studies in Media Communication*, 28 (3): 253–73.

Siddique, Haroon. (2018), 'Derry Girls Actor Offered Apology for "Overweight Girl" review', *The Guardian*, 15 June. Available online: https://www.theguardian.com/stage/2018/jun/15/derry-girls-actor-nicola-coughlan-apology-overweight-girl-review (accessed 10 May 2022).

Skeggs, Beverley. (2001), 'Feminist Ethnography', in Paul Anthony Atkinson, Amanda Coffey, Sara Delamont, John Lofland and Lyn H. Lofland, eds, *Handbook of Ethnography*, 426–43, London: Sage.

Small, Stephen. (1998), '"Serious T'ing": The Black Comedy Circuit in England'. In Stephen Wagg, ed, *Because I Tell A Joke or Two: Comedy, Politics and Social Difference*, 221–43, London: Routledge.

Smith, Angela. (2013), 'From Girl Power to Lady Power: Postfeminism and *Ladette to Lady*', in Claire Nally and Angela Smith, eds, *Naked Exhibitionism: Gendered Performance and Public Exposure*, 137–64, London: I.B. Tauris.

Smith, David. (2018), 'White House Correspondents' Dinner: Michelle Wolf Shocks Media with Sarah Sanders Attack', *The Guardian*, 29 April. Available online: https://www.theguardian.com/us-news/2018/apr/29/white-house-correspondents-dinner-michelle-wolf-stuns-media-with-sarah-sanders-attack (accessed 10 May 2022).

Sobande, Francesca. (2020), *The Digital Lives of Black Women in Britian*, Cham: Palgrave.

Solnit, Rebecca. (2014), *Men Explain Things to Me*, London: Granta.

Stanley, Liz, ed. (1990), *Feminist Praxis: Research, Theory and Epistemology in Feminist Sociology*, London: Routledge.

Stanley, Alessandra. (2008), 'Who Says Women Aren't Funny?', *Vanity Fair*, 3 March. Available online: https://www.vanityfair.com/news/2008/04/funnygirls200804 (accessed 10 May 2022).

Stebbings, Robert. (1993), 'The Social Roles of the Stand-up Comic', *Canadian Theatre Review*, 77: 4–7.

Steele, Claude M. and Joshua Aronson (1995), 'Stereotype Threat and the Intellectual Test Performance of African Americans', *Journal of Personality and Social Psychology*, 69 (5): 797–811.

Stott, Andrew. (2005), *Comedy: The New Critical Idiom*, New York: Routledge.

Superson, Antia M. and Anne. E. Cudd, eds. (2002), *Theorizing Backlash: Philosophical Reflections on the Resistance to Feminism*, Lanham: Rowman and Littlefield.

Symons, Alex. (2017), 'Podcast Comedy and "Authentic Outsiders": How New Media Is Challenging the Owners of Industry', *Celebrity Studies*. 8 (1): 104–18.

Tait, Amelia. (2018), 'We Must Try to Understand How Unwanted Virginity Leads Self-hating Incels to Murder', *The New Statesman*, 8 May. Available online: https://www.newstatesman.com/politics/2018/05/we-must-try-understand-how-unwanted-virginity-leads-self-hating-incels-murder (accessed 11 May 2022).

Thompson, Ben. (2004), *Sunshine on Putty: The Golden Age of British Comedy from Vic Reeves to The Office*, London: Fourth Estate.

Tomsett, Ellie. (2017), 'Twenty-first Century Fumerists: Bridget Christie and the Backlash Against Feminist Comedy', *Comedy Studies*, 8 (1): 57–67.

Tomsett, Ellie. (2018), 'Positives and Negatives: Reclaiming the Female Body and Self-deprecation in Stand-up Comedy', *Comedy Studies*, 9 (1): 6–18.

Tomsett, Ellie. (2019), *Reflections on UK Comedy's Glass Ceiling: Stand-Up Comedy and Contemporary Feminisms*. PhD Thesis. Available online. http://shura.shu.ac.uk/26442/ (accessed 20 September 2022)

Tomsett, Ellie. (2022) '"Less Dick Jokes": Women-Only Comedy Line-ups, Audience Expectations and Stereotypes' in Oliver Double and Sharon Lockyer, eds, *Alternative Comedy Now and Then: Critical Perspectives*, Cham: Palgrave Macmillan.

Tomsett, Ellie and Nathalie Weidhase (2020), 'A Sign of the Times: Comic Slogans and Imagery in Modern Day Political Protest', in Giuliana Monteverde and Victoria McCollum, eds, *Resist! Protest Media and Popular Culture in the Brexit-Trump Era*, London: Rowman and Littlefield.

Tomsett, Ellie and Rosie White (2024), 'Stand-up and Gender', in Oliver Double, ed, *The Cambridge Companion to Stand-up Comedy*, Cambridge: Cambridge University Press.

Tomsett, Ellie, Eric Shouse, Ignatius Chukwumah, Anastasiya Fiadotava and Cale Bain (2021), 'Special Editorial', *Comedy Studies*, 12 (2): 121–38.

Vinen, Richard. (2013), *Thatcher's Britain: The Politics and Social Upheaval of the Thatcher Era*, London: Simon and Schuster.

Wagg, Stephen. (2002), 'Comedy, Politics and Permissiveness: The "Satire Boom" and Its Inheritance', *Contemporary Politics*, 8 (4): 319–34.

Wagmeister, Elizabeth. (2022), 'Louis C.K. Sexual Harassment Accuser Slams Grammy Win: "Nobody Cares. That's the Message This Sends"', *Variety*, 12 April. Available online: https://variety.com/2022/music/news/louis-ck-grammy-win-sexual-harassment-accuser-1235230060/ (accessed 11 May 2022).

Watkins, Susan. (2018), 'Which Feminisms?', *New Left Review*, 109: 5–77.

Ways to Change the World (2018), [podcast] 'Reni Eddo-Lodge on Race, Social Injustice and Quotas', *Channel* 4, 4 April 2018. Available online: https://www.channel4.com/news/ways-to-change-the-world-a-new-channel-4-news-podcast-reni-eddo-lodge (accessed 9 May 2022).

Wheeler, S. Christian and Richard E. Petty (2001), 'The Effects of Stereotype Activation on Behavior: A Review of Possible Mechanisms', *Psychological Bulletin*, 127 (6): 797–826.

White, Rosie. (2018), *Television Comedy and Femininity: Queering Gender*, London: I.B. Tauris.

Willett, Cynthia and Julie Willett (2019), *Uproarious: How Feminists and Other Subversive Comics Speak Truth*, Minneapolis: University of Minnesota Press.

Willett, Cynthia, Julie Willett and Yael Sherman (2012), 'The Seriously Erotic Politics of Feminist Laughter', *Social Research*, 79 (1): 217–46.

Wood, Katelyn, Hale. (2018), 'Standing Up: Black Feminist Comedy in the Twentieth and Twenty-First Centuries', in Renee Alexander Craft, Thomas F. DeFrantz, Kathy A. Perkins and Sandra L. Richards, eds, *The Routledge Companion to African American Theatre and Performance*, 323–9, London: Routledge.

Zillmann, Dolf, and Joanne, R. Cantor (1972), 'Directionality of Transitory Dominance as a Communication Variable Affecting Humor Appreciation', *Journal of Personality and Social Psychology*, 24: 191–8.

Index

A. *Ant* (live performance) 157–9, 184
Abbot, Russ 34
abortion rights 150–2, 173
Acaster, James 44, 46
Adams, Jayde 43, 122
Adefope, Lolly 152–6
Adrienne Truscott's Asking For It (live performance) 146–50
advertising 69–71, 108–9, 139
aesthetic pressures 75–8
Ahmed, Sara 17, 21, 94–5, 107–8, 140, 226–7
Alexander, Dana 75–6
Allen, Fiona 40
Allen, Shane 166
All Killa No Filla (podcast) 122
Alma's Not Normal (TV show) 55
alternative comedy 138, 188
 movement of 1980s 5, 35–8, 77–8, 96, 214–15
 new alternative/DIY 44–6
Am I Right Ladies? (live performance) 166–8, 221
Amstell, Simon 44
Amusical (comedy night) 122
anti-Blackness 190
Appleby, Debra-Jane 43
arena comedy 38, 40, 92–3, 196
Arrowsmith, Gemma 122, 225
Arts Council England (ACE) 87, 108, 197, 206, 227–9
audience participation 65
audience perceptions of women-only comedy 26, 95, 100–4

Baby Cobra (Netflix special) 112
backlash to feminism 125, 173–6, 191, 209, 224
Baddiel, David 38
Bakhtin, Mikhail 142–3
Bamford, Maria 112, 114
Banet-Wiser, Sarah 138, 216
banter (concept) 175, 180, 196, 203
Baram, Daphna 70, 211
Barnes, Angela 145, 206
Baron-Cohen, Simon 7
Barraclough, Roy 35
Barreca, Regina 6, 8, 139–40, 157
Baruc, Rebecca 113
Bea, Aisling 129
Beale, Sam 29, 31, 32
Beard, Mary 124–5
Because You Demanded It (live performance) 157, 163
Bede, Jenny 120–1
Belanger, Jillian 113
Bergson, Henri 21
Best in Class (comedy night) 220
Beyoncé 139, 166–8
Beyond a Joke (website) 81
Bhaskar, Sanjeev 40
A Bic for Her (live performance) 157, 160–3
Bill Cosby Show, The (TV show) 199
Bing, Janet 9–10
Black, Bethany 87
Black, British and Funny (TV show) 40
Black comedy circuit (UK) 39–40
Blair, Tony 38–9
Bob, Kemah 222
body positive comedy 137, 146–8
body positivity 28, 150–1, 155–6, 168, 170–1, 223
Bourdieu, Pierre 21, 50
Boyle, Karen 111, 198, 201–2, 204, 208–9

Brand, Jo   36, 42, 75, 185–9
Branded (live performance)   55
Brexit   130, 174, 178
Bridget Christie Minds the Gap (radio show)   160
Brister, Jen   87
British Academy Film and Television Award (BAFTA)   6, 55
British Broadcasting Corporation (BBC)   40, 55–9, 103–5, 166, 190, 224–7
  BBCOne   166–7
  BBC2   40
  BBC3   117, 120, 166–8
  BBC Radio 4   40, 159, 177, 192
British Comedy Awards   185
British Comedy Guide   50
Brizendine, Louann   7
Bros: When the Screaming Stops (TV show)   130
Bryant, Aidy   113
Burch, Desiree   43, 222
Buress, Hannibal   200

Calman, Susan   43, 87
'cancel culture' (concept)   174, 179, 209
Caroline Aherne Bursary, The   224–6
Carr, Jimmy   147
Caulfield, Jo   104
Celebrity Big Brother (TV show)   183
Channel 4   40, 191, 217
Channel 5   183
character comedy   16–17, 53–4, 121, 135, 153–4, 157–9, *see also* Laughs, Dapper
Chawawa, Munya   121
Chortle (website)   50, 54, 177
Christie, Bridget   15, 43, 85, 112, 133, 156–66, 168, 170–3, 176, 179, 183–5, 191–2, 221, 227
Cisgender male universality (concept)   16, 46–7, 62–3, 127, 141, 154, 158, 190, 215
Cissie and Ada   35
class barriers   49–50, 72, 195
Clean (live performance)   179
Clinton, Hilary   8
Cohen, Danny   55–6, 225
Comedians, The (TV show)   34
comedienne   83, 212, 225
Comedy 50:50 (organisation)   207
comedy critics   49–55, 129, 153, 181–2, 215
comedy postures   160–3, 168–9
comedy promoters   5, 41, 59, 67, 69, 73–4, 85, 122, 207, 213–14, 218
Comedy Safety Standards Ireland (CSS) (organisation)   207
Comedy Store, The (venue)
  Manchester   44, 45, 100, 101
  Soho   35–7
Comic Relief (charity television performance)   189
Comic Strip, The (comedy group)   36
community   10, 63, 81, 85–8, 90, 133
compères   19, 62, 65–8, 76, 158, 212
confidence   64, 72, 119–20, 127, 220
confidence culture   139, 145, 171
Connolly, Janice (Barbara Nice)   17, 75, 77
'Cool Britannia' (concept)   12, 38
Cosby, Bill   147, 199–200, 209–10
Cosby Show, The (TV show)   199
costume   76–7, 158, 161, 223
Covid-19 context   74, 85, 118, 121, 174, 228
Covid-19 response from comedy industry   111, 131, 135, 200, 206
Covid Arms, The (online comedy night)   122
Creative Case for Diversity (ACE)   228–9

Crenshaw, Kimberlé 16
crowd funding 221
Cultural and Creative Industries (CCIs) 193-8, 202-3, 208
Culture Recovery Fund 85, 206, 228, 229

Dapper Laughs: On the Pull (TV show) 180-1
Davies, Sian 220
Dawson, Les 35
Day Today, The (TV show) 117
Death of Stalin, The (film) 117
Dee, Jack 184
Delaney, Steve 17
D'Elia, Chris 201
Dennis, Les 34
Department for Digital, Culture, Media and Sport (DDCMS) 193
Dessau, Bruce 81
Dexter, Felix 40
Diaz, Joey 201
dick jokes 95-6
Dilemma (radio panel show) 56
diversity initiatives 55-7, 94-5, 206, 217-20, 224-9
Dixon, Euridice 206
DIY comedy (concept) 44, 46
Donovan, Owen 206
Don Wong (Netflix special) 112
Double, Oliver 31-2, 34, 44, 45, 62-3, 182
drag performance 34
Duker, Sophie 190, 220, 222
Dunham, Lena 2

economic disparities 36, 61, 72-5, 83, 195, 213
Eddo-Lodge, Reni 95, 106, 154, 178, 191
Edinburgh Festival Comedy Awards 1, 46, 55, 85, 146, 156-7, 206

Edinburgh Fringe Festival, The 24, 49-55, 85, 150, 168, 179, 213
Edmonson, Adrian 36
El-Ghorri, Fatiha 153
Elton, Ben 36
empowerment 28, 138-9, 145, 164-8, 172, 222
Eurovision Song Contest, The, (musical competition) 130-1
Everyday Sexism (campaign) 2, 60
experiential knowledge 20-1
Eyre, Pauline 206

Facebook (Meta) 26, 114, 116, 133, 177-8, 221
Fagon, Annette 144
Fairburn, Rachel 122
fake laughter 8-9, 139-40
Feig, Paul 125
female bodies 137, 141-4, 150-2, 155-6, 165
female brains 6-7
Female Genital Mutilation (FGM) 162-3
feminism(s)
  3rd Wave feminism 152
  4th Wave feminism 111, 139, 152, 209, 212
  Black feminism 10
  Celebrity feminism 139, 165, 170, 212, 222
  Choice feminism 13
  Intersectional feminism 4, 16, 153, 124, 189
  Neoliberal feminism 138-9, 166
  White feminism 2, 13, 59, 125, 198-9
feminist comedy 1-2, 10, 62, 137, 146-56, 165, 172, 173, 183-4, 189, 191-2, 21-12, 215, 223-4, *see also* Christie, Bridget
feminist organising 86, 107-9
feminist research methods 3-4, 21-6
Ferdows, Saima 122

Fey, Tina   2, 14, 113, 114
Fine, Cordelia   5–7, 19
Fox, Kate   115
Frankie Boyle's New World Order (TV show)   190
Franzini, Louis   6
French, Dawn   36, 144, 167
Freud, Sigmund   21
Friedman, Sam   32, 33, 36, 46, 49–55, 220, *see also* T-Shirt comic
Frog and Bucket, The (venue)   45, 64, 70, 85, 92, 107, 218
funny for a woman (concept)   63–4, 216
Funny Women (organisation)   5, 41–3, 60, 73, 84, 108–9, 214, 217–18
Funny Women Awards   43

Gadsby, Hannah   112
gender
  binary   7–8, 14, 71, 83, 177, 209
  interpreted as genre   16–18, 71, 98, 156, 167, 216, 219
  segregation   37–8, 47–8
gendered behaviour   5, 8–9, 31
gendered language   5, 54–5, 65–6, 83–4
gender stereotypes   5–19, 34–5, 37, 47–8, 55, 63, 67, 70–1, 186
German, Lindsey   175, 183
Get Off Live Comedy (initiative)   207
Ghostbusters (2016) (film)   125
Ghosts (TV show)   153
Gideon, Llewella   40
Gilbert, Joanne   6, 20, 81, 153, *see also* comedy postures
Gill, Rosalind   13, 17, 171, 175, 180, 195–7, *see also* confidence culture
Gilligan, Mo   40
Gilligan, Nina   207

'girl power' (concept)   170, 223
Girls (TV show)   2
Glass Ceiling, the (concept)   3, 211, 228
Glee Club, The, (venue)   44, 45
Glitter Room (Netflix special)   112
Godliman, Kerry   57, 222
Graham, Ivo   44
Gray, Frances   6, 11, 29, 33, 178
Great People Making Great Choices (live performance)   151
Green, Chloe   219
grotesque   35, 142–3, 152
Gupta, Anil   40

Hagen, Sofie   43, 221
Hart, Miranda   1, 83, 105
Have I Got News For You? (TV show)   184–8
heckling   76–7, 101, 114, 127
Henry, Lenny   20, 196
heteronormativity   14, 168, 170
hidden labour (concept)   41, 122, 134, 195, 196
Hislop, Ian   185–7
Hitchens, Christopher   13–15, 158
Hole, Anne   144
Holt, Rosie   121
Home Safe Collective (initiative)   206
homophobia   17, 33–4, 41, 100, 174
Hughes, London   20, 112
Humitas (concept)   115
Huxley, David   12, 32
Hynes, Jessica   40

I'm Alan Partridge (TV show)   117
Ince, Robin   44, 159
Incel ideology   126, 174
Independent Television (ITV)   218
  ITV2   179–81
informal working practices   52, 194–5, 203, 213
Instagram   114, 118, 221

internalized bias 5, 52
Intersectionality 56, 59, 98, 153, 227-9, *see also* feminism(s), intersectional feminism
introductions from compères 61, 65-6, 85, 184-5, 212, 215
In Trouble (Netflix special) 112
irony 175, 180-3

Joe Rogan Experience, The, (podcast) 201
Johnson, Boris 174
Jones, Leslie 124-5
Jones, Rosie 222
Jongleurs, (venue) 44
Josh (TV show) 117
just joking, (concept) 1, 175, 180, 190, 203, 210

Kalviknes Bore, Inger-Lise 25, 113, 125
Khorsandi, Shaparak 143, 153
killjoys 9, 11-12, 107, 140, 204
King, Lara. A. 61-2, 144
Kirby, Brid 206
Kitson, Daniel 44, 133
Knowles, Beyoncé, 139, 166-8, *see also* Beyoncé
Kotthoff, Helga 6
Krefting, Rebecca 10, 24, 113
Kuipers, Giselinde 25, 51, 52, 79, 217

lad culture 179-80, 191
ladette 12-13
ladies nights (concept) 69-71, 219
Laughing Cows Comedy (comedy night) 5, 41, 64, 66, 70-3, 76, 84-5, 92, 214
Laughs, Dapper (comedy character) 179-92, 209
Laughter Show, The (TV show) 34
Lawrence, Andrew 176-9, 183, 191
Lee, Stewart 44-5, 133

Leigh, Kerry 66-7, 76-7
Le Mar, Angie 40
Lesbian, Gay, Bisexual, Transgender, Queer + (LGBTQ+)
  communities 71, 87, 89
  identities 10, 47, 99, 154, 214
  inclusion 108
  rights 88, 173
Lipman, Maureen 56
Live at the Apollo (TV show) 80, 104
Live Comedy Association (LCA) (organisation) 206, 218
Lloyd, Cariad 222
Lloyd, Marie 32
Lockyer, Sharon 20, 25, 35, 80, 90-2, 110
LOL Word, The, (comedy night) 219
Lolly 2 (live performance) 152-5
Long, Josie 44
Louis, C.K. 149, 200, 210
Lycett, Joe 118
Lyons, Zoe 43, 57, 87

Mabley, Moms 10
McCabe, Kate 87
McGee, Lisa 122
McKeague, Matthew 114, 117
Mackichan, Doon 40
McKinnon, Kate 113
McRobbie, Angela 13, 141-2, 165, 223-4
Maguire, Gráinne 150-2, 155
mainstream comedy circuit 44-6, 72, 85, 165, 214-16, 218, 228
  audience understandings of 93, 95-6, 100-2, 109-10
  as male space 175-6, 214, 219
  performer understandings of 62, 69, 75
Maitlis, Emily 181-2
Major, John 38
male brains 6-7
Manford, Jason 56

Manning, Bernard   34–5
Martin, Mae   44
masculinity   128, 175–6, 183, 196, 209
May, Theresa   139, 186
Mayall, Rik   36
menstrual cycles   143, 151, 155
meritocracy (the illusion of)   103, 105–6, 139
Merrill, Lisa   8
Merton, Paul   186–7
#MeToo   111, 198–202, 206–10
Michael McIntyre's Comedy Roadshow (TV show)   80
Millican, Sarah   1, 83, 104, 132
Mills, Brett   43
Mirza, Shazia   153
misogynoir   125, 190
misogyny   52, 77, 124–7, 160, 181, 216
  in comedy clubs   33, 63–4, 68–9, 101–2
  internalized   63, 98
Mitchell, Jodie   219
Mixed Bill: Comedy and Gender Research Network   103
Mizejewski, Linda   6, 14
Mock the Week (TV show)   104, 177
Mo'Nique   10
Moody, Alex   225
Moore, Thanyia   43
More More More. How do you Lycett, How do you Lycett? (live performance)   118
Morgan, Diane   43
Morrish, Ed   56, 58
Morton, Eleanor   121
Murray, Al   17, 132, 182
Music Hall   31–2

naked performance   146–8, 155
Nanette (Netflix special)   112
Neoliberalism   142, 168, *see also* feminism(s), neoliberal feminism

Nester, Eddie   40
Netflix (streaming service)   46, 112, 221
netnography (concept)   26
Newman, Rob   38
Newsnight (TV show)   56, 181–2
News Quiz, The (radio panel show)   56
Nice, Barbara   17, 103, *see also* Connolly, Janice
No More Page Three (campaign)   2, 163, 184
Norton, Graham   189–90
Notos, Soula   63

objectification   37, 76, 148, 187, 203, *see also* self-objectification
O'Doherty, Claudia   44
O'Doherty, David   44, 129
O'Keefe, Hazel   15, 22, 41, 60–1, 85, 214
Old Baby (Netflix special)   112
Omielan, Luisa   133, 156, 164–73, 189–90, 192, 221, 227
online abuse   122–8, 190, 220–1
online comic activism   150–2, 180
online communities   27, 111–18, 200
online gigs   200–1
online interaction with audiences   131–3, 135–6
online participatory humour   120, 130–1
online presence   128–9, 134–5, 177, 179
Operation Yewtree (investigation)   184
#OscarsSoWhite   154
Osho, Andi   43

panel shows   40, 78, 177, 183–9, 221, 227, *see also Have I Got News For You?*
  audience comments on   98, 105
  BBC announcement regarding   55–9, 104

comedians thoughts on   6, 57–8
Pappy's Fun Club (comedy
    group)   44
Papworth, Rebecca   225
Parker, Lynne   42–3, 57, 60, 61,
    108–9, 214, *see also* Funny
    Women
parody   118, 120–1
participant observer status   22–3,
    25–6, 193
Pascoe, Sara   43, 166, 222
Pegg, Simon   40
Penny, Laurie   125
period jokes   151–2, *see also*
    menstrual cycles
Perkins, Sue   56
Petts, Chloe   219
Phillips, Sally   40
podcasts   112, 113, 221
Poehler, Amy   2, 14, 113, 114
political correctness (concept)   174,
    177, 183, 224
Politics For Bitches (live
    performance)   126
Porter, Laraine   29, 34, 40
Porter, Lucy   56
Positionality (concept)   3–4
postfeminism   17, 71, 83, 108–9,
    139, 173, 175, 203
postfeminist audience
    attitudes   106–7
postfeminist comedy   137, 156,
    164–72, 222–4
postfeminist media culture   180
precarious labour   195, 197, 205,
    210, 213
Pritchard-McLean, Kiri   62, 64,
    68–70, 74, 122, 202, 207, 219,
    221
Private Eye (magazine)   185
Pub Landlord, The, *see* Murray, Al

Question Time (TV show)   124
Quirk, Sophie   45, 46

quotas   57, 70, 94, 102, 215

racism   10, 15–17, 64, 125, 127, 155,
    207
  on the comedy circuit   39–40,
    52, 189–90
racist comedy   33, 174
radio comedy   33, 38, 56, 122,
    159–60, 217, 225, *see also* BBC
    Radio 4
radio panel shows   188
Raised by Wolves (TV show)   217
rape culture   77, 126, 149–50, 155,
    195, 198
rape jokes   146–50, 180
Raskin, Victor   9
Ravens, Jan   56
representing all women
    (concept)   61–3
Res-erection (live tour)   181
retro-sexism   174
reviewers   54–5
right wing comedy   177–8
Rivers, Joan   162
Rowe Karlyn, Kathleen   143–4
Rudolph, Maya   2, 113
Ruffell, Suzi   87
Russell, Danielle   137–8, 141
Rutter, Jason   65, 68
Ryan, Katherine   43, 57, 58, 112,
    166, 222

Saha, Anamik   95
Saïd, Edward   29
Saturday Night Live (SNL) (TV
    show)   112–13
Saunders, Jennifer   36
#SaveLiveComedy (campaign)
    206
Sayle, Alexei   36, 159
Schneider, David   116–20, 127, 130,
    133–5
Schumer, Amy   2
segregated industries   196, 216–17

self-deprecatory comedy 137–45, 148, 171–2, 212, 222–3
self-objectification 76, 147–8, 171–2
sexism from industry professionals 67–9
sexism in workplaces 195–7
sexist comedy 33–5, 65–6, 95–6, 179–86
sexual assault/misconduct 149, 178, 184–5, 196–7, 203, 206–7, 209
sexuality 8, 10–11, 34, 99–100, 141, 165, 168–71, 190
sexual jokes/content 8–10, 33–4, 147
Shapiro, Michael 30
Shelf (comedy group) 219
Shifman, Limor (with Daphna Lemish) 164–5, 170, 223
Short and Girlie Show, The, (comedy group) 87
Shrill (TV show) 153
silencing (concept) 122–4, 132, 155–6, 229
Silverman, Sarah 14
Simmit, John 40
Sincerely (Recorded comedy special) 209
sitcom 11, 34–5, 40, 43, 112, 113, 117, 192, 217
sketch comedy 16, 35, 40, 112–14, 120–2, 153–4
Smack the Pony (TV show) 40, 43
Small, Stephen 29, 39
Smith, Allyson June 53, 57, 61, 66
Smith, Angela 12, 13
Smurthwaite, Kate 17, 62, 70, 71, 123, 127, 128
Sobande, Francesca 123, 136
social media 26, 49, 109, 111–36
Soho 35, 37
Soho Theatre (venue) 150, 159
Spaced (TV show) 40
spatial injustice (concept) 29–30, 33, 47–8, 175, 191, 209, 213–14

Spicer, Michael 121
Spittle, Alison 44, 129
Standard Issue Magazine 126
stand-up comedy (definition) 31, 62–3
Stand-up For Her (Netflix special) 112
Stanley, Alessandra 14
State of Play Report, The 81–4, *see also* Ticketmaster
stereotype threat (concept) 18–19, 66, 120
Stone, Frog 225
Stott, Andrew 30
Suspiciously Cheap Comedy (comedy night) 122, 219
Swift, Taylor 139
Syal, Meera 40
Symons, Alex 113

Taskmaster (TV show) 192
tastemakers 50–1, 58
Ticketmaster (organisation) 81–4
TikTok (social media application) 114, 121
#TimesUp (campaign) 111, 233
To Catch a Dick (Netflix special) 112
Toomey, Jessica 218
Tosh, Daniel 150
toxic masculinity (concept) 128
traditional stand-up comedy ('trad stand-up') 33–6, 48, 160
Trans Exclusionary Feminisms/Gender Critical Feminism 86, 174, 212
Trans Exclusionary Radical Feminists (TERFs) 86, 174
trans inclusion 4, 5, 86, 88
transphobia 86, 123, 174
trolling, *see* online abuse
Trump, Donald 115, 149, 174, 185
Truscott, Adrienne 146–50, 155, 200
T-Shirt comics (concept) 53, 59, 77, 222, *see also* Friedman, Sam

Twitter (social media application)   26, 112–34, 151, 167, 201, 208, 220, 221

UK Independence Party (UKIP)   177
An Ungrateful Woman (live performance)   157, 163
User Generated Content (UGC)   46, 114

Vagenda Magazine   2
vaginas   65, 95, 142–3, 148, 163
variety performance   31–2, 34
Vee, Sindhu   43
violence against women   77, 136, 147–9, 160, 175–9, 195, 198–202, 208
Virtual reality (VR)   116
Viz (magazine)   11–12

Wacky Racists (comedy night)   220
Walsh, Holly   57, 58, 222
Webb, Alice   225
Weinstein, Harvey   149, 199
What Now? (live performance)   157
What the Frock (comedy night)   84
What Would Beyonce Do? (live performance)   166–8
whiteness   56–7, 154–5, 163, 198, 226–7
white privilege (concept)   59, 70, 123, 155, 198, 226

Who Am I? (live performance)   157
Wiig, Kristen   113
Willan, Sophie   6, 7, 19, 54–5, 58, 67–8
Willett, Cynthia and Julie   11, 157
Winters, Dotty   126
'wokeness' (concept)   174, 177
Wolf, Michelle   114
'women aren't funny' (concept)   1, 13–17, 58
Women in Comedy Festival, The, (UK)   5, 22–7, 60, 71, 84–110, 214, 217, 218
Women in Film and TV (WFTV)   218
women-only comedy nights   79–110
  origins   41–3
women's rights   10, 13, 14, 31, 150–2, 155, 183, 212, 213
Wood, Katelyn Hale   10
Working Men's Clubs   9, 32–8, 44, 47, 69, 96, 175, 178, 211

xenofeminism   111
XS Malarkey   45

Yashere, Gina   20, 113
Younger, Maureen   65
YouTube   46, 112, 114, 120–1

Zehra, Sameena   206, 213
Zelenskyy, Volodymry   115